Unheard Voices

THE FIRST HISTORIANS
OF SOUTHERN WOMEN

Feminist Issues: Practice, Politics, Theory

Alison Booth and Ann Lane, Editors

Unheard Voices

THE FIRST HISTORIANS
OF SOUTHERN WOMEN

Edited by
Anne Firor Scott

University of Virginia

Charlottesville and

London

The University Press of Virginia
Copyright © 1993
by the Rector and Visitors
of the University of Virginia

First published 1993

Library of Congress Cataloging-in-Publication Data
Unheard voices : the first historians of southern women / edited by
Anne Firor Scott.
   p.   cm. — (Feminist issues)
   Includes bibliographical references.
   ISBN 0-8139-1432-9 (cloth). — ISBN 0-8139-1433-7 (paper)
   1. Women—Southern States—History. 2. Women—Southern States—
Historiography. I. Scott, Anne Firor, 1921– . II. Series:
Feminist issues (Charlottesville, Va.)
HQ1438.A13U54   1993
305.4'0975—dc20   92-26552
                                          CIP

Printed in the United States of America

For Will and Sarah
and Thomas
with love

Contents

vii

Illustrations
following page 26

The Young Voices

Virginia Gearhart Gray, c. 1928

Marjorie Mendenhall, 1920

Julia Cherry, c. 1920

Guion Griffis, c. 1922

Eleanor Miot Boatwright, 1936

The Mature Voices

Virginia Gearhart Gray, c. 1970

Marjorie Mendenhall, 1942

Julia Cherry Spruill

Guion Griffis Johnson and Guy Benton Johnson, 1959

Eleanor Miot Boatwright, 1950

Acknowledgments

I HAVE HAD splendid help from many people in the search for the elusive evidence upon which this essay rests. I am indebted to Betty Sue Beebe of Mary Hardin Baylor University; Ruth Boyce and Elizabeth Holston of the University of North Carolina Alumni Association; J. Frank Cook, Director of the University of Wisconsin-Madison Archives, and Judith Johnson of that staff; President Rhoda Dorsey of Goucher College; Jacqueline Goggin of the W. E. B. DuBois Institute at Harvard; Jane Knowles, Director of the Radcliffe Archives; William King, Director of the Duke University Archives; David Moltke-Hansen, Director of the Southern Historical Collection at the University of North Carolina, and Jill Snyder of that staff; and Carol Ronka of Bradford College.

Among those who shared their own research or memories are the late Ann Braddy, Florence Fleming Corley, Pamela Dean, John and Sallie Gray, Robin Harris, Jere L. Mendenhall LeGwin, Susan Levine, Martha Mendenhall, Robert Miller, Elizabeth Applewhite Pearsall, Emily Herring Wilson, and C. Vann Woodward. Elizabeth Pearsall was virtually a coauthor of the section on Marjorie Mendenhall.

I owe a great debt to Robert Connor and Kent Mullikin for offering the hospitality of the National Humanities Center during the spring of 1992. I am indebted to many members of the NHC staff for help, but most especially to Alan Tuttle, Rebecca Vargha, and Jean Houston of the Center Library who tracked down indispensable documents and provided copies with impressive expedition. I am grateful to Nancy Essig, Director of the University Press of Virginia, for encouraging me to undertake this study. At the eleventh hour Grace Guyer transformed texts of the essays written by the protagonists into typescript acceptable to the printer. Stephanie Yuhl was my cheerful coworker in the tedious task of proofreading.

Andrew Scott, Neal Salisbury, and Marjoleine Kars read the introductory essay in draft and pushed me to make it better. None of these helpful people are to be blamed for errors of omission or commission.

Unheard Voices

THE FIRST HISTORIANS
OF SOUTHERN WOMEN

PART I

A Different View of Southern History

Let any woman imagine for a moment a biography of herself based on those records she has left, those memories fresh in the minds of surviving friends, those letters that chanced to be kept, those impressions made, perhaps, on the biographer who was casually met in the subject's later years. What secrets, what virtues, what passions, what discipline, what quarrels would, on the subject's death, be lost forever? How much would have vanished or been distorted or changed, even in our memories?

—Carolyn Heilbrun, *Writing a Woman's Life*, 51.

Until very recently, and in many cases even yet, historians of the American South, including those who have produced pathbreaking books, articles, and monographs, have nearly all operated on the unexamined assumption that "history" is about what men do. Most have written as if the word *southerner* was a masculine noun.[1]

Sometime in the 1960s, in a context of feminist revival, a handful of historians, most of them female, began to take a new look at old records and began to create a "new history" of southern women. As they worked they were surprised to find that a small body of substantial research on the subject had been completed between 1927 and 1940, a time, so they had thought, when hardly anyone was paying the slightest attention to the history of women. When they looked more closely they found that the unpublished manuscripts, essays, and books in question had been written by five women who had lived, studied, or worked within a twelve-mile radius of each other in North Carolina.[2] Taken together their studies had set a comprehensive agenda for the study of eighteenth- and nineteenth-century southern women's history. Beginning in the 1920s, working in a field which provided few models, each of these historians had managed to do first-rate work, yet few of their findings had been incorporated into what would have been considered the mainstream of historical scholarship.

The women in question had played a double role: they were pioneers in establishing a new field of historical study, and they were pioneers as well in seeking acceptance in a discipline controlled almost entirely by men in a part of the country where women professionals were late on the scene. Their life histories highlight the hazards facing any new group seeking to make its way into a profession and tell us as well about the obstacles confronting the scholar who seeks to gain a hearing for a subject not yet recognized by the people in a position to define the parameters of a field.

Women as historians were not absolutely new under the sun. At least since the eighteenth century, when Hannah Adams wrote religious history for a living and Mercy Otis Warren published her history of the American Revolution, a handful of American women had aspired to be historians. In the first part of the nineteenth century, when the gentleman scholar dominated American historical writing, an occasional woman made a name for herself as a learned amateur, though none attained the stature of a Prescott, a Parkman, an Adams, or a Bancroft.[3] In the years after 1870, as colleges and universities began to appoint trained historians who then began to create a profession on the German model, a handful of unusually talented and persistent women had managed to take the newly important Ph.D. degree and to make a place for themselves among historical scholars.[4] These women usually made their reputations by doing meticulous research in well-established fields; English legal history was a particular favorite. In contrast to some of their amateur predecessors, none examined the history of their own sex.[5] The career patterns of these scholars differed markedly from those of men with similar qualifications. They remained single or married only when their childbearing years were past. No matter how excellent their preparation and publications, they could find jobs only in women's colleges or in small coeducational institutions somewhat out of the mainstream. Many worked in historical societies, libraries, and high schools. Very rarely one might be appointed at a state-supported coeducational university. The pace-setting eastern men's colleges had no use at all for women as faculty. Some male historians welcomed women as students but could not imagine them as potential colleagues. Others preferred not to have them around at all. Some women built careers as research assistants to established male historians, and a number of very well known men published the work of their female assistants as their own.[6]

A few women born in the 1860s and 1870s, most of them faculty members in the early women's colleges, achieved scholarly recognition: Annie Abel (b.1873) created the field of Native American history and won the Justin Winsor Prize in 1906 for her work on Indian removal. Nellie Neilson (b.1873), a Bryn Mawr Ph.D. who had studied with Charles M. Andrews, became one of the leading medievalists of her generation and was for a long time the only woman in the Medieval Academy. In 1930 Louise Kellog (b.1862), who had taken her degree with Frederick Jackson Turner at the turn of the century and whose thesis had also won the Winsor Prize, was chosen president of the Mississippi Valley Historical Association. Ten years later Neilson became the first woman (and the last for more than four decades) to head the American Historical Association.[7] In 1946 the Southern Historical Association chose as president a northern woman who taught at Goucher College. All of these "first woman" presidents had been born in the 1860s and 1870s and had taken their advanced degrees at prestigious institutions with very influential mentors. Two taught at women's colleges, and one was an archivist; all three were single and deeply committed to the profession. None were from the South. Indeed, of the thirty-four historians whose biographies appear in the four volumes of *Notable American Women,* only two were born south of the Mason-Dixon Line: Anna Julia Cooper, an African American from North Carolina, and Mary Wright (much younger than the rest) from Louisiana. The Berkshire History Conference, a tight-knit group formed in 1928 by a handful of women who had felt something less than warm acceptance in the American Historical Association, had no southern members at all. Even in what may be called the second generation of women historians, southern women were few, and it seems clear that those who tried to join the profession faced even more obstacles than did their contemporaries in the Northeast.[8]

In this area as in many others southerners had certain handicaps. Though even in antebellum times, as the essays reprinted here demonstrate, many southern women worked for pay, and many were teachers of children, few had any access to what were called the learned professions. After the Civil War poverty and the exigencies of Reconstruction limited the development of higher education for any-body, but especially for women. At the turn of the century except for Goucher College in Baltimore there was no southern woman's col-lege which approached the caliber of Vassar, Wellesley, Smith, Mount Holyoke, Pembroke, Barnard, or Bryn Mawr. For many young south-ern women state-supported normal schools provided the only oppor-tunity for education beyond high school (and even high schools only existed in the major cities). Opportunities for graduate study on their native ground were even more limited.[9]

This, then, was the context in which the five women whose work is here reprinted set out to become professional historians. They were born between 1895 and 1903 in four southern states: Maryland, North Carolina, Georgia, and Texas. All five earned the Master of Arts degree at a time when the number of women taking that degree in all fields, though rapidly rising, did not exceed six thousand a year nationwide; three were among the possibly five hundred women in the whole country who took the Ph.D. in history between 1920 and 1940.[10] Each went on to become a practicing historian and set out to achieve a foothold in the academic world.

The story of how they came to be historians in a particular place and time, and the kinds of careers they were able to create for themselves, can only be partly reconstructed. Like true southern ladies three of the five were excessively modest and did not make sure that the documents of their lifework would be preserved. Another left extensive records which were destroyed after her death. Those four provide a dramatic illustration of what Helen Vendler once called "the evanescence of personal history." The fifth—a native Texan—had few doubts of her value or the value of her work, and more than fifty boxes of her papers have survived. That scholars who had devoted so much of their lives to the study of documents should have been so careless of their own is another of the mysteries with which this study is punctuated. In spite of gaping lacunae in the data, a collective biography yields some intriguing insights along with many unanswered and perhaps unanswerable questions.

Members of this group were born within six years of each other,

4

all into middle-class Protestant families who put a high value on education. At least two had mothers of unusual education and ability. All were early identified as exceptionally able, and teachers and college classmates saw them as sure to succeed. Two graduated in the same class from the North Carolina College for Women; two others went to other single-sex institutions; only one took an undergraduate degree from a coeducational institution: Teachers College, Columbia. Three, possibly four, knew each other. Three married academic men, and two of these had children. All spent some time teaching, though only one ever held what today would be called a tenure-track job in higher education. One spent her entire career teaching in a girl's high school. Two had the common woman's experience of being sole caretaker for an aging mother; another helped to care for her own parents and those of her husband. Each spent some time outside the South in places where there was a lively intellectual and scholarly life. Two were outspoken feminists; the other three often wrote from a feminist perspective, though it is not clear how they would have defined themselves in that regard.

I knew four of the five in their late middle age. With what in retrospect seems an inexplicable lack of curiosity about their lives before I met them, I failed to learn, while there was yet time, what I would now give a good deal to know.

The lives here delineated, different in many ways, were chillingly similar when it came to their experiences in the historical profession. Their biographies as well as their work tell us a good deal about women in the American South. Each, of course, had her own particular life trajectory. We begin, not with the oldest of the group but with the youngest, who was first to publish.

Virginia Gearhart was born November 10, 1903, in Cumberland, Maryland, where her father worked for the Baltimore and Ohio Railroad. According to her children she grew up in "a very bright family with some strong minded women." In 1921 she enrolled in Goucher College, which had been created in the 1880s by the assiduous effort of an association of Methodist women concerned about the absence of educational opportunity for women in their city. By the time Gearhart enrolled it was probably the best woman's college in the South.

The years of her adolescence had been exciting ones for ambitious girls. Debate and discussion over women's roles had gathered strength through the first two decades of the century; the world war had brought an acceleration of women's activity in the cause of peace and social justice; and the year Gearhart entered college, white women nationwide at last won the right to vote.[11]

Baltimore was well supplied with "new women" for models. Like the northern women's colleges Goucher had provided a haven for able women. The faculty included at least three historians destined for more than local fame: Mary Wilhelmine Williams, Ella Lonn, and Katharine Gallagher. In 1921 Williams initiated what may have been the first course in women's history ever offered in an American college.[12] Other faculty members included people like Gertrude Bussey in the philosophy department, a fine scholar and committed social activist, who, along with Mary Williams, was a leader in the Women's International League for Peace and Freedom. In 1916 Goucher's proud neighbor, Johns Hopkins, had appointed Florence Bamburger as its first full-time woman faculty member.

The history department soon identified Gearhart as a promising scholar, and she became something of a protégé of Katharine Gallagher, a Vassar graduate with a Wisconsin Ph.D., a student of the Italian Renaissance who also published in American history and international politics. Gallagher had been recommended to Goucher in 1915 by Frederick L. Paxson as "the most competent woman student I have had." Nine years later Gallagher in turn recommended Virginia Gearhart to Paxson and his colleagues at Wisconsin for a fellowship in history, saying that the younger woman had the solid backing of the Goucher department and adding that she needed the atmosphere of a research university, since she was a bit diffident and "is now a little too much of the 'lovely girl' type, but . . . will develop very effectively I'm sure . . . she will be the best sort of a credit to you."[13] With this support Gearhart, who was graduating Phi Beta Kappa, was awarded tuition and $250.

At Wisconsin she came into a program in which women made up half of the fifty graduate students in history and a university where nearly 15 percent of the faculty (though none in history) were women.[14] The recognized leading scholar of upper middle western history, Louise Kellog, was at the State Historical Society in Madison.

Gearhart was one of six fellowship holders from the South; a considerable number of her contemporaries in the department would go on to become leaders in the discipline (Paul Gates, Hallie Farmer, Roy Robbins, Katherine DuPre Lumpkin, and Anne King Gregorie, for example; three of these five were southerners). In such a setting there would have been little reason for a woman of scholarly aspiration to lack confidence in her prospects. Judging by the letters they would later write, her mentors, Frederick L. Paxson, Carl Russell Fish, and Selig Pearlman, were as much impressed by her charm as by her mind.

Gearhart undertook to develop a broad background in European and American history, as well as in labor economics. She went through a rigorous course of study and was reappointed each year as an assistant with increasing levels of financial aid. In 1926, at the age of twenty-three, she passed a stiff preliminary examination which required twenty hours of writing on a wide variety of questions in European and American history. Six doctoral candidates took the examination that year: three women and three men. In 1927 with the strongest possible support from her Wisconsin professors she was awarded Goucher's Van Meter Fellowship, which relieved her of the need to teach sections while she wrote her dissertation.

All this is on the record, but how Gearhart came to write first a master's thesis and then a dissertation on southern women remains a mystery. None of her mentors had written about the South, and none had evinced any interest in the history of women. Fish, with whom she did most of her work, had studied in his undergraduate years with J. Franklin Jameson and was among the little group of social historians who were beginning to change the way history was taught in the colleges. While all of these men could teach her a good bit about methods of research, when it came to formulating questions presumably she was on her own, though it is possible that Fish, whose mother had come from Augusta, Georgia, was responsive to the idea of a study of southern women.[15]

Gearhart finished her dissertation in record time. As far as I can discover it was the first scholarly effort ever made to survey the life and work of antebellum southern women.[16] Though—as one would expect from a very young and inexperienced scholar working in the almost total absence of secondary literature—it has numerous failings, her work broke new ground in significant directions. Had it been noticed by the people who were training graduate students in southern history it would have given rise to dozens of other studies, and indeed might have brought social historians decades sooner to the use of certain very important kinds of sources.[17]

The general thrust of her argument was that the status and condition of southern women were changing through the antebellum period, whether the participants knew it or not. Gearhart's grip on southern demography and class structure was shaky at best, and at some points the modern reader must wonder whether her mentors read her drafts carefully, or if they themselves were inadequately informed on these questions. It is not clear that she understood that only a minority of southerners owned slaves. Occasionally she confused the experience of planter's wives with that of yeoman farmer's wives. Part of problem may have been that since there had not yet been much in the way of scholarly work on either class or demography she relied too heavily on travelers' accounts, accepting their impressions of southern society as accurate. She did not always notice when visitors contradicted each other or make any effort to resolve the contradictions.

Fish's biographer says that he "demanded accuracy of research," and certainly Gearhart was exceedingly diligent in her search for sources. Her most original contribution rests upon the data she drew from sources which were just coming to be used by innovative social historians but which had never been examined with an eye to discovering evidence about women: court records, state legislative records, census reports, and city directories, for example. She also used travel accounts, memoirs, manuscripts in the Library of Congress, plantation accounts, and the *Southern Literary Messenger*. These sources provided the basis for her picture of the lives of mostly (though not entirely) middle-class women.[18] She devoted one paragraph explicitly to the wives of yeoman farmers and in her introduction said she had given up a plan to write a chapter on poor white people for lack of material. She recognized, as not all southern historians were careful to do, the significant differences between the most successful plantations and the least. She understood that frontier society in Alabama and Mississippi was quite different from that of the seaboard states.

She also recognized the wide differences between plantation life and urban life and demonstrated that the planter's wife, unlike her urban counterpart, was an integral part of the southern economy. Juxtaposing ideology and myth with the material reality of women's lives, she wasted no time in discarding the image of the "southern heroine who never picked up her own hankerchief" and in deploring the prevailing tendency to romanticize southern women. She remarked that the "retiring modesty," said to be their chief characteristic, was "a pose which could be assumed or discarded at will." She recognized that marriage, believed to be every woman's goal, did not always provide a life of comfort and ease and quoted a realistic young woman: "One does not always have a great deal of good humor to spare after marriage."

She also found, from a detailed examination of newspaper advertisements, that whatever the law said, in practice married women were constantly buying and selling property. All this led her to look for other evidence that the status of antebellum women was changing. She examined premarital agreements and dower rights; everywhere she looked change was indeed taking place.

A chapter on education, which quite properly related the burgeoning of female seminaries to the first tentative beginnings of public education in the South, analyzed the curricula of such schools as existed and the textbooks in common use. Tracking petitions to the legislature for overdue pay, she discovered that there were an increasing number of women teaching in public schools in Virginia. She found a similar pattern in North Carolina where there was a primitive system of examining and certifying teachers. In all of this she was breaking new ground.[19]

In one of a number of provocative offhand comments which she neglected to develop, Gearhart observed that southern women often compensated for a quite inadequate education by an intense interest in conversation; family reunions, for example, she characterized as "occasions for exchanging opinions and diffusing intelligence," adding that "the real training school of the woman was the quiet grind of the plantation and of town life." She wrote, of course, in the heyday of Deweyite thinking on the nature of education.

Contrary to all conventional wisdom, Gearhart found antebellum women to be political actors. She discovered women themselves taking an active part in a political ferment over married women's property laws and showed Virginia women petitioning the legislature nearly five hundred times in the sixteen years between 1840 and 1856.[20] In the early years many of these were petitions for divorce. She also found women in several states working to change cumbersome divorce laws. This led her to a careful examination of legislative records dealing with divorce—possibly the first time this subject had been touched in the social history of the South. These records provided a window into the prevailing expectations and attitudes toward women. It occurred to her to use census data to trace the location of divorce petitioners, comparing Missouri, South Carolina, and Virginia. She found that men and women from slaveholding families, especially those living in river valleys, were more likely than their poorer neighbors to seek divorces. She offered no hypothesis to explain this pattern, saying that "it would be too dangerous to generalize on the material at hand." This finding, therefore, is chiefly significant as an example of her imaginative use of sources in the absence of many records made by women themselves. One of her successors would suggest that poorer people were likely to resort to desertion rather than divorce since the latter was expensive and required sophistication in dealing with the legislatures or the courts.

Gearhart challenged the popular notion that women had nothing to do with business; they were, her evidence showed, engaged in "all sorts of tasks of a business nature." She discovered many women earning a living, and recognizing the legal problem of deserted wives, she found a Virginia law of 1840 permitting a woman whose husband had left to resume the legal status of *femme sole*.

Compiling tables on women's occupations in New Orleans in 1860 she found 690 women in sixty-two different occupational groups. Poorer women, she wrote, "collected ferry rates and road tolls in the country or entered all sorts of manual labor in the cities. Necessity forced the gentlewomen into the world to make their own living by writing or teaching." She suggested that the constant talk about a "woman's sphere" in the antebellum South indicated that many women must be expanding its boundaries; otherwise why would so many men be telling them not to do so?

One of her major discoveries was evidence that southern women were active in organizing voluntary associations both inside and outside the church, including such controversial groups as the Daughters of Temperance.[21] Using city directories she established the existence of a wide variety of women's associations, and from James Buckingham's account she was able to draw something of a picture of the way these groups functioned. In Charleston she discovered, to name only a few, a Ladies Benevolent Society, a Female Education Society, several church groups, and the Seaman's Friend Society. She found women even in the small communities distributing tracts and Bibles, working to convert Indians, organizing missionary societies, setting up benevolent societies to care for widows and orphans. She noted the effect of such activity on women themselves and on their communities.[22] Though she concluded that, overall, organized women in the South were "less strenuous and less effective" than their sisters in the North, she found plenty of evidence of ferment, changing patterns, and a lively associational life.

Using the *Southern Literary Messenger* as a major source, Gearhart painstakingly compiled a list of women writers. She plowed through a good deal of bad fiction for a chapter on literary expression and concluded that "the southern lady was one of the most interesting of fictional characters." She searched travelers' observations for evidence about attitudes toward religion.

Gearhart took up the question of slavery in a gingerly way and decided that most southern women were unconscious of the moral issue, though profoundly involved with the actual working of the institution. There is very little in her study about the experience of slave women, and she made no effort to see the world from their perspective. She shared the assumption of her generation that "southern women" meant white women, that slave women were somehow in a different category altogether. Viewing the institution of slavery from the white woman's perspective, she defended slave owners against what she felt was unjust criticism: "That many of the incidents of *Uncle Tom's Cabin* and of the experience of Mrs. Kemble in the south were true has to be admitted; that slavery was morally wrong must also be granted; but the fact that these southern women spent their lives caring for the negroes was one of the elements of the question which has not been so carefully examined." Her choice of words shows her to have been quite in tune with most historians of the South in the 1920s and 1930s.[23]

On the subject of miscegenation, she was bolder, though she asserted without any contrary evidence that many foreign critics "exaggerated the prevalence of this type of immorality," adding that white mothers of mulatto children were rare. (She may have been the first white historian to recognize that some mulatto children had white mothers. Since this fact contradicted all of southern mythology, evidence for it was not easy for southern historians to see.) She also dredged up considerable data about women criminals—another area of real life which did not fit the prevailing myth.

She argued that while what she called the women's "tendency to a broader life" was greatly accelerated by the Civil War, the roots of change clearly lay in the antebellum period. What she chiefly lacked, working in Wisconsin, was access to women's own personal documents. With such documents in hand she could have confirmed and deepened her analysis of many areas she was the first to examine.

In her conclusion Gearhart described what she called the Charybdis and Scylla confronting the scholar attempting to write southern social history, especially one who sought to understand women's real lives. On the one hand, she said, the postwar generation had created an altogether misleading image of the glamorous antebellum lady, and on the other, northerners and foreign visitors had painted an extremely negative picture of these same women. Neither, she thought, represented the situation as it was revealed to the serious historian. She considered the critical views of outsiders less difficult to deal with than the glamorous image, which had become, she observed, itself a dynamic force in the history of the South for three quarters of a century "after the lady has gone with the passing years."

In her study the conscientious scholar appeared at times to be at war with the well-socialized southern lady. For example, after discussing the haphazard educational opportunity available to even the most prosperous southern woman, Gearhart felt it necessary to add: "Yet the charm of the southern woman in general was undisputed," as if in some mysterious way charm could compensate for ignorance. While she honestly reported the evidence that few women were troubled by the immorality of slavery, she felt called upon to stress the fact—clear from the petitions to the legislature—that a few women wanted to emancipate their slaves and were only prevented from doing so by laws forbidding free blacks to remain in the state.[24]

Taking it all in all, the original contributions in the dissertation outweigh its failings. There was a great deal in it which could have led to rethinking some of the major premises of southern history as it was being written at the time.

In 1928 Gearhart was awarded the Ph.D., and the university, as was its custom in the 1920s, demanded a $100 deposit to be held until she published something from her dissertation.[25] With this incentive she composed a précis of its most original findings and submitted it to the *South Atlantic Quarterly* then edited by William K. Boyd and published at Duke University. Unfortunately the *Quarterly*'s records for those years have vanished, so it is impossible to know what the editors suggested in the way of changes, or how they decided to publish what was in many ways a ground-breaking article on an unorthodox subject.[26] The essay summarizes some of the most original parts of the dissertation, though it hardly does justice to her work as a whole. Much of what she was first to say has become conventional wisdom; others of her findings are just now being "discovered" by energetic young scholars. Inevitably, with the development of women's history since the 1960s, a good deal of what she wrote has been corrected by later scholarship. So it must almost inevitably be with the earliest work in a field; she was first on the ground and a true pioneer, who seems not to have realized the importance of her own work.[27]

Given that all three of her mentors were men active and well connected in the discipline one would expect to find that in no very long time she would have been asked to appear on scholarly programs, and that her work would speedily have been incorporated in the various surveys of southern history then being written. While Gearhart was working under his direction, Carl Russell Fish was finishing *The Rise of the Common Man* for the History of American Life series. The book contains eight references to women, little enough though rather more than was customary at the time. Yet he took almost no advantage of all the careful research he was just then supervising. In one paragraph he summarized Gearhart's description of the plantation wife, citing her master's thesis, but he made no other use of her numerous findings, many of which would have added depth and complexity to his study had he been perceptive enough to include "common women."[28]

With the degree in hand Gearhart behaved like one of her own southern ladies. In a cafeteria line at the university she had met Irving Gray, a young zoologist six years her senior. As soon as she had defended her dissertation they were married and he took a job at Tulane. She departed for New Orleans equipped with glowing references from her Wisconsin professors. She had, according to one, "brains, character and personality . . . [and] is an unusually competent young woman." Carl Fish described her scholarship of "the very highest rank" and added the inevitable: "[She] has an extremely pleasant personality with great charm and culture. . . . I can recommend her without the slightest qualification and in the strongest way."[29]

Paxson, when he learned that she was moving to New Orleans, ignoring the potential of her unique knowledge of southern women's history, urged her to undertake a study directly related to his own field of interest, an examination of the Spanish period of New Orleans history. She dutifully fell in with his suggestion, and a letter she wrote to him in October 1927 provides one of the few glimpses into her mind at that time.

> From all I can see I'm going to have my hands quite full if I
> tackle the period 1763–1803. . . . The diplomatic side being
> more or less well done, it seemed to me that the thing to do was
> to settle down to reading the mass of Spanish manuscripts at the
> Cabildo which no one seems to have thought much about. There
> are also some Wilkinson letters there into which I'm just aching
> to get a peep. In fact a mine seems to be housed in the old mu-
> seum. . . . I want to get at the actual relations, the activities and
> the intrigues, which went on in the period. . . . of course a lot
> will depend on what I find. . . . As far as I have read . . . no one
> has approached the period from the angle I want to survey. . . . It
> will frankly be a frontier interpretation because I think the fron-
> tier theory applies excellently to this field.[30]

The tone of this letter suggests that marriage had not diminished her zeal for historical research—and that she was still taking her cue from her mentors. Two months later Paxson wrote that he had been intending for some time to tell her that the book he had suggested she write had just appeared from Houghton Mifflin (Arthur P. Whitaker's *Spanish American Frontier*). "Of course," he added cheerfully, "there are still plenty of open subjects in the same general field, but this particular one appears to be closed."[31] Again, not a word about her unique preparation to do a book that *nobody* else was likely to do.

With this particular rug so abruptly pulled out from under her, Gray accepted a chance to do substitute teaching at Sophie Newcomb College and went to work as a research assistant to Rudolph Matas who was in process of becoming a celebrated medical historian. She joined the American Historical Association, but whether she went to its meetings or was ever on a program I do not know.

Three years later when she was twenty-seven, Irving Gray was invited to join the faculty at Duke University. For awhile Virginia Gray was able to teach in the Duke Nursing School though her primary concern for the next few years was the care of three children. She met the usual responsibilities of faculty wives. Many people knew her, but none of those who survive remember that she revealed much about herself. Some people recall that she was active in local politics and occasionally worked as a poll watcher, once, at least, for the Socialist party. During the Second World War she taught English to naval cadets. Then, for the ten years, the record is blank.

In 1955, with her children growing up, Gray applied for a job in the Manuscript Department of the Duke University Library. Her application noted that she had a Ph.D. and experience in public speaking and in writing for publication and that she was an unskilled typist. She was appointed a part-time manuscript cataloger. Using her knowledge of medical history, she cataloged the famous Trent Collection. Five years later she became assistant curator of manuscripts at a salary of $4,500. Gray took on the task of organizing the massive Socialist Party of America papers and was soon recognized as the expert guide to their use. She also undertook the painstaking and demanding task of developing an accurate genealogy of the Duke family and in the process became knowledgeable about the history of Durham. She wrote essays for the library's *Notes* and served on the Historical Commission of the Presbyterian Synod of North Carolina. Colleagues in the Manuscript Department remember her as a woman of great intelligence who could wax enthusiastic about every new find in the documents. A woman who shared another of her enthusiasms (the collection of exotic recipes) said simply: "She didn't make you feel that she was learned; she was just an ideal good friend."

In 1962 I went to the Manuscript Department in search of data for what would become *The Southern Lady* (1970) and was immediately turned over to Mrs. Gray, as she was universally called. She was a walking bibliography of useful leads to manuscript sources. We talked many times about the questions I was trying to answer. From time to time she would send me a note about a source that she had just uncovered. Never once did she hint that she herself had written on the subject. She did not mention her *SAQ* article, much less her dissertation.

Years later, I puzzled over this extraordinary modesty. A hint of explanation may be drawn from one of the few surviving pieces of Gray's correspondence. In 1964 a book-writing friend from Baltimore for whom she had done a great deal of research wrote asking for "all your official college degrees, titles etc. for my acknowledgements. I want it to look as important as possible since I am giving you such a deserved and large portion of the credit." Gray responded by return mail: "Do not bother about me. . . . I am just Dr. Virginia Gray of the Manuscript Department."[32] Perhaps this self-effacing image of herself had prevented her from suggesting that I should read her dissertation. Or perhaps after thirty years, by then a far more sophisticated historian than she had been at twenty-four, she worried that her work would not stand scrutiny. It was only after her death (which occurred on a trip to England in 1971) that I came across her article and realized to my chagrin how many leads, especially source and methodological leads, it provided which had not occurred to me.

While Virginia Gray was raising children, teaching nurses and cadets, and eventually finding her niche in a manuscript collection, a few miles away in Chapel Hill three of her contemporaries were also undertaking pioneering work in southern women's history.

Marjorie Stratford Mendenhall, born in 1900 in Randleman, North Carolina, had grown up in Greensboro. Her mother, widowed when her eldest daughter was thirteen, had struggled against heavy odds to raise and educate four children. Perhaps it was financial pressure that pushed Marjorie to finish North Carolina College for Women in three years.[33] She sang in the chorus, played volleyball, chaired the literary society, made a reputation as a debater, earned high grades, and graduated at twenty. Her classmates labeled her "brainiest" in a senior class of eighty-eight young women.

The college was still, as it had been for almost three decades, a place where women were being trained to teach, on the ground that without good schools "there can be no progress in North Carolina."[34] Among faculty and students alike there was strong support for female ambition. Alumnae of those days often spoke of two historians who particularly inspired them: Harriet Elliot, then in an early stage of her distinguished career, and Walter C. Jackson, who later became president of the college. (Some years later when Marjorie Mendenhall applied to become a candidate for the master's degree at Radcliffe, Elliott and Jackson would be among those who wrote letters of support.)

Whatever may have been her ambitions at age twenty, the evidence suggests a need for immediate self-support; there were younger siblings still to be put through college. She found a job teaching history in a Roanoke Rapids, Virginia, high school. Beginning at an annual salary of $1,200, she moved up rapidly and by 1922 was head of the Department of History earning $1,800. In 1923, following the example of several of her college teachers, Marjorie enrolled for what would be the first of three terms in Harvard summer school.[35]

In 1924 she returned to Greensboro to live with her mother and teach history at her alma mater. Summers, she was back in Cambridge, studying history, education, economics, government, anthropology, and fine arts with Harvard professors; Arthur M. Schlesinger, Sr., was a particular mentor. The fall of 1926 found her teaching at Vassar, and in the spring term of 1927 she was in residence at Radcliffe, applying for a master's degree. Because she had done most of her work in summer sessions, Radcliffe required recommendations from professors and employers: ten in all from Harvard, Vassar, North Carolina College for Women, the University of North Carolina, and South Carolina College for Women testified to her competence as a scholar and success as a teacher.[36] Back in Greensboro the new degree brought her salary to $2,600 a year.

In 1929 Mendenhall's first published book review revealed a well-developed gift for critical analysis. Appraising a biography of Varina Howell Davis (wife of Jefferson Davis) she began by noting that the book "is bound in black moiré and lettered in gold. It will look well upon the library shelf. Unfortunately it will be found there in the future." Not content with an incisive critique of the book, she went on to indicate how a good biography might have been written, adding severely: "The opportunity to throw light upon social history is little exploited." The author, Mendenhall wrote, "has imprisoned the real Varina Howell and restrained her abounding vitality in a garment that is ill-fitting"; somehow this reminded her of Amy Lowell's "Patterns," which she quoted: "What is Summer in a fine brocaded gown? / I should like to see it lying in a heap upon the ground."[37]

In 1930, caught in a depression-related cutback, Mendenhall moved to Winthrop College in South Carolina at a considerably reduced salary. A year later a combination of fellowships from the Social Science Research Council and the University of North Carolina allowed her to embark on work for the Ph.D. in history at Chapel Hill. She had dreamed of returning to Radcliffe in 1932, but the economy continued its downward spiral and her aspiration was not destined to be fulfilled.

In October 1932 she reviewed Mary Beard's *On Understanding Women* for the *North Carolina Historical Review*. At thirty-two she had had ample opportunity to test the possibilities for bright young women in the depression South, and Mary Beard was one of the few scholars just then writing about women. Mendenhall's review suggests admiration for Beard, though she thought the framework of the book—which attempted to encompass the history of the world—excessively ambitious. Her conclusion provides at least a glimpse into her own mind at that moment.

> Mrs. Beard has discarded the almost outmoded feminist view . . .
> that women are becoming like men—the idea of the "comrade."
> Equality was no fetish with her. To her men are men and women
> are women and the greatest good for both will be the free ex-
> ercise of the different but complementary qualities of each. In the
> changing conception of the relation of women to life Mrs.
> Beard's volume is important for three reasons: (1) She discards
> the sentimental approach by the use of anthropology. (2) She ex-
> plains the holdover of an inadequate view of women by what
> Henry Adams calls the inertia of history, and attacks it by means
> of social history. And (3) she avoids the pitfalls of feminism.
> Henry Adams predicted that an understanding of the new
> woman would arrive by 1940. Towards that point Mary R.
> Beard's *On Understanding Women* has carried us several
> leagues.[38]

A year later in the same journal she reviewed a new textbook written by two men. Though she knew at least one of them well she did not hold her fire. She suggested that in their treatment of the Supreme Court the authors had "skirted propaganda and almost opened themselves to the charge of an uncritical use of material. . . . the impression was left that the Supreme Court is a static institution rather than a slowly changing one." Their chapters on "Life, Letters and Art" were, she said, "additions not component parts of the work," and she added that "it is *almost* a social history." Her closing judgment—designed, perhaps, to soften the overall effect of the review—was that the book "within the spheres of economics and politics will richly reward the serious student and thinking laymen with understanding of [their] own day." Reflecting perhaps her studies at Harvard with Arthur M. Schlesinger, Sr., she was highly critical of work which did not recognize the importance of what she defined as social history.[39]

By the following year Mendenhall had finished the course work for the Ph.D. including two courses in the Law School and some in economics. In print she was bold, yet in 1991 C. Vann Woodward, searching his recollections of their long-ago days together in the graduate program, wrote: "My vague memories are of a gentle, self-effacing person lacking in self-confidence and assurance. I remember reflecting about women scholars—what reason did they have for confidence and assurance in those days. . . . They could and often did marry and become "adjunct professors"—meaning no hope of advancement or tenure, no matter how productive, professionally or biologically. What a disgrace for the academy."[40]

Confident or no, while writing her dissertation Mendenhall was also again teaching at North Carolina College for Women, and in 1934 the *South Atlantic Quarterly* published "Southern Women of a Lost Generation." No evidence remains to explain how she came to write this article at a time when she was immersed in research on the origins of agriculture in South Carolina. Judging by the books she was asked to review we can guess that Walter Jackson or another editor at the *North Carolina Historical Review* had identified her as having a special interest in women. The article bears out that perception. Did she see it as a minor effort to do something that interested her while her real challenge was the dissertation? Did someone tell her that there was no future for a scholar interested in women's history and urge her to stick to agriculture? Or did she reach that conclusion from observation? One would give a good deal to know.

In any event, somewhere along the line, perhaps in connection with her teaching, she managed to conduct the research and write the essay.[41]

There is no hint in it that she had read Gray's article, or that they had met. She used only one of the same sources (Caroline Merrick's *Old Times in Dixie*). Oddly there is no mention of the work of Julia Spruill or Guion Johnson, which had begun to appear in articles, or of Elizabeth Anthony Dexter's book or those of Alice Morse Earle, which were virtually the only secondary works which might have offered some clues to the study of women's past.[42] Whether she found these works irrelevant because they dealt with the colonial and antebellum years or whether she had not heard of their existence is anybody's guess. In any case, Mendenhall used few secondary works of any sort; her principal sources were memoirs and writings of southern women themselves and summaries of tables she had constructed from census data. The tables themselves, she noted, were "too bulky to print." Gray's study had ended in 1860; Mendenhall began in 1865 and sought to delineate postwar women's work in home, church, and school and to provide evidence of the widening of women's sphere, a widening which Gray had suggested began in the 1840s.[43]

Since Mendenhall's essay rests on material outside her major area of research it is not surprising that it is a slighter piece of work than Gray's, built on a much narrower range of sources and demonstrating less clarity of perception. She was rather more unquestioning of certain southern attitudes than Gray had been. After a somewhat muddled introduction in which she first denied the existence of class stratification in antebellum days and then immediately differentiated between planters and "the plain people" (who had not yet been labeled as such by Frank Owsley and his students) she proceeded to a clear exposition of her major points. She saw postwar women of the "plain people," including many whose ancestors had been planters, as working hard to sustain southern society and set it on a new track. Foreshadowing scholarship in women's history forty years in the future, she dug out the evidence for the varieties of women's work and described home life as characterized by "isolation, inconvenience and drudgery." At the same time, she offered examples of women who, when it became necessary, exhibited great executive skill. She went on to describe the educational crusade in which women played so large a part and the gainful occupations in which women were increasingly employed. Much of her evidence pointed toward a gradual widening of woman's sphere, and her conclusion may be taken as a self-portrait of her own generation: "For the oncoming women a new mould was being formed. By the forces of their times they were to be urban, self-assertive, and competitive. They were to be critical of inherited patterns and traditions. In increasing numbers they were to accept and to further the widening of the interests of Southern women."

Perhaps Marjorie Mendenhall saw herself as "urban, self-assertive, and competitive," for at the time she wrote this article she was working hard to develop a scholarly career, to acquire the Ph.D., and to publish. Time and again the men who wrote letters for her spoke of her as "ambitious."

She was perhaps less "critical of inherited patterns and traditions" than she thought. In 1936 she edited for the *Yale Review* a plantation recollection written in the 1870s by the southern botanist H. W. Ravenel. The memoir is a graceful exposition of the most traditional upper-class apologia for slavery: in Ravenel's memory all slaves were well fed and clothed and treated with the greatest kindness. The only troublesome issue he recognized was slavery's potential for breaking up families. Even that he thought good masters avoided at almost all cost. Mendenhall apparently accepted his picture of the institution, and in her introduction she wrote: "The life of the Negroes—their customs, habits and superstitions—is here presented with the acuteness of observation which made H. W. Ravenel the leading American mycologist of his day."[44]

In 1937 also in the *Yale Review* she published an essay on "The Rise of Southern Tenancy."[45] In it Mendenhall effectively demonstrated that, contrary to the prevailing view, tenancy had existed long before the Civil War. She found tenants already living on credit in the 1840s and sketched a history of "the tenant class." (This is particularly interesting since only three years before she had appeared to deny the existence of antebellum social classes.) In 1940 Harvard historian Paul Buck created a stir with a paper presented to the American Historical Association entitled "The Genesis of the Nation's Problem in the South" in which he drew on Mendenhall's essay.

In 1938 a review of Howard Odum's *Southern Regions of the United States* appeared in the *Southern Review* over the names of B. B. Kendrick and Marjorie S. Mendenhall. "Not for the public," Mendenhall wrote several years later to a friend who was trying to help her get a job, "I really wrote this but since Dr. Kendrick had been asked to do it and since he criticised it, his name came first."[46] Two years earlier Kendrick had called her "an excellent scholar [with] a pleasing personality and splendid character." Obviously he also found her a useful assistant. The review itself reflected Mendenhall's profound knowledge of the history of southern agriculture. She complained that Odum's work had been written in a "partial historical vacuum."[47]

From time to time she updated her file in the Radcliffe Placement Office. The dean of the Graduate School at the University of North Carolina, the professor who directed her dissertation, a member of the law faculty, A. M. Schlesinger, Sr., Ulrich B. Phillips, and others wrote enthusiastic letters on her behalf. One of the standard questions on the Radcliffe Appointments Office questionnaire had to do with typing and shorthand. Mendenhall confessed only to hunt-and-peck skill, but, in answer to another question, she claimed to engage in "all active sports except swimming." In answer to "Salary expected" she boldly wrote "$3000." A New Woman indeed!

There is fragmentary evidence that with her Ph.D. almost finished Mendenhall applied for an opening in the rapidly developing history department at Duke University. In April of that year Frank Porter Graham, president of the University of North Carolina, wrote Duke president William Few in high praise of her work, calling her one of the "best young women in our graduate program" and detailing her publications. Clara Byrd, the alumnae secretary of what was by then called the Woman's College of the University of North Carolina, also recommended her to Few, writing: "For personal reasons she does not want to return to Greensboro. She is a superior person, and I wish we could at least keep her in North Carolina."[48] Though Few assured Graham that his history department was looking into the question, there is no evidence to support his statement. The correspondence of William LaPrade who was then head of the history department shows him busily recruiting several young men, two of whom were hired. A few years earlier he had responded to another young woman who had asked for an interview by saying that there was no room for more than one woman in any Duke department and since Alice Baldwin, the dean of the Woman's College, was a historian, no other would be considered.[49] It is painful to speculate upon what this promising young woman (whom U. B. Phillips described as one of the best he had ever taught, one of two to whom he had ever given an A+) might have been able to accomplish in a department that was rapidly establishing an enviable national reputation. Letters for the young men were plentiful and fulsome in their praise. The old-boy network, as later generations have dubbed it, was vigorously in action. Only Graham, a college president notable for his concern for the powerless, and Clara Byrd, a personal friend, spoke on Mendenhall's behalf. So while Duke ignored her, she went to a job at Bradford Junior College in Massachusetts to teach "social science."

In the fall of 1938 her paper on "James Henry Hammond as Planter" was one of thirty which made up the program for the fourth annual meeting of the Southern Historical Association. The record throws no light on the fact that the paper was read for her by her graduate school friend C. Vann Woodward.[50]

In 1939 Mendenhall finally achieved the Ph.D. Her dissertation on "A History of Agriculture in South Carolina, 1790–1860" was signed by a single member of the University of North Carolina history department: Hugh Talmadge Lefler. It is a fine piece of work and is still said to be the beginning point for anyone interested in the subject. It was checked out of the university library six times in 1990—an unusual record for a fifty-year-old unpublished dissertation. She included few references to women, but those few are interesting: she called South Carolina a "society of self-made men and active women" and quoted a contemporary diary on the assertive behavior of women in town for court day (p. 90). Years later she would note that she had been offered a subsidy to publish the work in the James Sprunt Historical Series, which included the best University of North Carolina dissertations in history, but that she had never had time to take advantage of the offer.

The degree seems to have made no difference in her job prospects. At thirty-nine she had held seven teaching posts; none except the last seemed to hold much possibility of permanence, and it was far from satisfactory for a scholar with a strong interest in research and writing. At Bradford she taught American History, American Government, Introduction to Economics, Introduction to Sociology, and a general course: Introduction to the Social Sciences. The latter was described as "study of the major problems of modern society which are of direct importance to women as citizens, consumers, and homemakers. . . . particular attention is devoted to the development of a scientific attitude in dealing with social questions."

Mendenhall continued to teach at Bradford until 1942 when she married a widower, Blake Applewhite, a landowner and merchant who lived in Wilmington, North Carolina. Kinship had brought them together: Marjorie Mendenhall's sister had married the first Mrs. Applewhite's brother. After an entirely traditional wedding she moved to Wilmington and took over the responsibilities attendant upon the wife of a busy and successful businessman. She charmed a bright teen-aged stepdaughter in whose education she took a great interest and became a "second mother" to her sister's children, two of whom had been named for her.

It was wartime, and the new Mrs. Applewhite volunteered for the Red Cross, taking messages from soldiers to families. She also worked with tenants on some farms her husband owned and tried to inform herself about the prospects for cattle farming in New Hanover County. As she would be all her life, wherever she lived, she was active in the Presbyterian church.

She did not abandon scholarship. Her stepdaughter remembers "the bookcases filled with her books, shoeboxes of notecards never quite hidden away under beds, journals neatly piled on tables and in various corners of rooms and a portrait of Erasmus."[51] Yet when this same stepdaughter talked of enrolling in graduate school Marjorie Applewhite advised against it, saying that women in graduate programs were put through too much unnecessary pain.

Blake Applewhite was proud of his wife's scholarly accomplishments. The happiness of their marriage was marred only when Marjorie's mother came for long visits during which she complained about her fate and made herself a burden. Fate had dealt hardly with Mrs. Mendenhall, and she had met it bravely. Widowed young, she had worked exceedingly hard to raise and educate her children, only to have a beloved eldest son die in medical school. She was frank to say that she had counted on her "old maid daughter" to see her through, and then the old maid daughter had inconsiderately married. Though she had plenty of reason to be discouraged, her bitterness made life difficult for the rest of the family. Then, suddenly, in 1945 Blake Applewhite died. The depressed mother became a permanent resident, while Marjorie Applewhite undertook to carry on her husband's business. In order to do so she learned to drive for the first time and wheeled around the countryside in a big old prewar Oldsmobile. Her efforts were not successful, and when her stepdaughter married in 1947 she sold the business and returned to Greensboro, with her mother in tow, this time to teach at Guilford College.

Apparently her disinclination to live in Greensboro continued, and in 1949 she accepted an appointment in the sociology department at Florida State in Tallahassee. Her mother did not like living in Florida; in addition she herself may have been embroiled with unsympathetic male colleagues on matters of curriculum. Whatever the combination of circumstances, she shortly moved back to North Carolina, this time to Chapel Hill where she bought a ramshackle old house and turned it into a boarding house for graduate students as well as into an apartment for herself and her mother whose condition had not improved.[52]

Jobs were not easy to find. Marjorie Applewhite reluctantly concluded that the men who ran the university had no interest in hiring women. The best she could manage were part-time assignments teaching political science to freshmen and some work in the extension program.

Even in this discouraging situation she continued to do research.[53] In 1958 she published a fine article on "Sharecropper and Tenant in the Courts of North Carolina" based on state supreme court cases.[54] It is an extension and rethinking of the *Yale Review* article published more than twenty years earlier. She had discovered one case dealing with tenancy dated 1811 and offered evidence that overseers had worked on shares as early as 1741. She concluded that "before the Civil War the terms, sharecropper, and cropper, were familiarly used in connection with agricultural crops as well as in connection with turpentine orcharding."[55]

In 1958 when my family moved to Chapel Hill, Mrs. Applewhite, as she was called (not Dr. or Professor as was common for the male faculty), was still teaching introductory courses in political science. The law courses she had taken years before had contributed to her research designs, as the article on tenancy demonstrated, and her varied experience had included teaching government as well as history. She welcomed us graciously, but—though I think she knew of my interest in southern women's history—like Virginia Gray she never mentioned her own work, and I only discovered her article on the subject after her death.

She died too young under troubling circumstances. A trip to Europe in 1960 and an appointment (worked out by an admiring former student) to the University of Maryland's overseas program in Germany rather than being a triumphant new beginning led to, or was coincident with, a major depression of spirit. She came home with her contract unfulfilled.[56] An experimental drug for depression relieved her symptoms, but unfortunately it also severely damaged her immune system. She died in August 1961 after six days' illness, following a fairly minor infection.

Records of her life which she had carefully preserved have since been destroyed; she exists principally in her published work and in the fond recollections of many family members. One grandchild, a Jesuit priest, when he was consulted for this essay reminded his mother that Erasmus, whose picture had accompanied Marjorie Mendenhall Applewhite on all of her travels, had also faced rejection and the displeasure of his colleagues and much of the scholarly world, but he had also felt that education was the means to overcome the barriers that separate people. He remembers his step-grandmother as a born educator who recognized and encouraged the interests and potential of each of the four Applewhite grandchildren. He guessed that she must have done this for many students as well.[57]

Family recollections picture an usually straightforward woman. Her stepdaughter has observed that she refused to flatter and dissemble "as women of her generation and mine have had so often to do." Nor did she tolerate fools very well. "I suspect that her honesty must have been off putting to many of her male colleagues," the step-daughter adds.[58] But it is not necessary to find personal peccadilloes to explain the hard time women, especially southern women, had

The Young Voices

Virgina Gearhart Gray, c. 1928.
(Courtesy of John Gray)

Marjorie Mendenhall, 1920.
(From Pine Needles, *the yearbook of the North Carolina College for Women)*

Julia Cherry, c. 1920.
(Courtesy of Robert Miller)

Guion Griffis, c. 1922.
*(From the Guy Benton Johnson
Papers in the Southern Historical
Collection, University of North
Carolina Library at Chapel Hill)*

Eleanor Miot
Boatwright, 1936.
*(From Maids and a Man,
the yearbook of Tubman
High School, Reese
Library, Augusta College,
Augusta, Ga.)*

The Mature Voices

Virginia Gearhart Gray, c. 1970.
(Duke University Archives)

Marjorie Mendenhall, 1942.
(Courtesy of Elizabeth Applewhite Pearsall)

Julia Cherry Spruill,
date unknown.
(Courtesy of Robert Miller)

Guion Griffis Johnson and Guy Benton Johnson, 1959.
(From the Guy Benton Johnson Papers in the Southern Historical Collection, University of North Carolina Library at Chapel Hill)

Eleanor Miot
Boatwright, 1950.
(From Maids and a Man,
*the yearbook of Tubman High
School, Reese Library, Augusta
College, Augusta, Ga.)*

being accepted in academia. The impressive thing in Applewhite's case is that despite periods of severe depression she never quite gave up.

Two other Chapel Hill women whose work appears here were friends and, though quite different in personality, shared many experiences. Julia Cherry had been born January 8, 1899, in Rocky Mount, North Carolina, where her father was postmaster and her mother—who has been a schoolteacher—was a Christian Science practitioner well known in the community for her gifts as a counselor of troubled people. She was also a supporter of suffrage and an advocate of birth control. Julia was eldest of three children, all of whom their mother encouraged to be good students. At sixteen she enrolled at North Carolina State Normal and Industrial School.[59] Following her mother's lead, she had been a suffragist in high school, and she was a campus leader in college. The 1920 yearbook pictures her in many different settings: the literary club, the chorus, the basketball team. In many of these she and Marjorie Mendenhall shared honors.[60] The yearbook took note of her friendship with Corydon Spruill, an outstanding student at the University of North Carolina, soon to be appointed Rhodes Scholar. She had known him for years, possibly since grade school. In those days Rhodes Scholars were not permitted to be married, so she stayed home in North Carolina and taught in Rocky Mount High School while he went off to England to study economics. When he came home in 1922 to become an assistant professor at his alma mater they were married. Two years later Julia was appointed to teach history and government at the Chapel Hill High School. In the small, close-knit faculty community of the 1920s she soon met two weighty University of North Carolina historians: R. D. W. Connor and William Whately Pierson. With their encouragement she embarked upon a master's degree in history, and in 1923 as the only woman in Pierson's seminar she wrote a prizewinning thesis on Orestes Brownson. On the strength of this Howard Odum made her a research assistant in the new Institute for Research in the Social Sciences for the purpose of writing a book about southern women. Her first thought had been to study changing attitudes toward women, a subject which would remain of concern though her long life. She realized, as she later said, that "only a very limited amount of research had been attempted in the whole field of social history of the South," and that she would have to lay the groundwork herself. For a beginning she decided to make a study of the life experience of women in the southern colonies. Turning over the sometimes crumbling colonial records gave her great pleasure, and she saw in them many things that had never before been noticed. Her work went forward when Corydon Spruill was invited to spend two years as a visitor at Harvard. Cambridge gave her access not only to the magnificent collections of Widener Library and the Massachusetts Historical Society but also to the encouragement of Arthur M. Schlesinger, Sr., who in 1920 had issued a clarion call for young scholars to undertake the study of women's past, and who was destined to have a major influence on her thinking about the nature of history.[61]

Doubtless trained as an undergraduate by the same Walter Jackson who had prepared and encouraged Marjorie Mendenhall and certainly by Connor and Pierson at Chapel Hill (themselves careful users of primary documents), she was a meticulous researcher. In the end she spent more than a decade reading every extant source that might throw light on colonial women's experience in the South, and in 1938, after five preliminary articles had appeared, the University of North Carolina Press published *Women's Life and Work in the Southern Colonies.*

Opening with a chapter called "Women Wanted" in which she showed just how they were valued in the early English settlements, she went on to cover such subjects as architecture, work, childbirth, courtship, education, reading, and the law. Possibly the most original chapters were those dealing with women's work beyond the domestic circle: in professional occupations and as shopkeepers, artisans, tavern keepers, and planters. Her bibliography, which listed only primary sources, filled twenty-five tightly printed pages.

The chapter included here is representative. Like all wise historians Spruill knew that prescription and experience are not the same; she discovered through careful study of manuscripts, newspapers, and court records that what she called the "prosaic businesslike manner in which marriages were often made" led sometimes to conjugal affection, loyalty, and happiness and other times to dissension and discord. She provided her reader with cases on both sides of the ledger, and concluded with typical restraint: "Many pages of court minutes are filled with altercations, scandalous accusations and recriminations, and patched-up agreements between husbands and wives, which indicate a state of matrimony somewhat out of keeping with the ideals set up by domestic conduct books and other guides to conjugal felicity."

Reviews of the book were mostly a chorus of praise. Spruill's friend Mary Beard provided a typically quirky discussion in *Social Forces*. Beard chose to take up a good bit of her space castigating a man who was quoted on the dust jacket as calling this book the very best ever done in the field. She doubted that he knew of any others and perhaps was miffed that he seemed quite unaware of her own work. Praising the book overall, she deplored its failure to deal with the intellectual life of southern colonial women, though she admitted that the evidence for such a life was meager in the extreme.[62]

Other reviews were more straightforward. Howard Mumford Jones, who had recently moved from the University of North Carolina to Harvard, wrote in the *Boston Evening Transcript:* "Such a book really creates a usable past, because it illuminates history in probable human terms and because one has confidence in an author who has gone to so much trouble in ascertaining what the facts were, not what she might wish they had been." Professor Schlesinger wrote that it was a "model of research and exposition, an important contribution to American social history to which students will constantly turn." Mary Benson, who in 1935 had published her Columbia dissertation on eighteenth-century women, also praised the book, though she complained of a certain amount of repetition. She singled out the chapters on women and the law, on conjugal felicity, and on women criminals for special mention. Eudora Ramsey Richardson, writing in the *William and Mary Quarterly,* thought it "a book for which feminists have been waiting. Men for the most part have been the authors of Southern histories and, interested as they are in martial matters and in statecraft, have expunged women's work from the record."[63]

Despite all this praise, the book rather quickly disappeared into libraries, where it was occasionally used by scholars of the colonial South, not always with adequate attribution.[64] In 1972, as women's history was being introduced in one college and university after another, W. W. Norton brought out a paperback edition which greatly widened its audience. Late in her life, in a moment of uncharacteristic self-congratulation, Spruill said to a newspaper interviewer: "I didn't cut any corners. I was a careful student. Nothing was thrown in. I knew all of it was right."[65] And so it was. Interpretations change; interest in the plain people has expanded; interest in the world seen through the eyes of slaves has developed; explicit theory has come to be highly valued. But despite all the excellent work that has been done since, *Women's Life and Work* remains the place to start for scholars interested in colonial southern women. It is also essential reading for any scholar interested in the social history of the colonial South.

Through her life Spruill persisted in defining herself as a "housewife who does a little writing and research in history." Until 1949 she taught at the University of North Carolina as a part-time instructor in social science, a task usually allotted to graduate students, but by that year her husband had become a senior administrator in the university and both sets of aging parents were in need of attention.

Duty was a major principle in Julia Spruill's life.[66] She took the responsibilities of the dean's wife with the utmost seriousness, inviting his advisees for dinner, but not before she had read each of their files so that she could treat each one as an individual. With the help of a highly competent housekeeper, who was her friend as well as her employee, she carried out the extensive social responsibilities attendant upon Corydon Spruill's position in the university.

Her interest in history and in women did not abate: she was vice president of two historical societies and president of the University Women's Club as well as of the local chapter of the American Association of University Women. She belonged for fifty years to The Club, a group of fifteen or so Chapel Hill women who met weekly to discuss books over lunch and sewing. She guided their reading, sometimes to history books.[67] As far as I have been able to discover she did not reach beyond the area to join either the Southern or the American Historical Association.

It was my great good fortune to meet Julia Spruill in 1959 shortly after I first discovered her book. She was delighted to find a younger scholar following her lead into southern women's history and shared her accumulated knowledge with openhanded generosity. She was as intrigued as I was by the gap between the image and the reality of southern ladies. In one conversation she reflected on the strange expectation that southern matrons should never seem to be busy but nevertheless were also expected to perform every household duty perfectly. "All those dinner parties," she sighed "when you prepare for three days and then when it happens it appears to occur by magic!" Though she never faltered in her admiration for her husband or her willingness to work on his behalf, there were times when she looked back with longing to her years of scholarship and wished that in the ensuing years there had been less responsibility for entertaining and more time for research. Corydon Spruill for his part was always proud of her accomplishments, and no one was more pleased than he when her book began to receive belated recognition in the 1970s.

One Sunday afternoon not long after the book was reissued my class in the Social History of American Women came for tea with Julia Spruill as the honored guest. At first she was so shy it seemed that she might simply sit quietly through the whole affair, but the students, who had just read the book, were full of questions about how she had accumulated so much evidence. Gradually she forgot herself and by the end of the afternoon was swapping stories with them as if she were a student again herself.

When the University of North Carolina belatedly conferred a distinguished alumna award upon her she was amazed—but grateful. By then in her eightieth year, she had developed what she considered to be an embarrassing tendency to drop off to sleep in public places. At the luncheon before the ceremony she was introduced to C. Vann Woodward, who was also receiving an award. When she confided her fear of falling asleep in front of a large audience, he promised to sit beside her and make sure that she did not disgrace herself on this great occasion. Of course (as one might have guessed) excitement did the trick, and the surveillance Professor Woodward had so graciously promised proved unnecessary. She smiled benignly on the audience, many of whom had never heard her name.[68]

In 1984 the Southern Association of Women Historians voted to establish a book prize in Julia Spruill's honor. Responding to the letter telling her of this recognition, she resorted to Pericles: "For it is only the love of honour that never grows old; and honour it is, not gain, as some would have it, that rejoices the heart of age and helplessness." Two years later, on January 27, 1986, she died. Corydon Spruill lived a few years longer and upon his death left an endowment to establish the Julia Cherry Spruill Chair in the history of women at the University of North Carolina.

Julia Spruill's friend Guion Griffis Johnson like Spruill, had been a wunderkind in college. Though they were friends and colleagues for more than sixty years, and though each was a superb scholar who made essential contributions to southern social history and the history of southern women, there were great differences in their approach to life as historians and as professionally trained women.

Guion Griffis had been born in 1900 in Wolfe City, Texas. She grew up in Greenville, Texas, where her mother was the only woman in town with a college degree. Guion and her sisters went to Baylor College for Women where she graduated at twenty with every honor the college could bestow. Like Marjorie Mendenhall and Julia Cherry, Guion Griffis was the star of her college yearbook—it is hard to find an activity in which she did not take part. She also wrote for the yearbook a bitter and powerful little short story "Birds and Beasts," dealing with an abused wife, which may suggest why her classmates voted her "most literary girl."[69]

Prominent among her activities was the editorship of the school newspaper. When she graduated Baylor College for Women immediately made her an associate professor of journalism, and in 1923, in order to qualify for the job she already held, she went off to take a degree in journalism at the University of Missouri. On her return she organized the Texas High School Press Association which would become a significant institution in the state. In the same year she married Guy Benton Johnson, a Baylor University graduate who had come back to teach after taking a master's degree in sociology at the University of Chicago. Years later she would say that they agreed before the wedding that she would continue with an independent career.

Guy, who was already achieving recognition for his work on the Ku Klux Klan, attracted the attention of Howard Odum who was in the process of organizing the Institute for Research in the Social Sciences at Chapel Hill. When Odum offered him one of the Institute's first fellowships Guion announced that she had no intention of starving in Chapel Hill and that unless Professor Odum had something for her she (and presumably Guy) would stay in Texas where both had jobs. Odum must have been anxious to attract Guy Johnson, for he worked out an assistantship for Guion—at the same rate of pay—sight unseen. In later life she would remember her early encounters with Professor Odum as occasionally stormy. He put her to work, she said, reading proof, which, as she told him after a few days, was not what she had come to North Carolina to accomplish. Before long she, like her husband, was enrolled in a Ph.D. program in sociology. After a year of puzzling over the thesis topic assigned by the sociology department, "The Press as a Social Force in North Carolina," which, based on her own experience as a journalist, she thought to be an impossible subject for research, she found her way to the history department, which suited her much better. Under the benign and thoroughly paternalistic direction of R. D. W. Connor (patron also of Julia Spruill and later to be the first Archivist of the United States), she was introduced to primary research. Connor sent her to the North Carolina Department of the Archives and History to read antebellum letters, and on her own she discovered the possibilities in court and legislative records. This, it turned out, was exactly what she had been waiting for. She had the born historian's profound love of documents and insatiable desire to accumulate evidence. She also had the gifted innovator's capacity to see more in her sources than had been seen before, as she soon began to demonstrate in a series of studies on the social history of antebellum North Carolina.

Somewhere along the way she wrote an essay on "Feminism and the Economic Independence of Women," which, though it won a prize and appeared in *Social Forces* in 1925, was not a good forecast of her more mature view of the world. With all the scorn young people are wont to heap upon their elders she criticized the feminists of the time for encouraging women to work for pay, though she made an exception of course for intellectuals "who alone can work under conditions sufficiently mild to enable them to couple motherhood and labor, and they alone have aspirations, ideals, illusions."[70]

By age twenty-seven Johnson had taken the Ph.D. and, to her amazement, in competition with three men had won the Smith Research Award. She had assumed a woman would not stand a chance. She began at once to expand her dissertation into a book, and as her research developed she sent off articles to the *North Carolina Historical Review*. In July 1929 a brief note appeared in the *American Historical Review:* "An article by Dr. G. G. Johnson of the University of North Carolina is another of those interesting and valuable studies which *he* has been making of life in North Carolina before the Civil War." It would not be long before southern historians, at least, would know that "Dr. G. G. Johnson" was not a man.

Her demonstrated research capacities inspired Odum to assign her to a study the Institute had agreed to undertake on the Sea Islands of the Carolinas. Published in 1930 as *The Social History of the Sea Islands with Special Reference to St. Helena Island, South Carolina,* Johnson's book is notable for its careful attention to the history of white women and slaves of both sexes. Writing at almost the same time as Virginia Gearhart and almost certainly having read Julia Spruill's manuscript, Johnson delineated the role of the white planter's wife more precisely than it had been done up to that time. She discovered that even in that somewhat remote agricultural community antebellum white women had their Dorcas Society, Tract Society, and Benevolent Society.[71]

In a chapter on "The Slave Community" she dealt at length with the daily life of black women, described the way black children had been cared for on Sea Island plantations, examined the nature of discipline, and suggested some thoughts about the relationships between black men and women. She provided an impressive bibliography of primary sources and appears to have examined every available document which might throw light on the history of the islands.

With the Sea Island study completed, Johnson turned back to work on the book which would come to be recognized as a classic, one that even yet has not been replicated for any other state, *The Social History of Ante-bellum North Carolina* (1937).

By concentrating on one state Johnson was able to look in depth at many of the social and cultural patterns Virginia Gearhart had identified as well as many others. The book was a model of the kind of study scholars such as Arthur M. Schlesinger, Sr., Dixon Ryan Fox, Carl Russell Fish, and Mary Beard were urging on American historians. As she had in the Sea Island study, Johnson used an enormous variety of sources to paint a picture of life as North Carolinians lived it in an era hitherto generally described in terms of the national struggle over slavery, over constitutional interpretations, the tariff, and westward expansion. Rather than using traditional political categories she examined religion, education, the social life of the slave, the free Negro, the court system, philanthropy, the press, and intellectual life.

Like Gearhart, Johnson dealt forthrightly with the issue of miscegenation and recognized that white women had indeed borne mulatto children.[72] For example, she found that one Thomas White had petitioned the legislature in 1800 to legitimate certain of his children. He said that he had been lawfully married, but when his wife gave birth to a black child he had left her to live with another woman, by whom he had had ten children. In 1832 a North Carolina court held that the birth of a mulatto child was not always sufficient cause for a divorce. In a remarkable opinion the judge said, in effect, that if a man married a woman who already was pregnant at the time of marriage he had to take his chances that the child would be a mulatto. Tabulating divorce petitions Johnson found that the third most common cause for such petitions in early nineteenth-century North Carolina had been "cohabitation with a Negro."[73]

The chapter on "Family Life" reprinted here paid close attention to the history of antebellum white women and children. Though she understood the expectations set before southern women, Johnson was well aware of the gap between expectation and reality. Combing manuscripts, legal documents, and newspapers she showed the extraordinary range of responsibilities that fell upon the women of well-to-do families. Her data yielded very little about the work of yeoman farmers' wives and daughters, but she, like Gearhart and Mendenhall, found masses of information about women wage earners. Some of what she found in legal records and census data about wage-earning women was quite similar to what Julia Spruill had discovered about eighteenth-century working women.

The section on children, beginning as it logically should with childbirth, has a great deal to do with women as well. Though Johnson refrained from outright comment on such things as the legal right to beat one's wife or the extraordinarily self-serving opinions of some North Carolina male judges, by clever juxtaposition she gave her readers plenty to think about. While she carefully documented the increasingly negative response of the North Carolina press to the women's rights movement as it gained momentum in the North, she added: "Nevertheless, southern women in their writings, their church activities, their education, and their daily work, were beginning also to cry, 'Equality!'" Quite independently (for though they lived only a dozen miles apart I can find no evidence that they ever met) she came to many of the same conclusions, based on far more research, that Gearhart had suggested a decade earlier.

By 1939 the Institute for Research in the Social Sciences was becoming well known for its studies in southern race relations, and in that year both Johnsons were recruited by Gunnar Myrdal to provide some of the basic research upon which he would base his magnum opus, *The American Dilemma*. Her assignment was to write about the development of racial ideologies. Here too, Guion Johnson was far ahead of most of her contemporaries. Four decades before "the social construction of race" became a common term among historians she was writing about "the invention of the Negro."

By this time the Johnsons had two children, and Guion Johnson demonstrated the same drive and ingenuity which characterized her scholarship in the organization of the dual-career family. The Johnsons moved to New York City for part of the time they were working with Myrdal. A nursemaid went with them, and when one of the children fell ill a widowed friend from North Carolina moved in to take charge of the children.

When the Myrdal work was over the family returned to North Carolina. When she had embarked on the Ph.D. in history Connor had assured Guion Johnson that there would be a job for her when she finished, but somehow it had not been forthcoming. Indeed her experience with some of the men in the department had been anything but encouraging. One announced in her hearing that women simply could not teach history.[74] Another, with equal certainty, had remarked that no woman was worth more than $125 a month.

The Second World War brought the opportunity the history department had refused to provide. Johnson was recruited to teach American History and Naval Strategy in the Navy V-12 Program because, she said, none of the men in the history department wanted to prepare such a course. She dived in with her usual energy, and fifty years later one of her former students wrote to say she had been a fine instructor, a good friend and adviser.[75] There were some returned veterans in her class who, as she remembered it, were astounded to learn from her what they had really been doing in North Africa.

In 1944 Guy Johnson went to Atlanta as director of the Southern Regional Council, an organization of southern liberals interested in economic reform and beginning to be concerned about race as well, and Guion, faced with a choice between a poorly paid teaching job at Agnes Scott College and a well-paid one as executive secretary of the Georgia Council on Social Welfare, chose the latter. Perhaps her study of social history had prepared her for work with all kinds of Georgians; in any case she traveled the state infusing the program with energy.

The war ended; the Johnsons again returned to Chapel Hill, and—as she told the story to an interviewer late in her life—Guion again confronted R. D. W. Connor with his promise that there would be a job for her if she finished the Ph.D. Connor patted her on the head, figuratively speaking, and announced that the history department was just then so filled with strife and bitterness that it was no place for a lady. He advised her to go back to her research. When she went over his head to the chancellor, saying that with a child at Harvard she needed to earn money, she got even more pointed advice. At that moment Guy Johnson's well-known liberal views on race had made him anathema to a little group of powerful men on the University Board of Trustees, and his job was at risk. The chancellor advised her to join as many women's organizations as she could find in order to make friends with the wives of influential men who might soften their husbands' views so that when the Board of Trustees had to vote on the reappointment of her husband there would be no problem.[76]

Whether this was the way it really happened there is no way to know, but what we do know is that Guy Johnson was not fired, and that Guion Johnson embarked on what would become one of the most distinguished careers of leadership in voluntary associations ever seen in North Carolina. She became, and remained for more than forty years, a vital figure in one organization after another, ranging across the spectrum from the Woman's Society for Christian Service of the Methodist Church to the YWCA, the American Association of University Women, and Chi Omega sorority. She created a comprehensive North Carolina Council of Women's Organizations which became a legislative force in the state and an important generator of public opinion.

Her leadership was not based so much on charisma as on a strong practical bent. In 1957, for example, working with the national American Association of University Women, Johnson helped to devise a strategy for supporting school integration in the southern states. She stood strong for principle but also offered sensible advice on the necessity for organizing support in advance if the AAUW was to take a stand in favor of implementing the *Brown* decision.[77]

In all of her work in voluntary groups Johnson preached the cardinal principle that members would work to carry out a program in direct proportion as they had had a hand in creating it. It is easy enough to formulate such a principle; Johnson had the necessary ability to put it into practice, which was one reason for her extraordinary success as a leader in so many associations.

By the 1960s when I first met Guion Johnson she was the preeminent figure in the eyes of women's groups all over North Carolina. She was the logical person to chair a committee on voluntary associations of the North Carolina Governor's Commission on the Status of Women, which she did with her customary intelligence and efficiency. The introduction to her segment of the commission's report is a deft summary of the history of women's associations, and the recommendations from her committee were possibly the most practical of any the commission made.[78]

Through it all, and busy as she was, Johnson never abandoned scholarship. In 1949 in a careful, thoughtful, and well-researched essay on "The Ideology of White Supremacy, 1876–1910" she dissected the rationale for white supremacy before and after the Civil war.[79] She followed this in 1957 with "Southern Paternalism toward the Negroes after Emancipation."[80] In 1965 in an essay called "The Changing Status of Southern Women" among other things she analyzed the part played by women's voluntary associations in bringing about social change, recognizing what few southern white historians seemed to know: that side by side with the complex structure created by white women there was a parallel structure of black women's voluntary associations which played a major role in black community life.[81] In 1967 the North Carolina Council of Women's Organizations published her excellent study called *Volunteers in Community Service*.[82] Though it was designed to be a handbook for would-be leaders of voluntary associations Johnson put the subject of voluntary activity in a broad historical context.

Together she and her husband wrote a history of the University of North Carolina Institute for Social Science Research, the organization with which both their careers had been so closely associated.[83] In a lighter vein, but thoroughly researched, was a splendid paper based on a series of letters written in the 1850s by Margaret Ann Burwell which she delivered in 1976 to the Historic Hillsborough Commission. In due course she along with her husband, too, received an alumna award from the University of North Carolina.

In her eighties Johnson continued to demonstrate the gift for research and writing which had made her Connor's pride and joy in her twenties.[84] By an odd coincidence in 1982 she presented a paper on the subject Marjorie Mendenhall had delineated so well in the 1930s and again in 1954: antebellum tenant farmers. She, like Mendenhall, described debt peonage as an antebellum phenomenon and showed that 29,000 free Negroes had been part of the "landless people."

Remarkable as *Ante-bellum North Carolina* was, and despite the positive reviews in historical journals when it was published, Guion Johnson did not feel that her work was well understood or much appreciated by the men who dominated the profession. Southern historians were slow to broaden their interests to include social history; she had been among the first to move in that direction.[85] Finally, in her eightieth year, came the kind of recognition she had craved. In a study of the historiography of North Carolina three well-known male historians in separate essays praised her book: one called it "one of the best . . . ever written about North Carolina," a second labeled it "monumental," and a third used the adjective "extraordinary." She wrote thanks to each of them.[86] Her thank-you notes are revealing:

> I am so glad that I have lived long enough to see *Ante-Bellum North Carolina* credited with being an honest historical effort. Most traditional historians of my acquaintance seemed affronted by it and a few were hostile. You can understand my gratification, therefore, at your . . . kind words on its behalf.[87]

Two years later the American Association of State and Local History gave her an Award of Merit.

Early in the 1980s a young North Carolina writer working on a project designed to allow older black women to tell their own life stories went to Guion Johnson for help.[88] Years later the writer recorded her memory of that visit: "Johnson was plump, dressed in a good dark Sunday dress, like my grandmother . . . and, like my grandmother somewhat mild at first, well-mannered, easy with a new person. . . . [She] offered to give me names of black women I might interview. . . . I remember a woman in Rocky Mount . . . who, because Guion Griffis Johnson had recommended me . . . was eager to see me. . . . She revered Johnson."[89] This acquaintance with a wide variety of black women (many of whom had been active in women's associations) was not surprising. Ever since the Myrdal study both Johnsons had been leaders in the small group of southern intellectuals who were trying to improve the condition of black people in the South. Their concern took many practical as well as theoretical forms.

Johnson died in her eighty-ninth year. In a long obituary the local newspaper noted that she and her husband had been the first research assistants at the Institute, and that she had done pathbreaking work under its auspices. When Guy Johnson died in May 1991 a detailed obituary in the *New York Times* praised his long life of work for improved relations between the races but did not mention his wife or their collaboration over many years.[90] If Guion, from her perch in heaven, got a glimpse of the obituary I am sure she told St. Peter: "You see, that's the way it always is; women are overlooked!"

In fantasy I like to imagine that in the summer of 1937 a woman who had come to the Duke University summer school, intent on earning an M.A. degree, somehow met Guion Johnson who was only twelve miles away. They would have had an exciting time together: Johnson was finishing her *Ante-bellum North Carolina,* and Eleanor Boatwright was embarking on a study of the status of women in antebellum Georgia. They shared an enthusiasm for primary research and shared, too, the sensitivity which permitted them to see women in their sources. Though there is no direct evidence that Boatwright had read Johnson's work (which was already becoming available in articles in the *North Carolina Historical Review*), they were much alike in their interests and findings and in the kinds of evidence they used.

In a logical world Eleanor Boatwright would have turned to Guion Johnson to direct her master's thesis but Johnson, though the best-qualified person in the country to undertake that task, had no academic affiliation and no widely recognized standing as a scholar. In the world as it really was Boatwright worked with a male historian, a scholar of great distinction, whose interest in women's history, judging by his published work, was minuscule.[91] But I am ahead of my story.

Whether purposefully or accidentally, Eleanor Miot Boatwright left few traces of her life for those who came after. Perhaps if we could ask her she would say that her legacy is to be found in the lives of thousands of young women who had studied history under her tutelage at the Tubman Girls High School in Augusta, Georgia, many of whom, half a century after her death, still speak with awe and enthusiasm about her teaching, the example she set, and the encouragement she gave them.

Whatever the reason, no papers seem to have survived, and a reasonably assiduous search for biographical data has turned up very few verifiable facts. She was born in Augusta, Georgia, in 1895. Her parents had earlier lost two sons in infancy. Her father, after trying a number of different careers, by the time she was growing up had a florist shop in North Augusta, South Carolina. She enrolled at the all-female Tubman High School, named for an early Augusta feminist, Emily Tubman, and considered to be one of the best schools in the state, one in which the most ambitious young teachers in Georgia hoped to find jobs. There Boatwright came under the influence of an extraordinary woman named Julia Flisch, who, identifying her as a talented young person and adopting her as a protégé, urged her to seek a university education. Since the University of Georgia did not admit women, Flisch recommended the University of Tennessee. Boatwright took the advice but later transferred to Teachers College, Columbia University, where she graduated in 1918. Meanwhile her father had died, and her mother had taken over the florist business. There are hints that Eleanor would have liked to stay in the larger world of New York City, but as a dutiful daughter she came home to live with her mother and shortly began teaching at Tubman herself. Since appointments to the school were so much in demand they usually went to women who had served a successful apprenticeship elsewhere in the state, often to women who had master's degrees from major universities.[92] We can infer that this young woman was already recognized as unusually able, or that Julia Flisch's influence opened the door, or both.[93]

She was early on recognized as a remarkable teacher and as a leader on behalf of women teachers. Julia Flisch remained her mentor on all fronts.[94] Sometime in the 1920s Flisch led a strike for equal pay for women teachers. Some of her contemporaries, now in their nineties, remember that in the 1930s Boatwright followed suit by organizing a teachers' strike over the issue of equal pay and retirement benefits for women.[95] In the process she helped lay the initial groundwork for the first teacher retirement program for the state of Georgia and was deeply involved in an effort to make sure that women teachers received benefits equal to those provided for men.[96]

A woman who had been her student wrote in 1992:

> Eleanor Boatwright was my first female historian role model. She encouraged me to study and enjoy history during my four years. . . . When I was a Freshman, I asked her for a world history book to study over the summer. . . . She found me a left over text. . . . I remember overhearing my mother talking to Miss B. about how much I studied, and Miss B. saying that I had not used one fifth (or some tiny amount) of my brain power yet. I was amazed. . . . She gave a pop quiz the first five minutes of every class . . . you had to be prepared to survive. I remember it as very interesting and I couldn't wait for the next installment.[97]

In 1934, by then sixteen years beyond the A.B., Boatwright enrolled in Duke University summer school to study history and made the highest grades the university bestowed. After several more summers in residence she presented a thesis for the master's degree called "The Status of Women in Georgia, 1783–1860." It was 296 pages of mostly excellent social history.[98]

The thesis is notable for its skillful use of a very wide variety of primary sources. Taking her cue from Julia Flisch, and doubtless also from Charles Sydnor who directed her research, she examined legislative records, court records from many different levels, wills, manuscript census returns, as well as manuscript personal documents from a variety of depositories. She combed the libraries for periodicals, published memoirs, essays by antebellum observers, and advice books and examined hundreds of newspapers. The work, in short, is thoroughly grounded in almost every source that any social historian would think of using. The charts she constructed from census data are models of their kind. Her definition of "status" was so broad that she could easily have called her work a social history of antebellum Georgia women. The thesis is better than many Ph.D. dissertations which have passed muster in the intervening years.

She wrote with delicate irony and an ever-present sense of humor. Her description of the situation of the first white women in Georgia is typical: "Indians and forests, and unplowed fields; toil, and danger, and unknown lands increased the weight of their chains without materially lengthening them." Introducing a chapter on courtship and marriage she wrote:

> In the State of Georgia prior to the Civil War an unmarried woman stood equal to her brother before the bar, but in her husband she found her legal grave and by his death her resurrection. The code under which she lived was biting with the acid of an old bachelor—St. Paul; and stinging with the vengeance of a henpecked husband—Lord Coke.

Many things she found in the case law and in other documents amused her, but she was not amused by the basic constraints laid upon women by law and social expectation. She made a thorough and sophisticated analysis of the legal disabilities women experienced. In the essay reprinted here she remarked:

> The ceremonial pledge of a man to his bride "with all my worldly goods I thee endow" did not have the legal significance of a valentine. For the civil law saw to it that the new-made husband lost nothing of his own at the altar and took away from it all his bride possessed—perhaps even the ring with which he made his vow.

Along the way she made many intriguing discoveries. For example, that advertisements for runaway wives were still common in antebellum Georgia. She understood the existence of the "plain folk" better than most southern historians of her generation, and her detailed attention to health and sickness showed that she had learned a good deal from Richard Shryock. She recognized the gap between law and custom, between image and reality. She confirmed Gray's evidence that women were politically active, that they were gradually getting control of their own earnings.

She reinforced Guion Johnson's assertions about the importance of miscegenation and made the point that not all interracial sex was restricted to the lower classes. For example, she discovered records of a magistrate in Charleston who had sent away a mulatto girl said to be the daughter of a white woman of a leading family. She also found a number of cases of slaves who gained their freedom by proving that their mothers had been white. Her data on the debate in Georgia over the definition of "Negro" has an extraordinarily modern ring. It seems quite likely that Johnson and Boatwright were the first white historians of the South to deal seriously with this set of issues, and almost certainly they were among the first to discuss the possibility that some mulatto children had white mothers.[99]

Using city directories to good effect, Boatwright confirmed the findings of both Gray and Johnson with respect to the widespread development of women's voluntary associations.[100]

In her section on women's work Boatwright (who had said at the beginning that her thesis would focus on white women) recognized that census data did not separate black and white. She, like Gray, found many women in business and discovered that the number of women planters was increasing through the antebellum period. Her concentration on white women distorts this section since black women were certainly, as Zora Neale Hurston once put it, the mules of the South. Though Boatwright like most of her white contemporaries was blind to this fact, from the general tone of her thesis one is tempted to believe that if she had lived into the 1960s her outlook would have broadened.

This brief summary cannot do justice to the thesis which was, for its time, a masterful piece of work. More than fifty years later a publisher is finally considering bringing it into print.[101]

In addition to studying and doing the research for her thesis, a fellow teacher who went to Duke with Boatwright remembers that they had a joyful experience. For a brief time she was away from the responsibilities of caring for her mother and her household, she met interesting people, and above all she was happy doing historical research. Though the state of Georgia promised a $1,000 increment to teachers who finished the master's degree, the doing itself seemed to be her primary motivation.[102] "She wanted," said her friend, "to be a *real* historian."[103]

A handful of surviving letters provide glimpses of her personality. Writing W. K. Boyd in May 1937 she had sought permission to take six semester hours in the summer, adding, "I know your standards are very high, but I work hard."[104] Evidently the fact that Boyd was in what would become his last illness led Charles Sydnor to answer her letter. On May 22 she wrote him, misspelling his name, to say that she hoped for an opportunity to work with him; "since I read your book I have wanted to." She announced her plan to stay for both summer terms, adding, "I have to get something started if I ever do, for: 'At last I am forty and ready to start / Beginning to live;—if I don't fall apart.' "[105] The next surviving letter, dated May 5, 1938, reported that she would return for the summer and asked Sydnor's approval for taking a history course and one in sociology. "I hope you won't put me out for I'm still sticking to my 'Georgia women' tho I sometimes doubt if they are worth all this fidelity." She said she was studying Spanish for her reading examination.[106] Sydnor replied approving her choices and advising her to work with E. Merton Coulter, who was to visit that summer, or with Richard Shryock, the medical historian. Since she eventually would thank Shryock for his help with her thesis perhaps she took the latter's course, but she also knew Coulter well enough to write joking letters to him, so she may have studied with both. In 1939 she again sent word that she would be coming: "This is just to forewarn you that my 'Women' and I are headed toward you for this summer . . . so that you may have ample time to organize your resources if you expect to avoid us." Her life had been busy:

> In addition to all the usual complications . . . now there is the state situation which leaves the schools without money. I without any qualifications other than strong lungs am almost continuously being sent somewhere to do something about it, and coming home with only another unpaid expense account.
>
> Sincerely hoping that you are unable to find a successful means of escape, I am Very truly yours,[107]

Sydnor wrote saying he had no wish to avoid her, but that he would only be on deck for the first term. She came, and the thesis was signed July 15, 1939.

By the following year she was seeking Sydnor's advice as to whether her study could be turned into a book. She herself thought the material good and hoped it might interest a university press, but she wanted an expert opinion. Sydnor replied in a long careful letter in which he said that she did indeed have something worth publishing, that her thesis was a superior one both in research and in thoughtfulness. He then suggested that if it was to be published there were some things that needed work: for example, there were a number of unsubstantiated generalizations. Although he said clearly that he thought the thesis, in whole or in part, deserved publication, she, as insecure graduate students are wont to do, gave his letter a pessimistic interpretation. Her summary of what he had said was "my thesis is not good enough, but too good not to be better. Perhaps some time something creditable may evolve out of the primeval ooze between those covers. Right now I don't feel that my back will ever be equal to the task."[108] Some weeks later he replied, explaining that he had broken his elbow in the meantime, saying that she had misunderstood and reiterated: "Your work does have very real merit and with some polishing ought to be published." He said he had only given her the advice he would have given himself in like circumstances.[109]

In March she thanked him for a copy of his essay "The Southerner and the Laws" and inquired about his broken arm. She reported discussing publication of her thesis with Robert P. Brooks, an economics professor at the University of Georgia who apparently at that time ran the University of Georgia Press. Brooks had given her work high marks but told her the press had no money; only authors who could afford to pay the costs were being published. She went on to say that she was "green eyed" over the success of some of her contemporaries, and that she had sent a finished copy to Richard Shryock (who by that time had moved to the University of Pennsylvania) hoping for some suggestions as to possible publishers.

Nothing came of her efforts to interest people in the possibility of turning the thesis into a book, and by January 1941 she had apparently decided to settle for publishing the much abbreviated version in the article reprinted here. She wrote Coulter, who was editor of the *Georgia Historical Quarterly,* that she had finally reduced the essay to the required length. After some discussion of forms of citation she went on: "I thought you said I could be a member of the Georgia Historical Society. What happened? Did I get black-balled? Don't mind telling me. I'm used to it. My best friend did as much to me in a bridge club recently. She said I was all right if I wasn't playing bridge. I was quite cheered up. I knew how I was when I was playing bridge, but I didn't know how I was when I wasn't." Coulter hastened to reassure her that she would be welcome in the historical society, and in her next letter she thanked him and told him of an "old lady" in Augusta who had some plantation records. She thought he might extract the records by a typical southern combination of flattery and references to kinfolks. She added, "Miss Sarah knows about you and admires your work, or at least admires your reputation, for I doubt how much reading she has been able to do for the past several years."[110]

The publication of her article proceeded apace, and in her last surviving letter to Coulter, Boatwright was again apologetic, this time for the fact that he had found errors in her footnotes. She commiserated with him about the budget cuts being instituted by Governor Eugene Talmadge. She enclosed an early history of the Augusta Presbyterian Church and an 1883 catalog of the Lucy Cobb Institute which she thought he might like to have.

While all this was going on she was teaching full time and playing an active role in the life of her school. She taught a Sunday school class. She continued to agitate for equal pay for women teachers and to work for an improved retirement system. Twice the young women at Tubman dedicated their yearbook to Eleanor Boatwright. They also gave her name to the Future Teachers club. The former pupil quoted earlier described her at that time as "always smiling, easy going, chuckling, and a good natured. . . . She sat on a stool when she taught, right in front of her pull-down maps and always pointing at them when she was teaching." Colleagues remember the joyful atmosphere of her classroom and that she was a person to whom other people went with their problems. Survivors speak fondly of her to this day.

Yet something about her life was not joyful. For years she had cared for an ailing mother and borne heavy financial burdens for the whole family which included her sister and a niece. She seems to have suffered considerably from arthritis. Her closest friend remembers that sometimes she was subject to depression. In early 1950 her eighty-four-year-old mother died; in October, Boatwright took her own life.

Her coworkers and her students were stunned. One friend remembered that Boatwright had long supported the right of people to commit suicide. There were speculations that her life had taken a turn for the worse when Tubman merged with the Richmond Academy (male) and she was remanded to a dreadful room on the fourth floor where, in addition to requiring her to climb four flights of stairs (a problem for a person with severe arthritis), there was too much noise from the music room next door for decent teaching. The male faculty were not, so memories say, very welcoming to the women from Tubman who were, on the whole, better educated than they. Half a century later one can only speculate that a situation such as her friends describe might have come to symbolize all the disappointed ambitions of a woman whose dream was to "be a real historian." Whatever her reason, her death was a great waste—the loss not only of a gifted teacher, but of a promising scholar.

What does this narrative, composed from the bits and pieces of remaining evidence, tell us about the history of southern women? We see before us five exceptionally able, well-trained, productive scholars, part of a wave of women moving into the professions in the early twentieth century. All five were pioneer social historians, years ahead of their time in their use of sources. One was beginning to see the need for studying slavery from the slaves' perspective; two had the courage to discuss miscegenation at a time when proper ladies were not supposed to know what the word meant. Two at least were outstanding in their use of the English language, and all five wrote well. All but one lived in an area generally recognized to be one of the centers of southern intellectual life, and the fifth studied there. With all these assets not one achieved a recognized position in the historical profession, and their work lay almost unnoticed for decades. How can this be explained?

The difficulties they encountered were common to women academics everywhere in the 1920s, but southern women had their own special obstacles.

First there was the matter of preparatory education. While the Northeast had at least seven or eight women's colleges whose academic programs were equal to those of the best male colleges, the South had few if any of this caliber. Most ambitious southern girls had access only to normal schools. The North Carolina Normal and Industrial College was exceptionally good for its kind and time, but its degree had none of the cachet attached to that of any eastern woman's college. When it came to seeking postgraduate education, the possibilities in the South were even more limited.

The state of higher education for women in the South also limited job opportunities. The best northern women historians found jobs in well-endowed women's colleges where they had time and support for research. Many were able to study in Europe. In the South women were also expected to find their careers in women's colleges. (Here as elsewhere men who welcomed women as admiring students were not so welcoming when it came to thinking of them as colleagues.)[111] But in the South there was no Bryn Mawr or Smith to which a young woman with a Ph.D. might aspire. The southern women's colleges whether private or state supported were poorly funded, and teaching loads were heavy. An ambitious scholar had little time to go beyond her daily responsibilities and had little chance to gain visibility from a post in any of them.

Then there was the matter of isolation. Though all of these women had spent significant periods of time outside the South—two at Harvard, one at the University of Wisconsin, and two in New York—they do not appear to have formed ties with any of the handful of outstanding women scholars who in the decades after 1900 had found their way to the faculties of the eastern women's colleges.

Perhaps, too, our five women were born a few years too late. They finished graduate work in the 1920s just in time for the Great Depression which limited opportunities for everybody but for women most of all. Marjorie Nicolson, born in 1894, was among the handful of highly successful academic women of her generation. Her field was English, not history, but her observations in a talk at the University of Michigan in 1937 are to the point: "My own generation will recall the suddenness with which [as a consequence of the world war] bars were

lowered and the rapid emergence of women into positions of prominence, as well as the great influx of women into lesser positions formerly held by men."[112]

But, she concluded, what had been taken as a permanent change
was only temporary:

> as I look back upon the records, I find myself wondering whether
> our generation was not the only generation of women which ever
> really found itself. We came late enough to escape the self-
> consciousness and the belligerence of the pioneers, to take educa-
> tion and training for granted. We came early enough to take
> equally for granted professional positions in which we could
> make full use of our training. This was our double glory. Posi-
> tions were everywhere open to us. . . . The millenium had come;
> it did not occur to us that life could be different. . . . Within a de-
> cade shades of the prison house began to close. . . . in the higher
> professions women reached their peak about 1926 and since that
> time a decline has set in, not upon the growing boy, but upon the
> emancipated girl.[113]

As she went on Nicolson reflected on the various ways in which, as
she saw it, academic women were increasingly being limited, both in
the opportunity for study and in the chance to find jobs commensu-
rate with their training. She wound up with a stirring call to the
"great coeducational universities of the country" to give women an
equal opportunity, both for study and for jobs. There is no evidence
that the institutions in question heard, or if they did that they responded.

Nicholson's pessimism would have been reinforced had she read
a study called *Women and the Ph.D.* conducted by Emilie Hutchinson of Barnard College and published in 1929. Based on over fifteen
hundred replies to a questionnaire sent women who had taken the
Ph.D. between 1877 and 1924, it spelled out the difficulties women
faced in excruciating detail. Comments from historians in the group
were mostly sad: one said that the openings for women were too few
to justify the time and money required for a Ph.D.; another said that
there was little opportunity for women to "get just rewards." Another thought that only exceptional women gained recognition; still
another wrote that opportunities were few and when they existed
were in colleges with such a heavy work load that there was no time
for research.[114]

An even more depressing picture—especially of male attitudes—emerges from an article on "Women Doctors of Philosophy in History" which appeared in the *Journal of Higher Education* in 1942. It offered statistics which the authors, one of whom was a distinguished historian, interpreted to mean that on the whole women with advanced degrees in history, compared to their male colleagues, had failed woefully as teachers or as scholars. With barely concealed pleasure the authors concluded: "The list of distinguished women scholars in history is not long; the record of the average woman who persevered in academic study until she attained the doctorate is not impressive. She has seldom held high or responsible positions in the teaching profession, and she has not proved a productive scholar. . . . Women who took the Ph.D. in history hold poorer positions, are more likely to be unemployed, and are less likely to do research than men."[115]

Few women would have argued with the description, but the implication that this proved women to be quite incapable of becoming good scholars and highly regarded teachers was, to say the least, superficial. It seems not to have occurred to the men writing the article to look behind the figures to the situation of women in academia. They might have reflected, for example, on the fact that though Margaret Judson's book in English constitutional history was universally praised she never received any job offer from a coeducational institution, while a man who had published less well on the same subject at the same time was immediately offered a full professorship at Wisconsin.[116] Or they might have examined the case of Alice Felt Tyler at Minnesota, a specialist in American diplomatic history, who was relegated to the survey course in Western civilization and then denigrated by colleagues when she wrote a best-selling text for the course! She was "intellectual mentor" to the young women at the university but had a hard time gaining tenure.[117] Had they bothered to talk with the most distinguished women holders of the Ph.D. in history a far different interpretation of their data would have been required.

Like women elsewhere, these southern women were often treated as marginal workers. When the depression hit Johnson and Spruill were the first research associates at the Institute for Research in the Social Sciences to be cut off. Spruill and Mendenhall as mature scholars were allowed to teach only the kinds of courses the regular faculty disdained. Only the exigencies of wartime allowed Gray and Johnson to teach in the universities to which they were attached.

Though all of these structural constraints were important in limiting opportunities in the South, they were not peculiarly southern. Many of them operated, though perhaps not quite so powerfully, in other parts of the country.[118] This little group of southern women had an additional disability: they had chosen to work in a field which male historians simply did not recognize. Women were not deemed to be part of "history" as it was usually defined. People who work on invisible subjects rarely become visible themselves. Certainly it was not the quality of their work that prevented Johnson and Spruill from being recognized until they were in their eighties: few historians of their generation or later ones did better work. Boatwright and Gray have never been recognized, and while Mendenhall's work in agriculture gained some attention, her article on southern women was ignored. The wonder is that some of these women continued to write, for it is difficult indeed to maintain self-confidence if the external world gives you no positive feedback. It is a truism that talents not used will grow rusty or evaporate.

The prevailing culture made it difficult for women themselves to see their own careers as paramount, as more significant than family responsibilities or their husband's careers. Indeed, it was often true that a professional woman had great difficulty being taken seriously if she married. Even a single woman or a widow found it hard to put work above care of aging parents. In this group only Guion Johnson insisted through her life that her career was as important as her domestic responsibilities. The most successful of the five, she also had the sturdiest ego—she continued to fight for her rights through her life, and when she met an insurmountable obstacle she executed a flanking movement by way of the voluntary association.

The responses of the others differed as their personalities differed. Marjorie Mendenhall worked on and on. In 1942 the chance for a highly respectable marriage briefly allowed her a way out, but when her husband died after three years she was back in the struggle again, and it continued for the rest of her life. In the end she slipped into depression and was overwhelmed. Boatwright was also a fighter, but for her also, apparently, the obstacles were overwhelming. Gray found a niche in which she could do historical research and made a place for herself by becoming an expert in the work she was assigned to do. Spruill adapted as a graceful southern lady, and no one now knows whether she did so with a whole heart or with a profound sense of potentialities that had died for lack of opportunity to develop.[119]

It is impossible to measure the cost to the world of scholarship of their marginality (and that of so many others) . . . or the cost to themselves.

Notes

1. Of course, women were not the only invisible southerners in most history-as-written. Slavery as an institution, slavery as a political issue, slavery as a form of economic organization were all studied, but the actual lives of slaves and especially the world as seen through their eyes or those of the freed blacks after the war were to be found only in the fiction of an occasional writer such as Charles Chesnutt, not in the formal histories of the South.

2. Two of the five lived in other places for part or all of their adult lives but studied in the area—one at Duke in Durham and the other at Chapel Hill. The other three spent their entire adult lives in one of the two towns.

3. Frances Caulkins and Elizabeth Ellett, for example.

4. These included Katherine Coman and Mary Barnes, born in the 1850s; Louise Kellog, born 1862; Lucy Maynard Salmon, Annie Abel and Nellie Neilson, all born in 1873; and Helen Sumner, born in 1876. The difficulties facing a woman who wished to become a scholar were such that only the strongest personalities and intellectually most able persisted and succeeded in this first generation.

5. One exception might be Elizabeth Anthony Dexter, author of *Colonial Women of Affairs* (Boston: Houghton Mifflin, 1924), but though she taught briefly at Skidmore College, Dexter's career was principally in the Unitarian church and various peace movements, not in academia. Lucy M. Salmon published a study of domestic service in 1897 which was largely based on contemporary data gathered through a voluntary association. An interesting study could be made of the way academically trained women used voluntary associations to provide opportunities and support they could not find in institutions of higher learning.

6. Frances Victor, for example, prepared at least eight of the volumes for Hubert H. Bancroft's massive history of the Pacific states. All were published over his name. Helen Sumner was a key person on the research team of John R. Commons, and a great deal of her research went into his two-volume *History of*

Labour, yet she was unable to find an academic post and wound up working principally for the federal government. Louise Kellog's contributions to Reuben Thwaites famous *Early Western Travels* were inadequately acknowledged. See the essays on these three women in Edward and Janet James, *Notable American Women* (Cambridge: Harvard University Press, 1971), vols. 2 and 3.

7. Jacquelin Goggin has analyzed the long campaign on the part of other women historians which finally led to Neilson's election. See "Mary Wilhelmine Williams: Feminist, Activist, and Historian," paper presented at the Eighth Berkshire Conference on the History of Women, Douglass College, June 1990. Also in 1940 there was a single panel called "Some Aspects of the History of Women" at the annual meeting of the American Historical Association. One paper was on American feminism, the other on "The Influence of the Mexican Revolution on the Status of Women."

8. James, eds., *Notable American Women,* and Barbara Sicherman and Carol Hurd Green, eds., *Notable American Women the Modern Period* (Cambridge: Harvard University Press, 1980). The Jameses' volumes are weak on the South. The fourth volume includes southern women in many of its categories, but among the historians there are only these two.

9. For contrast with the situation in the Northeast, see Mabel Newcomer, *A Century of Higher Education for Women* (New York: Harper and Brothers, 1957), chap. 10. Three other southern women's colleges with high aspirations were Randolph Macon in Lynchburg, Virginia; Agnes Scott in Decatur, Georgia; and Sophia Newcomb in New Orleans.

10. For perspective: in 1970 roughly 82,000 women took the M.A. and about 8,000 the Ph.D. in all fields. Over the fifty-year period from 1920 to 1970 the number of females counted by the census had more or less doubled; the number taking advanced degrees was thirteen times larger than it had been fifty years earlier. See *Historical Statistics of the United States: Colonial Times to 1970* (Washington, D.C.: GPO, 1975), 385. The first woman who took a Ph.D. in history, Kate Ernest Levi, did so in 1893 at the University of Wisconsin. See Jacquelin Goggin, "Challenging Sexual Discrimination in Higher Education," *American Historical Review* 97, no. 3 (June 1992): 768–802, for detailed analysis of the problems faced by women historians.

11. One can only guess as to what influences may have come to bear on this bright young woman from a small Maryland town who came to Goucher at the age of sixteen. Certainly Maryland, and especially Baltimore, presented many examples of active, effective women in a wide variety of civic organizations, suffrage groups, and peace organizations as well as in academia. See Winifred G. Helmes, ed., *Notable Maryland Women* (Cambridge, Md.: Tidewater Publishers, 1977) for brief biographies of many such women.

12. Goggin, "Mary Wilhelmine Williams."

13. Paxson, telegram to Dean Eleanor Lord, Goucher College, May 29, 1915, Gallagher to Paxson, Dec. 9, 1923, Goucher College Archives. Gallagher's work, Paxson added, "shows unusual powers of investigation and arrangement

and she is an experienced and successful teacher." He also said that he would have urged his own department to hire her had there been a vacancy, and that "her appearance is good and her personality is vigorous" (Paxson telegram, May 29, 1915). All of the letters of recommendation I have read for this study dwell on personality and appearance. Carl Russell Fish, for example, recommending Virginia Gearhart for a Goucher fellowship: "Doubtless local acquaintances in Baltimore will speak of Miss Gearhart's extraordinary personal charm. It has made a distinct impression here, and will give her always the opportunity to make her attainments most effective" (Fish to President William Guth, Goucher College, Feb. 8, 1926, University of Wisconsin-Madison, Department of Archives).

14. It should be noted, however, that university-wide only about 10 percent of the students holding fellowships were women.

15. It is intriguing to speculate as to what each of these three may have contributed to her innovative use of data: Paxson was a student of the westward movement, and Fish had published a study of the Civil Service and was writing *The Rise of the Common Man*. Perlman worked on the history of trade unionism and had worked with Helen Sumner.

16. Virginia Gearhart, "The Southern Woman, 1840–1860" (Ph.D. diss., University of Wisconsin, June 9, 1927). Gearhart herself noted that as far as she could tell she was the first scholar since Mary Forrest, *Women of the South Distinguished in Literature* (New York: Derby and Jackson, 1860), to study the history of southern women.

17. For the historian of higher education it is interesting to note that in contrast to the high quality of the substance, the physical dissertation is, by today's standards, deplorable—misspelled words, missing words, words marked out or erased, a missing page of bibliography all characterize the library copy. Yet the University of Wisconsin was obviously one of the leading graduate departments in the country. On the other hand, the qualifying examination appears on paper to be far more demanding than what would normally be expected today.

18. Louise Kellog, "Carl Russell Fish" in *Dictionary of American Biography*, Supplement 1, (New York: Charles Scribner's Sons, 1944).

19. Thomas Woody's massive two-volume work, *A History of Women's Education in the United States* (New York: Science Press, 1929), had not been published when Gearhart wrote. In the preface Woody would write about "the comparative silence—in some educational histories, almost complete—on the subject of women's education; and equally striking, the scant attention given her emancipation and education in the general histories of the country." Essentially Gearhart had to do her research from primary sources. The wonder is that, working principally in Wisconsin, she did as well as she did. She did some research in the Library of Congress but none in southern archives.

20. Now, more than sixty years later, scholars are rediscovering the political involvement of antebellum Virginia women. See Suzanne Lebsock, *The Free*

Women of Petersburg (New York: W. W. Norton, 1984). See also Elizabeth Varon, "Women & the Law in 19th Century Virginia: Antebellum Legislative Petitions, 1810–1861," *LEX Claudia* 10, no. 2 (Fall 1991): 5–7, 26–31. Varon found divorce petitions continuing long after the legislature had tried to hand over the issue to the courts.

21. As recently as 1985 a respected scholar could still write: "Until the late 1870s southern culture . . . discouraged female association" (Jean Friedman, *The Enclosed Garden: Women and Community in the Evangelical South, 1830–1900* [Chapel Hill: University of North Carolina Press, 1985], xi). Four of the five essays reprinted here offered contrary evidence, but it was lost to sight for a long time. See also Anne Firor Scott, *Natural Allies: Women's Associations in American History* (Champaign: University of Illinois Press, 1992), chaps. 2 and 3.

22. David Elsberg, writing an honors paper at Duke University in 1992 on southern women's education, was struck by the number of references he found to the Daughters of Temperance and a variety of other voluntary associations.

23. Compare her view with that implied in Marjorie Mendenhall's introduction to the H. W. Ravenel memoir. See below, p. 21.

24. Gearhart was not alone in wishing to believe that many southerners would have freed their slaves but for the laws requiring that freed people leave the state. It is doubtful that people who comforted themselves in this way had consulted the slaves themselves, many of whom took extreme risks to get to the North. Women who petitioned the legislature on the subject were a small but striking minority. Here as elsewhere Gearhart failed to reckon with the diversity of southern women's behavior.

25. Gearhart defended her dissertation in June 1927; she did not actually receive the degree until June 1928. Meantime she had married, moved to New Orleans, and written the article reprinted here.

26. In 1962 the same journal accepted my first article in southern women's history, "The 'New Woman' in the New South" *South Atlantic Quarterly* 61 (Autumn 1962): 473–83. Years later at a historical meeting I met a young woman who had been on the staff of the *Quarterly* in 1962. "What a fight we had," she recalled; "many people said your article was just political, not history at all." Needless to say I would like very much to know whether Gearhart's article had aroused similar controversy in 1928.

27. Early in two senses: she was first to tackle the subject, and she did so very early in her scholarly career. Few graduate students of twenty-four are capable of so much original thinking, even though the dissertation is uneven. It is indeed a little bit like the little girl with the curl: when it is good it is very very good, and when it is bad it is awful.

28. Carl Russell Fish, *The Rise of the Common Man* (New York: Macmillan, 1927), 18.

29. University of Wisconsin-Madison, Department of Archives. I am in-

debted to Mr. J. Frank Cook, Director, for supplying all the extant records of Virginia Gearhart's years at the University of Wisconsin.

30. Virginia Gearhart Gray to Frederic L. Paxson, Oct. 18, 1927, ibid.

31. Frederic L. Paxson to Virginia G. Gray, Jan. 31, 1928, ibid.

32. Alexandra Lee Levin to Virginia Gearhart Gray, Feb. 3, 1964, and Gray to Levin, Feb. 7, 1964, Department of Special Collections, William R. Perkins Library, Duke University, Durham, N.C.

33. What had originally been called the North Carolina Normal and Industrial College became in 1920 the North Carolina College for Women. Later it was the Woman's College of the University of North Carolina and is now the University of North Carolina at Greensboro.

34. Annie G. Randall "Training Teachers in North Carolina," *State Normal Magazine* 5 (1901): 59, cited in Pamela Dean, "Learning to Be New Women: Campus Culture at the North Carolina Normal and Industrial College, 1892–1920," paper delivered at the annual meeting of the Southern Historical Association, November 1990. This paper foreshadows Dean's dissertation in progress.

35. Dean, "Learning to Be New Women."

36. Letters in the Archives of Radcliffe College, provided by Jane Knowles, Archivist, with the permission of President Linda Wilson.

37. *North Carolina Historical Review* 6, no. 1 (Jan. 1929): 115–17. Amy Lowell, herself an archetypal new woman, had published "Patterns" in 1915.

38. Ibid., 9, no. 4 (Oct. 1932): 397–99. Since Mary Beard's *On Understanding Women* (London: Longmans, Green, 1931) is seldom read today it may be worth quoting a little of its closing summary: "Looking backward toward the horizon of dawning society what do we see . . . Woman—assuming chief responsibility for the continuance and care of life. We are in the presence of a force so vital and so powerful that anthropologists can devise no meter to register it and the legislator no rein strong enough to defeat it. . . . From this elemental force in the rise and development of civilisation there is no escape and more of human history can be written in its terms than any of Clio's disciples have yet imagined" (see p. 513 ff.).

39. *North Carolina Historical Review* 10, no. 2 (April 1933): 144–46.

40. C. Vann Woodward to Anne F. Scott, July 23, 1991.

41. In a letter of recommendation written in 1935 William Whately Pierson, then dean of the Graduate School at the University of North Carolina, wrote: "She has also from time to time during several years been engaged in a study of the Social Status of Women in the South from 1860 to 1900" (Few Papers, Duke University Archives). Since this was a year after the publication of the article Pierson, at least, thought it to be part of an ongoing study.

After this book was in press Jacqueline Goggin presented a paper suggesting that as late as 1936 Mendenhall saw the history of women as her major focus and claimed to be studying agriculture in order to comprehend the society in which southern women functioned (Jacqueline Goggin, "Arthur M. Schlesinger and the

Feminization of American History," paper presented to the History of Education Society, October 1992). The mystery deepens: why, then, did she never again write about women though she continued to publish essays in agricultural history?

42. The work of Spruill and Johnson is discussed below. Elizabeth Anthony Dexter, *Colonial Women of Affairs* (Boston: Houghton Mifflin, 1924); Alice Morse Earle, *Colonial Dames and Goodwives* (Boston: Houghton Mifflin, 1895) and *Home Life in Colonial Days* (Houghton Mifflin, 1913).

43. The absence of *South Atlantic Quarterly* records for the years before 1937 means that we cannot discover whether the editors—several of whom were new since 1928—made the connection with the earlier article, or whether it was they who persuaded Mendenhall that her tables were "too bulky" to publish.

44. *Yale Review* 25 (Summer 1936): 748–77.

45. Ibid., 27 (Sept. 1937): 110–29. She was in good company for the same issue contained articles by Alvin Johnson, H. S. Commager, Hajo Holburn, and Walter de la Mare.

46. Marjorie Mendenhall to Clara Booth Byrd, Nov. 18, 1954, Alumnae Files, University of North Carolina at Greensboro. I am indebted to Pamela Dean for retrieving this letter.

47. "The South: Region or Colony," *Southern Review*, Spring 1937, 633–46.

48. C. C. Byrd to W. P. Few, March 22, 1938, Alumnae Files, University of North Carolina at Greensboro.

49. Though any judgments made in hiring faculty must be subjective, only one of the two men hired came close to Mendenhall in ability. Both however had finished their degrees. All the correspondence that I have seen between Few, William Wannamaker (the dean), and LaPrade speaks of searching for men.

There is ample evidence of William LaPrade's dislike of the idea of women as historians. In 1992 an award-winning historian told me that when, in her youth, she applied for admission to graduate work at Duke he had castigated her for two hours for such an unnatural ambition. His earlier rejection of another young woman, in which he cited Baldwin's presence, reads: "Circumstances make it necessary that the University have only a limited number of women students. . . . it is manifest [therefore] that the University can use only a limited number of women instructors. . . . In view of the fact that Dr. Alice Baldwin, Dean of Women, is here a member of the Department I am afraid we shall not have an opening for another woman in the near future" (W. T. LaPrade to Mary Bosworth, Dec. 5, 1927, LaPrade Papers, Duke University Archives). Baldwin, as a dean, had very little time to serve the history department.

50. The day was long gone when women did not read their own work in public; perhaps the explanation is simple: the expense of traveling from Massachusetts to New Orleans.

51. Elizabeth Applewhite Pearsall to Anne F. Scott, March 10, 1991.

52. All the evidence from the family suggests that however difficult Mrs.

Mendenhall became late in life, she had performed heroically in her youth and all her children felt that they owed her a great deal.

53. A younger cousin who greatly admired her, trying to formulate her memories of Marjorie Mendenhall, writes: "What a gentle person she was. I always saw the piles of papers, heavy study. . . . Grace would be a good word to use. Also thoroughness in her research" (Martha Redding Mendenhall to Anne F. Scott, Nov. 20, 1991).

54. *North Carolina Historical Review* 31, no. 2 (April 1954): 134–49. It may be revealing that while the other contributors to this volume of the journal were identified as professors or librarians she chose to say simply: "Dr. Marjorie Mendenhall Applewhite of Chapel Hill has contributed to various historical journals."

55. Ibid., 136–37.

56. Two poignant Applewhite letters from this period have survived, as well as a letter describing the situation written by the man who had arranged for her appointment. I am indebted to Jere Mendenhall LeGwin for copies of these revealing documents.

57. Elizabeth Applewhite Pearsall to Anne F. Scott, March 10, 1991.

58. Ibid., Nov. 3, 1991.

59. Dean, "Learning to Be a New Woman."

60. *Pine Needles,* 1920. This is the yearbook of the North Carolina College for Women.

61. Arthur M. Schlesinger, *New Viewpoints in American History* (New York: Macmillan, 1922), chap. on "The Role of Women in American History." It is interesting that women, who were pushed to the margins of the profession, were among the first southern historians to begin thinking in terms of social history. Mildred Thompson, who was the only woman in the group of Reconstruction historians trained by William A. Dunning at Columbia, was also the only one of his protégés who included much analysis of society in her work. As will be apparent, every one of the women in this study did pioneering work in social history at a time when politics, diplomacy, and war were the predominant interests among the male historians.

62. This somewhat halfhearted praise from Beard is puzzling in view of the fact that she had read and made suggestions when the book was in manuscript, and her copy of the book itself is inscribed by the author: "With a heart full of love and appreciation, J.C.S." Perhaps as reviewer she was wary of seeming to puff the work of a good friend. After Beard's death the book was sent back to Julia Spruill and is now one of my proudest possessions.

63. Significant reviews included those by Philip Davidson, *Journal of Southern History* 5 (1939): 254; Mary R. Beard, *Social Forces* 17 (March 1939): 450; Reba Strickland, *Mississippi Valley Historical Review* 25 (March 1939): 556; Eudora Ramsey Richardson, *William and Mary Quarterly,* 2d ser., 19 (April 1939): 248; Howard Mumford Jones, *Boston Transcript,* Feb. 18, 1939, 1.

64. I believe the University of North Carolina Press nominated *Women's Life and Work* for a Pulitzer Prize in History. Julia Spruill commented on the irony that the book that actually won the Pulitzer was on the subject of her master's essay and one which in private she thought somewhat inferior to her own work: Arthur Schlesinger, Jr.'s *Orestes Brownson*.

65. Anne M. Cooper, interview in the *Chapel Hill Newspaper*, Feb. 11, 1983.

66. From childhood Julia was a "good girl." A family anecdote has it that when she and her sister Mildred were in grade school the irate mother of a little boy came to complain that Julia had hit her son. Mrs. Cherry stoutly denied that the incident could have happened. Finally the mother wavered. "Perhaps it was Mildred," she said. "Ah," said Mrs. Cherry, "now *that* is possible!" Along the same line, Julia was voted "most diplomatic" by her college classmates.

67. As any examination of this generation of women historians makes clear, the American Association of University Women was an important institution for academic women. At a time when the male-dominated professional societies were less than welcoming, the all-female AAUW, with its high standards and interest both in scholarship and in public affairs, offered a way for able women to make themselves felt. It was also one of the very few organizations which offered fellowships exclusively for women. Three of the five women of this study are known to have been active members.

68. Chapel Hill friends who had known Julia Spruill well expressed surprise when they read her obituary: "I never knew she was such a distinguished person!" several said.

69. *The Bluebonnet 1921* (published by the Senior Class of Baylor College, Belton, Texas), 244–45. The story has a remarkably modern theme.

70. Guion Griffis Johnson, "Feminism and the Economic Independence of Women," *Journal of Social Forces* 3, no. 4 (May 1925): 612–16. (It may be significant that Johnson did not list this article on her mid-life curriculum vitae.)

71. Chapel Hill: University of North Carolina Press, 1930.

72. A comparison of Johnson's work with Gearhart's makes clear the immense advantage of having access to a large number of relevant manuscripts, as she did in North Carolina. Johnson's was also the stronger, more analytical mind.

73. Johnson, *Ante-bellum North Carolina*, 220.

74. The irony is that his books now lie unopened in the library; hers is about to be reissued more than half a century after its original publication.

75. Charles D. Murrell to Guion G. Johnson, March 15, 1984, Johnson Papers, Southern Historical Collection, University of North Carolina at Chapel Hill.

76. Oral History Interview with Dr. Guion Johnson, Southern Historical Collection, University of North Carolina at Chapel Hill. We all know to be cautious of recollections. This has all the earmarks of an oft-told tale, perhaps invented or modified in retrospect. Nevertheless it is intriguing when one realizes

that Guion Johnson developed what was probably the most distinguished career as a volunteer ever seen in North Carolina.

77. Susan Levine, who is writing a history of the national AAUW, found records of several of Guion Johnson's efforts in the organization. The one cited here came at a meeting of the national Social Studies Committee in October 1957 (microfilm reel 113 of the AAUW Papers, AAUW Headquarters, Washington, D.C.).

78. *The Many Lives of North Carolina Women*, Report of the Governor's Commission on the Status of Women (Raleigh, 1964). As chairman of the commission I found myself working very hard to persuade many committee members to fulfill their responsibilities. This was never the case with Guion Johnson: she did what she had agreed to do promptly, efficiently, and with impressive results. Probably she should have been chairman of the commission. I have never known why Governor Terry Sanford chose me, who had only lived in North Carolina for four years, rather than she who had certainly earned the right to the job if anybody had.

79. Fletcher Melvin Green, ed., *Essays in Southern History* (Chapel Hill: University of North Carolina Press, 1949), 124–56.

80. *Journal of Southern History* 23 (Nov. 1957): 483–509. She also wrote an article for the *Journal of the American Association of University Women* in May 1958 on "The Changing Status of the Negro."

81. John C. McKinney and Edgar T. Thompson, eds., *The South in Continuity and Change* (Durham: Duke University Press, 1965), 418–36.

82. Guion Griffis Johnson, *Volunteers in Community Service* (Chapel Hill, N.C., 1967). This book deserves to be in every bibliography on volunteerism.

83. *Research in Service to Society: The First Fifty Years of the Institute for Social Science Research at the University of North Carolina* (Chapel Hill: University of North Carolina Press, 1980).

84. See "The Landless People of Antebellum North Carolina," paper delivered at the annual meeting of the Federation of North Carolina Historical Societies, Nov. 18, 1982, Johnson Papers, Southern Historical Collection, University of North Carolina at Chapel Hill.

85. Authors rarely receive all the recognition they hope for, and Johnson exaggerated the degree to which *Ante-bellum North Carolina* was not recognized. The library copies I have examined in various parts of the country have always been well-worn, usually to the point of being rebound. What was not much recognized even by the people who used the book was the innovations she introduced when she included women as vital creators of social history.

86. Jeffrey J. Crow and Larry E. Tise, eds., *Writing North Carolina History* (Chapel Hill: University of North Carolina Press, 1979), 65, 93, 125.

87. Guion Griffis Johnson to Robert Calhoon, May 20, 1980, Johnson Papers, Southern Historical Collection, University of North Carolina at Chapel Hill, quoted by permission of Edward S. Johnson.

88. The study became Emily Herring Wilson, *Hope and Dignity: Older Black Women of the South* (Philadelphia: Temple University Press, 1983).

89. Emily Herring Wilson to Anne F. Scott, June 14, 1991.

90. *New York Times,* May 25, 1991.

91. Boatwright would cite Virginia Gearhart Gray in her thesis, but whether she ever discovered that Gray was in Durham I do not know.

92. In 1946—two decades after Boatwright was hired—there were forty-four women faculty members, including at least eight who had master's degrees. Nearly all had the A.B. degree, from such places as Vanderbilt, Smith, Syracuse, and the University of Chicago as well as from a variety of southern colleges.

93. Flisch deserves, and may soon get, a biography of her own. Born in Augusta in 1861, she graduated from Lucy Cobb Institute in Athens, Georgia, in 1877 and applied for admission to the University of Georgia, which would not admit women for another forty-two years. Rejected, she wrote a dramatic letter to the *Augusta Chronicle* deploring discrimination against women in Georgia. After teaching at the Georgia State College for Women for many years and writing novels, as well as many articles for newspapers and magazines, in 1906 she went to the University of Wisconsin for an M.A. By that time she was an active member of the American Historical Association. She appeared on its program in 1905 and again in 1908. Her carefully researched paper on "The Common People of the Old South" and an equally careful "Bibliography of the Public Records of Richmond County, Georgia," were published by the association (see the *Annual Report of the American Historical Association* for 1906, vol. 2 [Washington, D.C.: GPO, 1908]). Both of these were cited in Boatwright's bibliography. Later Flisch returned to Augusta to care for an aging mother and taught at Tubman High School, where Eleanor Boatwright came under her influence. It is generally agreed among the survivors of the Tubman faculty that it was Flisch who set Boatwright on the road to being an historian, and it is quite plausible to suggest that Boatwright's choice of thesis topic also bore the marks of Flisch's interests and her approach to historical research. Boatwright used many of the documents first collected in Flisch's "Bibliography"; Ann Braddy, Boatwright's closest friend, says flatly, "Miss Flisch chose Eleanor to be her Sword Bearer." When Augusta Junior College was organized in 1926 Flisch became dean of women. She lived until 1939 and until recently had dropped entirely out of historical memory. Robin Harris at Georgia College in Milledgeville, Georgia, is writing her biography. Her novels contain useful social history.

94. I asked Ann Braddy, "Why did Boatwright not go on to the Ph.D.?" Braddy's response was quick: "Money, and anyhow with Julia Flisch for a teacher who needed a Ph.D.?"

95. Robin Harris, the assiduous biographer of Flisch, can find no record in the Augusta newspapers of either of these strikes. The anecdotal evidence comes from women who were teachers at the time; apparently the newspapers were loath to encourage such goings-on by writing about them.

96. Eleanor Boatwright to J. Harold Saxon, Nov. 12, 1947, to J. L. Yaden,

Nov. 16, 1947, in files of Teachers Retirement System of Georgia. I am much indebted to Dorothy Hughes, Administrative Assistant, for providing this and other data about Eleanor Boatwright's encounters with the Retirement System.

97. Florence Fleming Corley to Anne Firor Scott, March 8, 1992. Professor Corley, a distant cousin of Boatwright, graduated from Tubman in 1950.

98. Boatwright finished her thesis just as Spruill and Johnson were publishing their books. They would have found her work fascinating and reinforcing; she could have learned a great deal from them. As far as I know neither they nor she ever knew about each other. She did cite Gray's article.

99. Of course black historians were far more sensitive to this issue, but their concern was overwhelmingly for the black woman, usually a slave woman, who was forced into sexual relationships with a white man. In the 1960 edition of John Hope Franklin, *From Slavery to Freedom: A History of Negro Americans* (New York: Alfred Knopf), we find this paragraph: "The extensive miscegenation which went on during the slave period was largely the result of people living and working together at common tasks and the subjection of Negro women to the whims and desires of white men. There was some race mixture that resulted from the association of Negro men and white women, but this was a small percent of the total" (204–5). In 1970 James Hugo Johnston, *Race Relations in Virginia and Miscegenation in the South* (Amherst: University of Massachusetts Press), which had been a dissertation at the University of Chicago in the 1930s, finally found a publisher. Johnston is an African American. In 1980 Joel Williamson published *The New People* (New York: Free Press), the first definitive work on the subject of miscegenation. Williamson, consulted for this note, confirmed my view that southern historians were not dealing with the subject at all in the years when Johnson and Boatwright were writing. He tells me that anthropologists, psychologists, and sociologists were beginning to think about it in the 1920s, but not the historians. And as far as I can determine only the women among white scholars dealt with the white woman–black man aspect of the phenomenon. Thus Johnson and Boatwright in this as in so much else were ahead of their time.

100. As I have studied the essays reprinted here I continue to be puzzled as to how the idea ever got started that southern women did not organize their own associations. Thomas Woody, *Women's Education in the United States*, vol. 2 (New York: Science Press, 1929), was well aware of the kinds of evidence that would be used by Gray, Johnson, and Boatwright on this question. "In the South, female societies were *no less common* [than in the North]. Perhaps they were more so." He went on to list several and added, "All the foregoing are but a handful of the vast number incorporated in the states named and elsewhere during this period." He cited the laws of Virginia and indicated that he had found similar evidence of incorporation of voluntary associations in other states.

101. Ralph Carlson Publisher of Brooklyn, N.Y., is making arrangements to publish it with a long introduction and commentary which will place the work in the context of its time.

102. Just as well. From the record it seems that her salary of $1,800 a year did not change between 1938 and 1943. It did improve after that, though money remained a problem for the rest of her life.

103. Marie A. Hurlburt of Augusta, Ga., interview, Sept. 5, 1991.

104. Eleanor Miot Boatwright to Dr. William Kenneth Boyd, May 9, 1937, Charles Sydnor Papers, Department of Special Collections, Perkins Library, Duke University, Durham, N.C.

105. E. M. Boatwright to Charles Snyder [*sic*], May 22, 1937, ibid.

106. E.M.B. to C.S.S., May 5, 1938, ibid.

107. E.M.B. to C.S.S., March or April 1939, ibid.

108. Boatwright wrote Sydnor on Jan. 14; he replied Jan. 23, and her second letter is dated Jan. 27, 1940.

109. His reply is dated Feb. 24, 1940.

110. The letters to Coulter are in the Coulter Historical Collection, Hargrett Rare Book and Manuscript Library, University of Georgia. I am indebted to Professor John Inscoe of that university for searching these out for me.

111. Even when a male mentor thought of proposing a woman for a job his colleagues quickly set him straight. A poignant case in point is thoroughly documented in the Alice M. Baldwin Papers, Duke University Archives. Andrew McLaughlin at the University of Chicago had directed Baldwin's excellent dissertation; he admired her work and her general abilities and wanted to bring her in as a permanent member of his department but was forced to write her that there was simply no chance that he could persuade his colleagues. "You and I agreed in our conversation that whether it be just or not, the fact is that in the university there is not much opportunity for women. I should not want to have such a sentiment proclaimed aloud from the house-tops. . . . But you know the conditions as they actually exist." He advised her to take a job as dean of women at Trinity College (which would later become Duke University) and registered his regret both for her and for the University of Chicago that this seemed to be the best thing to do. She took his advice and had to bargain very hard to secure an appointment as assistant professor of history along with the job of dean of women. She eventually rose to full professor of history. McLaughlin's own talented daughter, Constance McLaughlin Green, experienced many of the problems outlined here. Margaret Judson, who is generally very diplomatic in her memoir, noted with some bitterness that when she published a book in English constitutional history which was widely reviewed and favorably contrasted with another book on the same subject by a male scholar, he was at once invited to a full professorship at Wisconsin while no jobs were offered Judson. She remained at the New Jersey College for Women (later Douglass College) for her entire career. See Margaret Judson, *Breaking the Barrier* (New Brunswick, N.J.: Rutgers University, 1984).

112. Marjorie Nicolson, "The Rights and Privileges Pertaining Thereto . . . ," in *A University between Two Worlds: Michigan, 1837–1937* (Ann Arbor: University of Michigan Press, 1938), 413.

113. Ibid., 414–15.

114. Emilie J. Hutchinson, *Women and the Ph.D.: Facts from the Experiences of 1,025 Women Who Have Taken the Degree of Doctor of Philosophy since 1877* (Greensboro: North Carolina College for Women, 1929), 182–83.

115. William B. Hesseltine and Louis Kaplan, "Women Doctors of Philosophy in History," *Journal of Higher Education* 14 (1943): 254–59.

116. Judson, *Breaking the Barrier,* 109–10.

117. Ruth Bordin (author of *Frances Willard* and *Women and Temperance*) to Anne F. Scott, March 20, 1992. "I feel," Bordin wrote, "that Alice Tyler, even more than Mary Beard perhaps, is the mother of us all. She almost invented the practice of the social history as women have practiced it during the last fifteen years." Tyler's *Freedom's Ferment* was published in 1944 by the University of Minnesota Press.

118. Newcomer, *A Century of Higher Education for Women,* chap. 10, is especially relevant at this juncture. Not only does much of Newcomer's research reinforce the argument here with respect to women's career patterns in general, but by detailing the importance of educational opportunities she by implication highlights the difficulties of southern women. See also Willystine Goodsell, "The Educational Opportunities of American Women—Theoretical and Actual," *Annals of the American Academy of Political and Social Science* 143 (May 1929): 1–13.

PART II

The Pioneering Essays

These essays are reprinted here just as they appeared when first published, with only an occasional correction of an obvious typographical error. They provide among so many other things interesting evidence of how standards of scholarly documentation have developed in the ensuing years.

VIRGINIA GEARHART GRAY

Activities of Southern Women: 1840–1860

South Atlantic Quarterly 27 (1928): 264–79

While some of the language of this essay and some of its sweeping generalizations ring oddly more than half a century later, its initial publication was a contribution to knowledge of the first order. Gray used a wide variety of sources never before examined for this purpose to call into question a number of myths about antebellum southern women. Even today a close reading of this essay may yield ideas for research that has not yet been undertaken.

Her discussion of womens' associations, for example, along with similar points in three other of these essays, suggests just how much we don't know about this phenomenon in the South. Where did they flourish? What kinds of work did they do? Who led, who belonged, how did the early organizations transform themselves during the Civil War? Why were the postwar developments in the South so far behind those in the North? And so on.

The analysis of the political participation of antebellum Virginia women now underway would come as no surprise to Virginia Gray since she had collected many scattered pieces of evidence on the subject. If her evidence was drawn largely from the top of the pyramid it was because that was what she had to work with in Wisconsin. Hardly anybody in the early 1920s had devised good methods for illuminating the lives of invisible women. Her use of legislative documents was a tiny step in that direction.

Her data on women's wage work could be developed far more than she was able to do. Of course a modern discussion of the subject would make far more careful distinctions among different kinds of southern women and would certainly not fail to look first at black women who constituted a majority of southern women wage earners.

As with wage work and voluntary associations, so with education in the South. Though some studies exist, there is still room for much more work.

Historians, of all people, should not lose sight of their intellectual forebears. Many excellent ideas are born before their time, lost to sight, and need to be rediscovered when we are ready to see them.

TO THE MAN of the street in the decades just preceding the Civil War, woman developed into as perplexing a problem as her daughter of today, the flapper. New and puzzling demands arose, such as never troubled the minds of past generations, because wives had never thought aloud concerning their rights. To the more pessimistic of the old school, the meeting of the group of northern women at Seneca Falls, New York, in 1848, and their Declaration of Rights must have seemed an unnatural attack upon a very comfortable system of home life. Women belonged beside the hearth be they married or single. Only there, asserted American masculinity, were they able to lead lives of usefulness; and the approved departures from such circumstances must be cloaked by the mantles of religion or of dire necessity.

The southern man faced a less dismaying situation. His wife and daughters had not arrived at the audible stage, even if they were aware of their disadvantageous position. With that silence which seemed to characterize the southern woman in touching upon her activities, she left no direct evidence of favorable thoughts towards the new status of women. Condemnation alone was recorded. The most telling indications that northern sounds were not unheeded came in a highly indignant poem in *The Southern Literary Messenger:*

And this is progress!—Are these noisy tongues—
In fierce contention—raised and angry war—
Fit boast for womanhood?[1]

The years have left to the United States one of its most beautiful traditions in the form of the southern belle. Seen through the eyes of romantic fiction and saddened recollection, a glittering lady with billowing hoop-skirts made her curtsy graciously from the background of a golden age. She was the heroine who developed into the perfect mother. She was the belle. Behind her hoop-skirts—which hostile opinion tried to tinge with indolence—many types of southern women, perhaps less gracious, have been hiding; and the glamor of her aristocratic charm has rendered hazy her own more practical characteristics. Undoubtedly the southern woman was not straining after her rights; yet whether she realized it or not, the wind was stirring in the magnolia trees. From the Kentucky belle who presented colors to her regiment to the Virginia woman who was arrested for selling liquor without a license, activity other than domestic affairs claimed a share of feminine attention. With the Census of 1860 significant employment statistics first were printed; and the innovation was not explained by improved methods in compiling the report. Growth was also evident in the employment lists of directories of many southern cities between 1840 and 1860. In spite of modern protestations of the period, the current which swung the modern southern woman into prominence had it ante-bellum beginnings.

Every young lady discovered certain conventional ways of using her leisure. Plantation management bequeathed little time to its mistress.[2] One must turn to the women of the stimulating urban communities to glimpse activities beyond the home. Here the small, elegant household did not absorb the lady's leisure; and increasing cost of living drove younger families into the hotel, in spite of criticism on the part of their elders.[3] The city and the town also formed the background for a class of poorer women with no counterpart in the poor whites of the country who supposed that manual labor placed them with the slave.

The retiring manner tended to retreat before the practical demands of life, if indeed it ever had existed, as the fashionable theorists insisted. Reserve was quite often the natural result of quiet plantation life. Maria McIntosh, the southern novelist, claimed that influence was not to be exerted by public debates, associations, and petitions, but in the old state of Virginia and the newer creation of Missouri women had no feminine hesitancy in petitioning for redress of grievances.[4] Whether for pensions or merely for aid, the more or less deserving claimed state aid. Women did not shrink from exposing their desires for the title to escheated property or for payment for slaves executed or transported by the government.[5] In 1841 and 1842 Sally Niles, widow of the famous Hezekiah, asked Virginia to purchase her husband's interest in the *Register*. Even divorce was brought for legislative review, although few cases appeared in South Carolina because of the unfavorable attitude of the government.

Perhaps one of the most typical expressions of the lady on the question of public appearances was declaimed in an introduction of an address upon the horrors of war:

> To some it may appear strange that a lady should come forward in public, and address a mixed audience, and give her sentiments on a subject in which it cannot be supposed she has had any experience. Some, if not many, of my sex, may fancy that I am rather transgressing the boundaries of strict female reservedness, and that it is wrong for a lady to speak in a public assembly. Were I alone and unprotected, it would scarcely conform with that delicacy which a female ought always to cultivate and maintain, but when I do it in the presence of my liege lord to whom I am accountable for all my actions, and when it is on war a subject in which he has all his life been interested. . . .[6]

Society was not shocked when Octavia Le Vert took up the cause of Mount Vernon. This very charming woman of Mobile collected a thousand dollars in one day; and the project reminded her, she declared, of Italy's accomplishment in preserving Ariosto's home as a shrine. So noted was her refinement that the Governor of Alabama appointed her as commissioner from the state in 1855 to the Paris Exposition.[7]

An example of the demurring but steady entrance of southern women into public affairs developed with the temperance movement. From its incipiency, Virginia men had opposed "the union of females in the pledge"; and the hotheaded threatened violence to any man who asked their wives to take the vow. The old arguments of the advocates of woman's modest participation in moral and elegant affairs finally prevailed. Because of their powerful influence in moulding the social customs of a country and because of their heavy suffering from the evils of intemperance, they gained in number until they equalled the male participants in the movement. Finally, a branch of the Daughters of Temperance was founded in Richmond, but it did not spread to the other parts of the state.[8] The crusade was not reflected to any large extent in literature written by southern women. The most striking effort for the cause was composed by Caroline Lee Hentz as a poetical address for the Tuscaloosa Fourth of July celebration. The Total Abstinence Society of Alabama was regaled with horrors of the moral python, intemperance, and were urged to cling to the merits of "water, cold water."[9]

Approved forms of feminine edification were tinged by religion. Many women found that exertion with a pious intent received the public smile. Preaching alone was excluded; Martha Moffett of Baltimore, so designated in 1859, indeed must have performed singular duties.[10]

About 1840 an epidemic of fairs broke out among the southern women whose activities were later rivaled by famous benefits in the northern cities during the Civil War. The New Orleans *Daily Picayune* spoke lightly but very favorably of one held to raise a "house over the homeless orphan." Ladies industriously plied their needles to provide many articles for "the fair," so that the immense crowds in the St. Louis ball room might view the belles dispensing fancy work for an admission of twenty-five cents. The corner-stone for the new house was laid amid flattering newspaper publicity. One grateful orphan even wrote a poem to the worthy ladies.[11] Not to be outdone by feminine New Orleans, Vicksburg women also held a benefit of the same nature to complete the Episcopal Church building. While results of the New Orleans venture and a similar one for the orphans of St. Louis remain unrecorded, the Baltimore ladies raised twenty-five hundred dollars for their orphans.[12]

As early as 1838 the indigent females of Richmond had aroused public interest, so that a joint stock company contributed a capital of five thousand dollars based on twenty-five dollar shares. The investment went for the humane purpose of purchasing materials for poor females to make into garments to be sold to the association, and so the treasury was to be replenished from the profits of future operations.[13] Julia Mayo Cabell published in 1858, *An Odd Volume of Facts and Fiction, in Prose and Verse,* to aid the establishment of a Richmond work-house. Even a soup kitchen serving as high as six hundred Baltimoreans daily, was founded by Mrs. Thomas Winans.[14] The directory of Baltimore revealed that such organizations as the Female Humane Impartial Society were practical attempts to aid less fortunate women. The establishment of homes and the work of the benevolent societies were early instances of philanthropy which assumed new forms in the social service work of a later generation of American womanhood.

Of all activities, feminine participation in politics was the most hotly debated. Woman's political recognition received publicity, but made little actual progress towards public approval. No southern lady retained the respect of her associates if she actively ventured upon so unfeminine an interest as politics.[15] Indeed, most of the travelers of the period insisted with Susan B. Anthony that no female participation in politics existed.[16] Exclusion from the franchise combined with lack of property rights by married women was a serious handicap, but many southern women did not feel the vital necessity of changing their position. Maria McIntosh wrote: "There is political inequality ordained in Paradise, when God said to woman, 'He shall rule over thee' and which has existed ever since."[17] Man theoretically represented their family interests; and the most common argument for masculine dominance plead woman's influence over the judgment and the will of man through the heart.

Southern women did influence political activities, but their effectiveness has never been gauged with absolute accuracy. They accepted their situation, but they never lost interest in the circumstances of southern life. The record of their attention to public affairs is scattered in incidents of no great importance, but which, if grouped together, paint a different picture. Mrs. John Tyler's letters, though from a northern woman, portrayed what a southern president's wife knew and thought about politics. Speaking of a local defeat in which she was interested, Mrs. Tyler wrote: "The only thing to compensate for this disappointment will be the defeat of Clay. Was there ever an election like this? A sword by a hair seems suspended over each party."[18] To her sister Margaret, she referred to the appointment of a Mr. Guillet to a consulship, but she did not intend to give him such a choice one as Marseilles. After the retirement of the Tylers from the White House, political comment continued in her letters. From Polk's conduct to rumors of Buchanan's appointment to the Supreme

Court, she turned to give her views upon the presidential aspirants. Believing that they all studied the best means to get the chair rather than the most righteous and patriotic methods, she concluded, "So I go this election, for men not principles, and prefer the person of Gen. Zack Taylor."[19]

Mrs. Polk of Tennessee was the medium by which James Polk sent his political instructions to one of his followers, Major Graham. Further, she interviewed a political friend to see that the congressional campaign was in order. Writing from Campbell's Station to her, Polk expressed the wish that any factor be prepared which would influence his political success in 1841.[20]

In 1838 Kentucky gave the franchise to all widows with children of school age; and many indications other than idle flattery may have prompted the campaign orators and the newspapers to speak so graciously of the fair daughters in the same breath with the patriotic sons. No southern Fourth of July celebration was complete without its toasts to the fair. Sometimes women themselves sent in toasts to be proposed. In the early forties a well-dressed young lady attempted to sell political pamphlets on the train at Frederick, Md. Certainly the most respected young ladies knew such favorite campaign songs as the one for Clay quoted by Mrs. Pryor:

> Get out of the way, you're all unlucky,
> Clear the track for old Kentucky![21]

Mississippi songs of "Tippicanoe and Tyler, too," were supplemented by aprons and handkerchiefs embroidered with log cabins and cider barrels. Under banners for the torch light parades made by ladies, Virginia children scrambled into wagons to form tableaux representing Liberty and the original thirteen colonies.[22] The presidential contests meant real occasions, even though the female ballot was an object of the most remote possibility to many of the women. The enthusiastic ladies waved their handkerchiefs for Yancey of Alabama as he arose to address the Democratic Convention at Charleston in 1860.[23]

Local politics were also impressed upon their minds, often as the result of an election at polls held in their homes. From Georgia and Mississippi echoes of the famous old barbecues attracted people for miles to break the isolation of plantation life. "Ole Mistis" and the young ladies came with their colored maids to celebrate by testing the ability of the neighboring housekeepers.

But the most renowned of the southern circles was that formed in Washington in the fifties. Beauty made a "sort of female Congress," wrote Prince Murat. [24] Mrs. Pryor's experience with its leaders led her to believe that inevitably graceful taste and inherited ability secured the reins of social control to them. Mrs. Yulee, the wife of the Senator from Florida, and her sisters, Mrs. Merrick and Mrs. Holt, together with Mrs. Robert J. Walker and Mrs. Jefferson Davis, formed the nucleus of the little circle so influential in Buchanan's administration. [25]

From such activities the southern woman made an easy transition to other occupations capable of producing a livelihood. The character of her academic training pointed to writing or teaching. As long as she did not venture beyond the conventional moral novel or sentimental poem, her works were reasonably certain of publication. For the more modest or for those whose verses were a pastime, a nom-de-plume such as "Tenella" was considered appropriate. *The Southern Literary Messenger* devoted pages to the work of these anonymous authoresses. Modesty prevented the publication of the admirable French of the Creoles; Emilie Evershed's *Une Couronne Blanche* went to Paris for publication. [26]

Under the spur of necessity the talented lady contributed such slender volumes as that of young Carrie Bell Sinclair, of Georgia, or poured forth a torrent of novels like those of Mrs. Emma D. E. N. Southworth. An amazing number turned northward to the columns of *The National Era, The Saturday Evening Post,* and the New York *Ledger.*[27] The picturesque Mrs. Southworth stood forth as a popular, voluminous, and impassioned novelist whose literary style never equalled the rapidity of her publications. Her charming Georgetown home was a resort of the distinguished of the nation. Maria McIntosh wrote from an entirely different angle; and her novels published in the North were considered jewels of moral worth.

Three centers in the South itself encouraged feminine talent. In the justly famous *Southern Literary Messenger,* edited by Richard Thomas, many poems of comparatively unknown women were printed; and its comments upon more experienced contributors were none the less critical because of past achievements. In a lesser way the *Literary Gazette* of Charleston performed the same service under Mr. Richards. But the third great center was in the West. George Prentice, of the Louisville *Courier-Journal,* stretched a helping hand to the budding poetesses of the Mississippi Valley. One of his friends, famous as "Amelia", published a volume of poems in 1845 which went through fifteen editions.[28] Not all editors were as favorable as these three. The New Orleans *Daily Picayune* refused by special editorial all poetical contributions.[29]

From conventional channels women ventured into other literary enterprises. Miss Blount edited a paper published in Bainbridge, Georgia, for two years; and Mrs. Gilman guided one of the first of southern juvenile journals, *The Southern Rosebud.* Originally a native of Massachusetts, this "past master in the order of American female authors" remained in the South, and was so identified with the section that Mary Forrest grouped her with its most famous women in 1860. Still another type of writer was represented by Sally Rochester Ford, a "leading light of the Baptists," in *The Christian Repository.*[30]

Combining the authoress with the teacher, Almira Lincoln Phelps deserved more fame than has been accorded to her. Only two women had been honored by membership in the American Association for the Advancement of Science: Maria Mitchel and Almira Phelps. The latter came from the North to the southern city of Baltimore. Mrs. Phelps' work absorbed so much of her interest that she wrote a successful series of text-books upon botany, chemistry, and natural philosophy. No less than a million copies had been circulated by 1860. Her home in the late fifties became the center of communications from former pupils from all over the South.[31]

Southern women conducted many private schools; and the reaction against them was negligible. While the headship of a seminary was not generally trusted to a woman, yet many women became principals of schools in the larger cities of the South. Real controversy arose over their teaching in what was loosely termed the public school. While northern tutors taught the wealthy southern youths, poorer children resorted to the old fields schools or to state institutions. The poor schools attached a stigma abolishing social status. In the early forties woman's employment aroused some discussion, but she won her place in primary work. In South Carolina a free school position indicated a lack of qualification for a better position. But in spite of obstacles women gained an entrance. Hence the pressing problem of proper professional training for teachers arose, but it had not developed beyond discussion before 1860.[32]

Female activity in the education of indigent children in Virginia was disclosed by certain petitions to the Legislature for unpaid salaries.[33] Compensation was miserably small, while discrimination in favor of male teachers was a common practice. North Carolina alone tried to improve this situation in the fifties. C. H. Wiley, its great superintendent, reported in 1854 that better salaries were drawing women into state employment. The almost unknown practice in the South of certification and examination of women teachers was initiated. By 1855 the monthly salary of the female teacher in the Tar Heel State had risen to eighteen dollars, a payment second to none, Massachusetts and Indiana giving approximately fifteen dollars a month to their women teachers.[34]

Perhaps the least appreciated of feminine activities was the performance of business duties. In controversies over the higher education of woman constant reference was made to the impracticality of mathematics for her; and yet records unconsciously revealed her in all sorts of business transactions. The Virginia legislative journals tell the story of loans to women and from them.[35] Jane Polk gave evidence of close attention to business details in her borrowing, payment of bills, and budgeting of expenses. Other women were interested in small investments in railroad stock.[36]

In legislative reports of 1840 upon the status of the Mississippi Union Bank and its branches, cotton notes contained names of women as endorsers as well as drawers for amounts ranging from five hundred to seven thousand dollars.[37] The same story repeated itself in 1851 in the statements of the Bank of Missouri and its branches, but in this instance the names were neither so numerous nor the amounts so large.[38]

Southern women also fulfilled the duties of the executrix. One of the largest class of petitions by women to the Virginia Legislature concerned such offices.[39] They sold property, paid debts, and acted as guardians of their children. Left with a plantation, Mrs. Polk kept an overseer and a factor, and saw that all details remained in order.[40]

Some women hired their Negro slaves for monthly or yearly compensation. Mrs. Polk let a Negro for one year for $47.62.[41] Scattered through the Virginia legislative journals are accounts of such transactions by women who hired their Negroes' services to state institutions.[42] Three such slaves were employed by the Eastern Lunatic Asylum, the payment varying from five to thirty dollars, while the University of Virginia hired the slave Aaron from Elizabeth Woodley for seventy dollars for one year. The extent of this practice has not been definitely measured, but its existence can not be questioned.

From activities meeting the requirement for a lady, transition passed through occupations tending towards the manual to arrive at those debarring from social standing. No definite line was established, but the invisible wall between these classes was insurmountable. The southerner lost all interest in recording the happenings in the life of the poorer class of women. Because they were so lowly, they themselves left slight evidence of their habits and occupations, which, if humble, were at least necessary to the southern community. Their prosaic life and small numbers did not invite historical attention. A nucleus sprang from the old apprenticeship laws upon the southern statute books; even the Missouri constitution of 1821 included such regulations. Any homeless infant, with the court's consent, became an apprentice until the age of sixteen; and a living parent was also permitted to bind out a daughter. The master was ordered to teach the girl reading, writing, and the ground rules of arithmetic, together with compound rules and the rule of three. At the expiration of her term of service, she was provided with suitable clothing worth twenty dollars, a bible, and ten dollars in the current money of the United States.[43]

That women did seek situations was evident from the columns of the New Orleans *Daily Picayune:* "Situation wanted. A white women, good cook, washer, and ironer wants a situation."[44] Chambermaids, nurses, seamstresses, and even a New York governess were rivaled by frequent appeals from the boarding house keepers; and the mid-wife, Mme. Cochrane, did not hesitate to employ the newspapers. Mantua and other dressmakers, together with the milliners, went to the directories for publicity.

The profession of the actress seemed to be shunned, as was the general field of public entertainment. Few galleries were controlled by women. Mrs. Charles Howard owned an Athenaeum and Gallery of Fine Arts in Baltimore, but the active management was given to men. While "Old Sol" Smith, New Orleans producer of 1840, was begged to test the histrionic ability of a young lady of St. Louis, the existence of the southern actress remains hidden. More ordinary but none the less interesting, the fortune teller, the somnambulist, and the planet reader appeared in New Orleans in 1860. Baltimore and St. Louis had fortune tellers, too, but none as perplexing as the lady phrenologist of New Orleans.[45]

No reliable statistics upon the occupation of southern women have been collected. For the more lowly employments, two chief sources have been left in the directories of cities and in the United [States] Census for 1860. Silence cloaked any organizations, although the late thirties brought echoes when the tailors of St. Louis and Louisville struck, demanding that tailoresses be no longer employed.[46] Women needle workers at Fells Point, Baltimore, organized a short-lived society in 1833. Another in 1835, under the name of the United Seamstress Society of Baltimore, blended into the movement producing the United Men and Women's Trading Society.[47] Benefits became a chief objective, the Baltimore *Republican* of October 15, 1835, announcing a benefit performance by the great actor, Mr. Booth. Later in the same year Baltimore clergymen were urged to appeal to their congregations in behalf of the seamstresses.[48] While their remuneration was unrecorded, that of women needle workers in general was small. Mrs. Tyler wrote in 1845 that eight dollars a month should command the best.[49] Records for payment for making clothes for the Virginia lunatic asylums indicated a higher wage, varying from eleven and a half to ninety-nine dollars, but statistics are sadly insufficient.[50] The most numerous occupations involving labor with the hands were centered in needle workers, who were classified in the directories under many heads. Perhaps the most prevalent were the dressmakers, about one hundred and sixteen appearing in Baltimore and one hundred and twenty in New Orleans around 1859.[51]

While the greatest number of seamstresses were employed in Baltimore, and were distributed through the country, the tailoresses were scarce. Few vest makers received mention in 1860, but the millinery shops claimed a large portion of women. No city lacked its fancy shop; and the embroiderer had risen to importance. Professional corset makers and artificial flower makers never gathered in large groups. The blanket term of clothier designated the largest class of female workers in Missouri, according to the Census of 1860.[52] Only one case, that of Mrs. Lytle and Mrs. Shipley, witnessed the existence of a "Gents Furnishings" conducted by women.[53] The Census listed workers on men's clothing as the second largest group of women employed in the South, their number constituting six thousand of the seventeen odd thousand engaged in all occupations.[54] In contrast to these figures the workers on women's clothing were officially numbered at ninety-three. Census figures recorded only those engaged in factory or semi-factory employment, because the number of dress-makers in New Orleans alone totaled more than one hundred.[55]

A new type of working woman arose in the mills, even before the industrial revival of post-bellum days and the full development of the factory system. Adolphus Meier's company in St. Louis ran a cotton mill with one hundred and fifty workers, largely women and children.[56] Census statistics revealed that most southern women factory workers produced cotton goods; and their number outranked even that of the men in this work. The seven and one-half thousand females so occupied were concentrated largely in Maryland, North Carolina, and Georgia. Woolen mills employed less than cotton factories, Georgia alone containing over two hundred of the nine hundred women so listed.[57]

This prosaic record contrasts strongly with the chronicles of the belles and their balls in its revelation of thirty-seven different kinds of employment in New Orleans for the less wealthy. The ever-present grocery, the boarding and rooming houses, and the variety store have continued to the present day. And although a single clerk was discernible, the upholstress, the shoemaker and the book binder and seller, and the china-store keeper swelled the list of Baltimore workers. Even jewelry stores were conducted by women.[58] To the female cigar sellers, Missouri added a hundred tobacco manufacturers. Nurses were not regarded with as high professional esteem as today, but all the South praised those aiding Norfolk during the yellow fever epidemic in 1855. Mid-wives and the "doctresses" of Petersburg,

Virginia were essential to the community. In Baltimore the cupper and leecher still lingered, although a female physician had arrived. The state asylums and institutions for the blind called for matrons and attendants. From baking and dairy work to washing and cooking, southern women used their abilities to make an humble way in the world. They were not the belle type, but their presence in the heyday of the modest and retiring lady is illuminating.

The operations of female liquor dealers in Baltimore was supplemented by the arrest of two Virginia women for the sale of ardent spirits without license.[59] Coffee houses, inns, taverns, and hotels—these were not without their female chatelaines in southern communities. Glimpses are brief, yet indicative that slave labor was not the sole dependence of the South. Inaccurate figures conflict, but the impression remains.

All southern women were not ladies in the accepted and narrow sense of the fashionable novel; and certainly the South was not blessed with more indolent women than any other section, considering its climate and social circumstances. If one searched for a parallel trait of the lady to that mellowness which characterized the best of the gentlemen of the Old South, that quality would have been an innate refinement which did not have to hide behind a cloak of assumed modesty, a culture which was derived from old traditions, a standard which permitted the gentlewoman to lead an active life. This southern woman of the upper class as well as her humbler sister, accepted what life gave. She did not struggle. Hence the women of the ante-bellum South adapted themselves to all manner of activities, old and new.

Notes

1. L. S. M., "Woman's Progress," in *Southern Literary Messenger* (Nov., 1853), p. 700.

2. An excellent general picture of the duties of the plantation mistress is contained in the portraits drawn by: Emily Burke, *Reminiscences of Georgia* (N. P., MD CCCL). Caroline Gilman, *Recollections of a Southern Matron and a New England Bride* (Philadelphia, 1860). Caroline Merrick, *Old Times in Dixie* (New York, 1901).

3. Frederika Bremer, *Homes of the New World* (2 Vols., New York, 1853), II. 226.

4. Maria McIntosh, *Woman in America, Her Work and Her Reward* (New York: MDCCCL), p. 118.

5. Virginia Legislature, *Journal of the House of Delegates* (Richmond, 1840–1860), see petitions. The Journals of the states of Mississippi, Missouri, and South Carolina may also be consulted. The author has traced the various kinds of petitions for and by women in these volumes.

6. Mrs. Myra Gaines, "The Horrors of War," in *The New Orleans Book* (New Orleans, 1851), p. 96.

7. Virginia T. Peacock, *Famous Belles of the Nineteenth Century* (Philadelphia, 1901), p. 116.

8. Anonymous, "Temperance Reform in Virginia," in *Southern Literary Messenger* (July, 1850), p. 433.

9. Caroline Lee Hentz, "An Address Delivered before the Total Abstinence Society of Alabama," in *Southern Literary Messenger* (Dec., 1843), pp. 1745–1746.

10. John W. Woods, *Directory of Baltimore for 1858–1859* (Baltimore, 1859), p. 268.

11. New Orleans *Daily Picayune*, Dec. 12–25, 1839.

12. *Ibid.*, Jan. 10, 1840.

13. Philadelphia *Public Ledger*, March 2, 1838.

14. J. T. Schaff, *Chronicles of Baltimore* (Baltimore, 1874), p. 563.

15. Maria Child, *History of the Condition of Women in Various Ages and Nations* (2 Vols., London, 1835), II. 265.

16. Harriet Martineau, *Society in America* (2nd. Edt., 3 Vols., London, 1837), I. 291.

17. McIntosh, *Woman in America*, p. 22.

18. Mrs. John Tyler to her mother, Washington, August 19, 1844. The collection of Mrs. Tyler's letters is in the Library of Congress.

19. *Ibid.*, Nov. 7, 1844.

20. James Polk to Mrs. Polk, Campbell's Station, May 9, 1841. The collection of Mrs. Polk's papers is also in the Library of Congress.

21. J. S. Buckingham, *The Slave States of America* (2 Vols., London, 1842), II. 136–257. [*Editor's note:* Widows with school-age children could vote in school elections, not in general elections.]

22. Mrs. Roger Pryor, *My Day, Reminiscences of a Long Life* (New York, 1909), p. 82.

23. James F. Rhodes, *History of the United States from the Compromise of 1850* (8 Vols., New York, 1909–1913), II. 441–447.

24. Achille Murat, *America and the Americans* (Tr. by J. S. Bradford, New York, 1849), p. 248.

25. Mrs. Roger Pryor, *Reminiscences of Peace and War* (New York, 1905), pp. 81–84.

26. Alicée Fortier, *Louisiana Studies* (New Orleans, 1894), p. 50.

27. Mary Forrest, *Women of the South Distinguished in Literature* (New York, 1861). The last chapters are filled with examples of the more obscure authors.

28. *Ibid.,* p. 386.

29. New Orleans *Daily Picayune,* Jan. 4, 1840.

30. Forrest, *Women of the South,* pp. 41; 55; 67.

31. *Ibid.,* p. 185.

32. Missouri Legislature, "Message of the Governor," in *Journal of House,* 1847–1848, pp. 26–29.

33. *Ibid.,* 1840–1852.

34. Edgar W. Knight, *Public School Education in North Carolina* (Boston, 1916), p. 170.

35. Virginia *Journal of the House,* 1842–1843, Doc. 4, The Report of the Second Auditor, p. 5.

36. The Papers of Mrs. Polk, 1841–1843. Virginia *Journal of House,* 1846–1847, Doc. 44, "Proceedings of the Joint Committee Charged with Investigating Rail-roads Companies," p. 77.

37. Mississippi, *Journal of House,* 1840, pp. 577–613.

38. Missouri, *Journal of House,* 1851–1852, pp. 70–90.

39. Virginia, *Journal of House,* 1842–1843, Doc. 6, "Proctor's Report on the University of Virginia," p. 8.

40. Papers of Mrs. Polk, receipts for the year 1842.

41. *Ibid.,* Doc. 9400, 1842.

42. Virginia, *Journal of House,* Doc. 34, "Report of Board of Directors of Eastern Lunatic Asylum," p. 21, 1842–43.

43. *The Revised Statutes of the State of Missouri,* edt. by W. C. Jones (St. Louis, 1845), pp. 116–117.

44. New Orleans *Daily Picayune,* Jan. 4, 1840.

45. Woods, *Baltimore Directory;* Robert Kennedy, *St. Louis Directory* (St. Louis, 1859); Charles Gardiner, *New Orleans Directory for 1860* (New Orleans, 1860); W. N. Haldeman, *Pictures of Louisville* (Louisville, 1844). These directories contained the names and the occupations of the women of the cities. No generalities can be made upon the nationalities involved except to state that there were many Irish and some French names represented.

46. Evans Woollen, "Labor Troubles between 1834–1837," in *Yale Review* (May, 1892), p. 98.

47. J. R. Commons, *History of Labor in the United States* (2 Vols., New York, 1918), I. 354.

48. Baltimore *Republican,* Sept. 14, 1835, Baltimore, Md.

49. Mrs. Tyler to her mother, Sherwood Forest, Oct. 6, 1843.

50. Virginia, *Journal of House,* 1840–1847. The reports of the directors of the various lunatic asylums are not included after the last named date.

51. See note 47. R. P. Vail, *Mobile Directory* (Mobile, 1842); W. L. Mon-

tague, *Richmond Directory and Business Advertiser* (Richmond, 1851); and W. E. Ferslew, *First Annual Directory for the City of Petersburg* (Richmond, 1859).

52. "Manufactures in the United States in 1860," in *The Eighth Census* (Washington, 1865), pp. 295–314.

53. Woods, *Baltimore Directory*, p. 267.

54. Census Report, Manufactures, 1860, pp. xxi–cxxi.

55. Gardiner, *New Orleans Directory*.

56. James Hogan, *Thoughts about the City of St. Louis* (St. Louis, 1854), p. 55.

57. Census Reports, Manufactures, 1860, p. xxxv.

58. See directories cited in notes 47 and 53.

59. Virginia, *Journal of House*, 1852, p. 269.

MARJORIE STRATFORD MENDENHALL

Southern Women of a "Lost Generation"

South Atlantic Quarterly 33 (1934): 334–53

The first paragraph of this essay reveals the assumption which nearly all southern historians shared in the years before 1960: that southern history meant the history of white people. In this case "Southern women" meant southern white women. So, too, the opening pages are based on perceptions of the antebellum period common to many southern historians writing in the 1930s.

Marjorie Mendenhall had been one of U. B. Phillips best students, but she had also been part of the graduate student group at Chapel Hill which included C. Vann Woodward and other young iconoclasts. Echoes of both exposures can be found here. No sooner does she tell us that in the days before the war all white people stood together (hence no hierarchy) than she also offers something similar to Woodward's own view about the hegemony of the merchant-farmers who moved to town in the years after 1865 and includes some recognition of the Populists whom he would bring so forcefully to the attention of historians a few years later.

It is only when she turns to women that we find her own significant contribution to the historiography of the South. Like Gray, Mendenhall dealt with subjects not usually examined in the context of southern history. Much of what she discovered has since been amplified and modified, but—again like Gray's essay—this article suggests a number of lines of research which still await their historian. Even less work has been done on late nineteenth-century women's education in the South than on the situation in the years before the Civil War, and we have no detailed study of the part women played in the great educational crusade of the eighties and nineties. Nor do we have the comprehensive study of nineteenth-century southern women wage earners which might have followed from the work of four out of five of the scholars whose work is collected here. And just as prewar voluntary associations have been virtually ignored, so, too, there is no broad study of late nineteenth-century developments in this area.

A close reading of this essay reveals a good deal about Mendenhall herself as well as about her subjects.

A FTER THE political maneuvers of the ante-bellum period and the agony of "the war" the white people of the South stood together—united in poverty and in a search for a new way of life. This poverty and search both conditioned and motivated the lives of Southern women from the end of the war to the nineties.

The literary evidence of post-bellum Southern poverty is voluminous, but for stark reality and comprehensiveness the essay of James L. Sellers in *The Mississippi Valley Historical Review* of 1927–1928[1] is unexcelled. Mr. Sellers has shown that the economic incidence of the Civil War on the South revealed itself in a shortage of agricultural capital, a reduced area under cultivation, a diminished agricultural production, depreciated land values, a stifled industry, a demoralized commerce, and totally inadequate banking and currency facilities. If to these one adds the national debt, which in proportion was to the South exactly what its name implies, and pension and tariff systems which constituted an unavoidable indemnity of at least a billion dollars, the picture is fairly complete. Superimpose on this the outgoing trail of those who preferred to invest their strength where the odds were less, and the trail of a smaller group who proposed to invest their funds where interest rates were high, and a society in which women outnumbered men will be seen facing a future of so little hope and so much hardship that one is moved to ask whence the strength that bore them through it.

The search for a new way of life was the inevitable result of the

passing of the plantation system. In ante-bellum days Southern society was not stratified. The life of that day was fluid and vigorous
and practically free of class antagonism. The medium that held its
unruly vitality together was a general acceptance of the plantation
system as a necessity and a positive good. To the initiated it becomes
increasingly clear that the system was no system at all. In the phrase
of Ulrich B. Phillips, who knew it well, it was "less a business than a
life."[2] But system or no system when it was gone the old order was
gone.

The planter was on the whole a secular figure, mingling the
chivalric virtues of hospitality, pride, courtesy, and regard for women
with the antique virtues of urbanity, nicety, and distinction. He
wanted to live a "good life" after the manner of the English country
gentleman or the Greek idea of καλος καγαθος. The plain people
who were to work out the destinies of their section were distinguished from the planters by a patriarchal character religious in its
foundation.[3] They were stern and hard, patient and persistent. Fri-
volity and decoration, felicity and an expressed affection were dis-
counted or distrusted by them. In the stress of the times the survivors
of the old "aristocracy" toned down their hospitality, pride and
emphasis on the amenities toward a kindliness, a gravity, a Puritan
decorum, and a quiet faith that blended with the high shrill faith of
the simpler folk. This carried them through the hard days and has
remained in varying intensity a constant in the character of the people
of the New South.

In less happy efforts to isolate that factor that gave to pre-war
society its unity and characteristic quality no byproduct was more
curious than the dualistic interpretation which divided Southerners
into planters and poor whites. Today the term "poor white" has a
diminishing significance. And as the delusion of the dualism of Southern social classes fades there appears more and more clearly on the
historical horizon a non-articulate, but powerful and numerous,
plain people who were to give to the New South the imprint of their
lives. Their new way came to be at once a greater repudiation of
farming as a mode of life than the acceptance of the old order had
been, and a register of the unceasing hold of the frontier ideal of
"getting ahead."

In the days just after the war the old ways and the old manners
lingered on, manifesting themselves at greater and greater intervals,

in brief flashes that attested the latent power of a recessive strain. With recovery slow everywhere and almost imperceptible in the rural regions vitality more and more reasserted itself in the form of an exodus to the West or to the towns. The latter was perhaps more successfully effected than the transfer to the West which in many cases was an "out of the frying pan into the fire" movement with a defeated return often its end. The man who turned the trick of transfer to town with the greatest ease was probably the merchant-farmer. It does not seem too much to say that he and his wife became the characteristic figures of the eighties and nineties. They more and more set the tone and determined the direction that Southern life was to take for a time. They were transitional figures. For that and other reasons description is difficult and may best be postponed.[4] Yet more difficult is the interpretation of the tone which they lent to society. The direction is however quite clear. They turned the eyes and interests of the men and women of their day away from life on a mere subsistence basis toward a life where comfort and companionship seemed probabilities, away from life on a frontier basis toward life on more sophisticated levels—away from the country and toward the town. These people were not cherishing much of the Old South. Their gods were the gods of the new day. A few of those who did not join their procession lived in the past. Many turned their minds toward a revolt against farm conditions. Like the usual society this one had its apathetics as small and inconsiderable perhaps as the "poor whites" of an earlier day but with a ghost that is just as difficult to lay.

In the meantime (that is, between 1865 and 1890) Southern women were with unanimity and industry working through the home, the churches, and the schools to make life livable for their families. The limits of their lives were clear and restrictive. But as the thread spun out the social strata widened and differentiated for them as for the men. At the top and the bottom they were working out a larger and more complicated design. In the less fortunate groups they were stepping into renumerative occupations. In the favored classes they were slipping into the professions and identifying themselves with movements, such as temperance, women's clubs, and suffrage. It is the purpose of this paper tentatively to describe (1) their work in the home, the churches, and the schools, and (2) the first evidences of the widening of the Southern woman's sphere.

The post-bellum family was patriarchal by inheritance and the sanction of religion. The inheritance was from both the genteel and the farming classes. From the latter came peculiarly the insistence on the religious justification. In post-war homes as in pre-war homes all great and grave decisions, all final commands were made by the father or older brother. Each family must present itself through a masculine head, though in many cases there must have been a mere reign and not a rule. The brilliant managing of Mrs. Allston of South Carolina had as its aim the return of the family to some of the ancestral lands where Charles, the son, might direct the family.[5] Mrs. Caroline E. Merrick, who grew to womanhood in the period just prior to the war and who was "emancipated" by the nineties, early "ascertained that girls had a sphere wherein they were expected to remain, and that the despotic hand of some man was continually lifted to keep them revolving in a certain prescribed and very restricted orbit."[6] Mrs. Marietta Minnegerode Andrews, first child of a post-war marriage, noted that all the women of her family spoiled their husbands as her mother spoiled her father.[7] Children were brought up in the admonition to honor their parents, and, since the mother particularly assumed the duty of training the young, the father received especial reverence and respect.

If the father was the titular head and sovereign the mother was generally the ways and means committee. Within the domestic unit she was the primary agent of cultural continuity, transmitting ideals, religious convictions, and opportunity to the children. For the adults she had hope and courage and inspiration and, more often than not, good sound advice. Isolation, inconvenience, and drudgery were her lot, accepted and often glorified. A whole literature of privations has grown up about her. She planned the meals and often cooked them. She "kept" the house. She "kept" a kitchen garden. She "kept" the milk sweet and clean. She raised chickens. She made, mended, and sometimes washed and ironed the clothes for the family. This was a job in the days when ready made garments were rare. She canned and dried the surplus fruit. She admonished and instructed the children, of whom there were seldom less than four and often as many as fourteen. She settled disputes and devised means of discipline. She went to the Ladies' Aid Society and she "took" the family to church. She did a thousand other things. With a genius worthy of a broader field she skimped and saved and schemed to accumulate a surplus so that the older children might go to school and bring back a skill that might in turn provide the means for the education of the younger ones.

All this was accomplished in homes that were either modeled upon or built for a régime in which servants were plentiful, or in the rude and poorly planned homes of poverty. Susan Dabney Smedes, speaking of the difficulties at Burleigh, says that "the arrangement of both house and plantation had been planned to employ many servants as was the custom in the South. Everything was at a long distance from everything else. As time went on an effort was made to concentrate things. But without money it was impossible to arrange the place like a Northern farm with every convenience at hand."[8] A house with a hall through it and a hall across it, "the middle porch," and with the kitchen in a separate building, had been one of the ideal ante-bellum arrangements that had gradually to be discarded. Sentiment and poverty, masculine control of building, ignorance, and the lack of leisure in which to compare and plan explain the retention beyond 1890 of an unsuitable house plan.

A succession of homely duties, of cares and anxieties, early robbed the mother of her girlish beauty and settled in her face a look of selflessness and disciplined character. In the daguerreotypes and occasional portraits of the period there is little joy and charm but a faithful record of strain and stress, sincerity and spirit, purpose and pride. One man explained that pride as loyalty. The quick response was: "Loyalty, it is not loyalty which makes us proud but pride that makes us loyal! Who could help being proud to belong to a State which could claim as its own such families as made the South what it was, and are making it what it is—families whose women no less than its men have borne themselves always, even amid the downfall of their country as conquerors not as conquered!"[9] Intensely local, definitely provincial in outlook, these strenuous mothers and maiden aunts concentrated on maintaining continuity and existence to such an extent that some of them became "contemporary ancestors."[10] By far the most of them felt in their grave way that the past was past and could never return; that the present with all its drawbacks and disappointments was full of the materials for creating a new order, just and inspiring for all classes, and in its potentialities not definitely inferior to the old order.

Throughout the period women preferred to work in "woman's sphere," quietly coöperating with the men in social and economic rehabilitation, but wherever necessity required they publicly displayed a varied executive ability. There is, for instance, the story of Miss Frances Butler, who during the greater part of ten years was actively in charge of several rice plantations on the coast of Georgia. Miss Butler adjusted the domestic economy and met labor troubles with particular ingenuity. She must have enjoyed her labors, for just before her marriage to an English clergyman she wrote to a friend, "I have worked so hard and cared so much about it, that it is more to me than I can express to know that I have succeeded."[11]

Then there is the story of Mrs. Robert Allston of South Carolina[12] who had to arrange for one hundred people on the farms in North Carolina and five hundred on the plantations in South Carolina. In a short time she had grasped the full extent of the situation and was exhibiting a remarkable patience and capacity for detail. After several thrilling experiences with the overseer and the negroes Mrs. Allston found that more than mere economy would be needed to save any of her property. As a result she set up a school for girls in Charleston. The school was a great success, but when the son was graduated from Charleston College the family returned to Chicora Wood where Charles could direct the rice planting. Every year for three years Mrs. Allston had invested one thousand dollars from the school. This sum provided for the mending of fences and the house and for the buying of seeds and implements.

Mrs. Marietta Minnegerode Andrews described several women of the period. Her Aunt Ida managed an estate in all particulars and with the greatest serenity. She knew all about raising corn and planting wheat and breeding stock and poultry; she knew all about the care of forests and the proper conservation of timber; she knew all about cooking and preserving and sewing and gardening; "and she knew all about God. A remarkable women!"[13] Then there was Aunt Katy, who, young and inexperienced as she was, managed Oatlands with its immense acreage and its swarm of ignorant and dependent blacks, so as to spare Uncle George, who had "not only the kindest heart in the world but the sort of training that unfits a man for effort or to assume responsibility."[14]

The churches of the South in the post-war period were organized after the fashion enjoined by Paul (I Tim. 2:9–15). Such an organization was in harmony with the general patriarchal order of this rural society. In the churches women "took fast hold on the solemn realities and relied on the divine consolations of religion." They brought the young into the church early and exerted a loving pressure upon the older pagans with so great a success that few were left out of the fold and the churches were able to give a puritanical tone to dress, amusements, manners, and morals. Many women in those days could echo the thankful sentiments of Susan Dabney Smedes: "The crowning blessing of our lives came in those days of poverty and toil. The beloved head of the house took his baptismal vows on himself and became a regular communicant in the Church."[15]

The Ladies' Aid Societies and the Ladies' Auxiliary were of great help to the churches and became centers for one of the great preoccupations of the period—the foreign mission movement. As if the local demands on their sacrificial energies were not enough these women collected funds from numerous and varied sources in order that the heathen might have the one true faith. It appears probable that the women of the South were especially interested in sending missionaries to foreign lands, whereas at the same time the women of the North were especially interested in the home mission movement in the South.

Near the end of the period women began to assert themselves more definitely in the churches.[16] Some of the interesting modifications are suggested in a chapter called "Women Preachers" in Dr. John Brevard Alexander's *Reminiscences of the Past Sixty Years.* "A half century ago it was uncommon for a woman to occupy a prominent position as a leader of music in our churches, but she would keep quiet till some man would start the hymn and wait until at least two lines were sung before she would join in. This was a time of rare modesty, but peculiar to our own Southland. No one [woman] ever thought of speaking in public, or entering the ministry or addressing a mixed audience. But customs and fashions have changed; New England can no longer claim the sole right of permitting women to enter the lecture field."[17]

Corra Harris felt the change in the church and in the women of the church somewhere in the latter years of her husband's ministry (in the nineties) when he "stepped out of one generation into another where the ideals of the Christian life were more intelligent but less heavenly."[18] During this time towns and villages were growing. As they grew the churches gave them tone. Social groups were formed about the churches and women moved in the groups so strictly that in the latter part of the period and in certain places individuals might be more easily classified by church membership than by family name.[19]

The interest of Southern women in education after the Civil War amounted to a veritable passion. It might involve actual teaching or agitation, or both as in the case of Mrs. Cornelia Phillips Spencer, who kept her little village school in Chapel Hill and at the same time worked most effectively through the press and her friends for the reopening of the University of North Carolina.[20] So general was woman's interest in education that the Reverend Amory Dwight Mayo, who worked in the field of Southern education for twelve years of the period under investigation, named as the one feature that most compelled his attention, "the push to the front of the better sort of Southern young womanhood, everywhere encouraged by the sympathy, support, sacrifice, toils and prayers of the superior women of the older generation at home."[21]

In the years from 1865 to 1890 four definite things were brought about in education that were of particular interest to women. First, the old seminaries and academies (largely of religious foundation) were revived and temporary private schools were established. Second, women largely displaced men as teachers in the elementary grades of the new public schools. Third, the movement for the establishment of women's colleges by the states was gotten under way. Fourth, coeducation was introduced into several of the state universities.

The education of Southern women before the war was accomplished in the homes or in the academies and seminaries maintained generally by the churches. In the more economically favored classes there was produced a rarely cultivated and gracious type of woman, remarkable for administrative capacity and tact.[22] These women devoted themselves with a double energy to meeting the emergency in education caused by the demoralization and poverty attendant upon war. They wished first of all to guarantee to the young good breeding, self-control, and a measure of skill sorely needed in the disorder of the times. Attending this wish was a determination to enforce quietly an opposition to the imposition of an educational system which was not controlled locally.[23] "Hundreds of the most cultivated and distinguished women; many of the widows, daughters and sisters of men once eminent in civil and military affairs before and during the great conflict found their way to the schoolroom. It would be easy to show that almost every celebrated family in the old Atlantic Southern States was represented there by some woman of high social standing, good culture, and eminent character. . . . It can readily be seen what an elevating and powerful influence this must have been in the opening era of this work of rehabilitation. . . . It brought the highest religious, literary and social womanly culture in these states in contact not only with the daughters of the superior families, but often in the new private and public schools with the children of both sexes, and all classes, gathered in from the highways and byways."[24] The revived denominational schools, such as Greensboro Female College, Salem Academy, and Limestone College, have had a continuous expanding part to play in the education of women since the war. The private schools lasted, on the whole, not much later than the eighties.[25] A description of one of the latter, in operation from the fall of 1865 through the spring of 1869, has been preserved.[26] This school, organized in Charleston by Mrs. Robert Allston, was a boarding and day school for girls ranging from beginners through the early teens. It was organized like a real home, with no rules, a scheme which worked exceedingly well, since Mrs. Allston was a very wise and respected person. There were four teachers, and in the last of the period five. Miss Allston, Mrs. Allston's daughter, taught the elementary subjects. A cousin taught French and literature. Later Mlle. le Prince came to live in the house and to encourage the speaking of French. Mrs. Allston herself taught all the classes in history. Professor Gibbes of Charleston College came over to teach Latin and mathematics. The school was a great success—so great a success that many deplored its closing, none more than Mrs. Allston's daughter who loved teaching and the life of Charleston.

During the eighties the small private schools declined and locally controlled public school systems received the support of increasing majorities.[27] From the beginning public schools have been directed by men, but the actual teaching has been done increasingly by women. In the Southern schools of 1870 there were more men teachers than women. By 1880 women had gained a slight lead. In 1890 that lead had been greatly increased. When it is remembered that administrative positions constantly held by men are included in the figures below the increase in the number of women teachers becomes even more impressive.

Teachers in the Southern States, 1870, 1880, 1890

	Male	Female	Total	Percentage Male	Percentage Female	Proportionate increase Male	Proportionate increase Female
1870 . . .	11,890	9,942	21,832	54.47	45.53	1	1
1880 . . .	19,878	20,916	40,832	48.73	51.27	5	6(c.)
1890 . . .	27,822	39,658	67,480	41.08	58.92	5	8(c.)

The simple explanation for the invasion of the field by women seems to be that for a low salary[28] a careful and capable woman could be secured. Young men of the times were engaged in a more definite restoration of the economic fabric. Many of them were emigrating.[29] One suspects that on the whole there were greater discrepancies and variations in the education of post-war boys than in that of the girls.

In the early days of the locally revived schools a host of "elect ladies" taught, but this army could not last forever. It became clear that some provision had to be made for the education of teachers. This was clearly recognized by the able administrators of the Peabody Fund, Dr. Sears and Dr. Curry, who became leaders in the teacher-training movement. As a temporary relief institutes and summer schools were started. For permanent relief the Peabody Normal School was established at Nashville, Tennessee, in 1875. Then the states were encouraged to establish normal schools. Mississippi responded first in 1884. South Carolina and North Carolina followed. The movement gained prestige as other states fell into line. While it is possible that most of these schools were at first "starveling institutions . . . long on piety and short on good manners and good sense,"[30] many of them have since developed into colleges of some note.

Colleges with less specialized aims and with curricula similar to those of men's colleges began to appear. The Woman's College, Baltimore, was founded in 1884; Sophie Newcomb appeared as a part of Tulane University in 1886; Agnes Scott was established in 1890.[31] Older colleges began the modification of their organization to meet national standards. That this was slow was the result of meager endowments rather than of conservatism. By 1890 the following Southern universities had become coeducational:[32] Missouri, 1870; Mississippi, 1882; Texas, 1883; and Kentucky, 1889.

As the new education got well under way comparisons with national standards brought out many weaknesses and non-conformities in Southern colleges. Independent colleges began to emulate more advanced institutions. Out of the comparison and discussion was to grow an organization of woman's colleges with the purpose of securing higher standards.

Teaching was for the women of the period by far the most important remunerative occupation. There is, however, definite evidence that they were entering other fields. Mayo estimates that in 1890 there were in the United States 346 economic opportunities for women while in the South there were only between twenty and forty.[33] So strong was the hold of the idea of "woman's sphere" that only those remunerative occupations that could be pursued in the home were approved. Boarders were spoken of as "paying guests," and often the process of paying a board bill required all the tact of a diplomat. Many an impoverished woman soothed her sense of guilt at having betrayed the ideal of womanly dependence by accepting for painstaking sewing a mere pittance. Miss Kearney, representative of a younger group, wished to work publicly, but her father objected strenuously. She secretly sewed for the Negroes, securing thereby some of the necessities that were not forthcoming otherwise.[34]

Throughout the period there were large groups of women gainfully employed. So much the census tells us, but when more particular details are sought difficulties are met. From 1870 to 1890 the technique of census taking and recording was undergoing a change. The grouping and naming of occupations shifted. And Negroes and whites were not separated except on the basis of the whole United States. Many of those enumerated as gainfully employed were Negroes engaged in agricultural labor, domestic service, and laundering.[35] Since among males engaged in agriculture, laborers and owners are in a ratio of 1:1 or 2:1, whereas among females in agriculture the owners are few (for instance, in Georgia in 1870 there were 53,000 female laborers to 1,000 owners), and since white female agricultural laborers were unknown in the South, the conclusion is inescapable that agriculture was the field of the colored women and that from two-thirds to four-fifths of the Southern women engaged in gainful occupations before 1890 were Negroes. Many white women were undoubtedly engaged in agriculture, but public admission of the facts was evaded.

In manufacturing is found a larger number than in trade or professional service. This is to be explained by the number of milliners and dressmakers.[36] The number of dressmakers increased from 17,860 in 1870 to 71,319 in 1890. Although the number of dressmakers and seamstresses is large the fact should receive no great emphasis from the feminist viewpoint because the sewing was done in most cases in the homes. The number of female cotton mill operatives was still small in 1890 (17,433); yet it was six times as large as the number in 1870.[37] More significant than numbers is the fact that in 1870 the number of male operatives exceeded the number of females while in 1890 the positions were reversed.[38] Invasion or precipitation, whichever it be, children had also entered the textile industry.[39]

The same development that characterized teaching and that was beginning to appear in manufacturing appeared in that division of the occupations known as trade. Women by 1890 had already begun to settle into the subordinate positions. Whereas in 1870 the number of female traders and dealers was larger than the number of clerks, by 1890 this was reversed.[40] The same tendency is seen in boarding-house keeping and in hotel management. By 1890 more women "kept" boarding-houses and more men "ran" hotels. Of course boarding-house keepers could also keep the illusion of "women's sphere."

In 1890 there were in the South among women 12 lawyers, 89 journalists, 108 professors, 120 clergymen, 221 authors and literary and scientific persons (whatever that may mean), and 434 physicians and surgeons.[41]

It appears that women had barely begun to make their way into the professions and that they were "edging" into the lower ranks of the other occupations. The old ideas of propriety were still very strong in 1890; yet a questionnaire of 1892 dealing with the propriety of self-support in women showed the older women giving a qualified approval to the idea as a second best resort of a woman, while the younger women gave unqualified approval to the idea.[42]

Turning from a subject of doubtful propriety to one of impeccable reputation, at least in the feminine mind of the period, we find that the temperance cause was an importation. The Woman's Christian Temperance Union, originally a Northern reform movement, was enlarged in 1880 to include Southern women. In 1881 Miss Frances E. Willard, president of the organization, made her initial Southern trip.[43] Within three months the members of her party had visited one hundred towns and cities.[44] Between 1881 and 1887 Miss Willard came south four times, "attending in different years a State Temperance Convention in almost every one of the fourteen Southern states."[45] The temperance movement was in its very nature appealing to Southern women. With its puritanical foundation it was easily allied with church activities, especially at first before it was seen to lead to a demand for the suffrage. Furthermore it offered a respectable and appealing outlet for the energies of the women of leisure who were beginning to appear in the eighties. The women who followed Miss Willard so eagerly at first were somewhat taken aback when they realized in 1882 that the society was about to take a stand for woman suffrage. The conservatives withdrew from the organization and invited the Southern delegates to go with them. The invitation was declined, however, with the remark that they "had seceded once and found that it didn't work."[46] Upon this evidence it can hardly be said that Southern women accepted suffrage so early!

One of the characteristic figures of the temperance movement was Miss Belle Kearney.[47] She became a temperance worker shortly after experiencing Christian conversion. In her work she necessarily became a supporter of the Prohibition party and a suffragist.

The story of Mrs. Caroline E. Merrick's attachment to the "cause" is a singularly interesting one. Miss Willard's interest was aroused by the reading of an account of an address given by Mrs. Merrick, in which she treated the gentlemen to "some of the extemporaneous sugar plums which they had been accustomed to shower upon women."[48] An acquaintance between the two grew into a friendship which led to Mrs. Merrick's acceptance of the presidency of the W.C.T.U. in New Orleans "not from deep conviction of duty on the temperance question but because she could not resist the inspiration of Frances E. Willard's convictions."[49]

Organizations for more varied purposes appeared in the eighties. Some of these were established for humanitarian ends, some for self-culture, and others to secure the ballot. Mrs. Merrick tells of the formation of the first woman's club in the South.[50] Organized in New Orleans in 1884, it estimated its scope thus: ". . . the vital and influential work of our club must always be along sociological lines. . . . In the aggregate we are breaking down and removing barriers of local prejudice; we are assisting intellectual growth and spiritual ambition in the community of which we are a dignified and effective body—for the immense economy of moral force made possible by a permanent organization such as ours is well understood by the thoughtful."[51] Affiliation with the general movement came shortly, for in 1889 delegates attended the Convention of Women's Clubs held in New York under the auspices of Sorosis.[52] By 1890 there were in New Orleans headquarters for the Louisiana State Suffrage Association and for five local clubs, the Woman's Club, the Arena Club, the Portia Club, an offshoot of the Portia Club, known as the Era Club (Equal Rights Association), and the Woman's League for Sewerage and Drainage. Other cities could probably have shown a similar roster.

The beginnings of the club movement indicate a falling away from the old conception of a "woman's sphere." There is a more subtle manifestation in the relaxation of the reverential attitude toward the masculine head of the family that amounted almost to worship, or the admission of the presence of an indelible character in the "stronger" sex. In the latter part of the period there accumulate, among the older and the younger women, instances that show a diminution in the attitude of reverence, Mrs. Andrews, who was seventeen in 1890, remembered from her childhood that her mother's "lady cousins" were better able to adjust themselves after the war than were the "gentlemen" cousins.[53] She noticed, too, that the Lost Cause lost a great deal of its lustre upon close observation of the ex-heroes.[54] Now a woman who had been seventeen in 1865 might have seen these things. She would hardly have written them. Miss Kearney, born too late to be a slaveholder, let her father's objection to her intention of earning her own living hold her for several years in poverty and secret employment, but in the eighties, after a series of violent and protracted interviews, she became successively a teacher, a lecturer, and a suffragist.

Then there are the two interesting cases of Mrs. Cornelia Phillips Spencer and Mrs. Caroline E. Merrick, both born in 1825. In reconstruction days Mrs. Spencer virtually accomplished the reopening of the University of North Carolina without once projecting her own personality, and she seemed to have been astonished when she was honored for it. Her mind was active upon many lines, and it is no surprise to find her views on woman suffrage in the Young Ladies' Column of *The North Carolina Presbyterian Standard*. She was thoroughly opposed to the idea at first. But as time went on and she became aware that the refusal of men to include women in the groups that formulated educational policies was promoting the growth of the woman suffrage movement, she admitted a lack of conviction concerning the old viewpoint that is most suggestive in its implications:[55]

> I must confess to being so blind and bigoted that only lately has it occurred to me that there might be some good on the other side of Woman's Rights. Only lately have I looked at it dispassionately and I find to my disgust that the female reformers out yonder in Wyoming, or in Chicago, or New York—where not save and except down South—have really an argument or two on their side. No use shutting our eyes or closing our ears till the flood is upon us, or I am afraid we shall all be swept away. Violent denunciation and contempt are no answer to argument. There are surely two sides to this great question. Yes, I feel cross! And yet a house mother—one of those quiet women who keep society from going to pieces—is she not as valuable to the world as a Mme. de Stael—or more so? Still, I feel *cross*!

Mrs. Merrick tacitly admits having conformed for the greater part of her life to a pattern dominated by the masculine influence,[56] but by the eighties she was developing a flippancy on the subject, and in the nineties she became a confirmed exponent of the idea of equality for women, using her influence to secure for them a voice in the counsels of the churches, the schools, and the nation. Who can conceive of a woman of the sixties saying what she said in 1881?[57]

> Lest they should feel overlooked and slighted, I will say a word to the men. God bless them. Our hearts warm toward the manly angels—our rulers, guides and protectors, to whom we

confide all our troubles and on whom we lay all our burdens. Oh, what a noble being is an honest, upright, fearless, generous, manly man. How such men endear our firesides, adorn and bless our homes. How sweet is their encouragement of our timid efforts in every good word and work, and how grateful we are to be loved by these noble comforters, and how utterly wretched and sad this world would be, deprived of their honored and gracious presence. Again I say, God bless the men.

The last word in a controverted matter in the days of which we write would probably have been spoken by a clergyman. These are the words of the Reverend Amory Dwight Mayo: "It was apparent that the day when the father of the house and the parish minister could draw a hard and fast educational and social diagram of the Southern woman was passing."[58]

The white women of the South in the years from 1865 to 1890 had mended the war-broken homes and conspicuously revived the churches. They had made a major contribution to education. True to their ideal of "being a good influence" they had espoused the temperance cause. Many who lacked economic security had ventured into the occupations. A few had entered the professions. Still in the majority in 1890 were the valiant rural women of the generation that has been called "lost," the women who were frankly submissive to the masculine portion of their world, who were more conscious of being wives, mothers, daughters, and sisters than of being women in a cosmopolitan society. For the oncoming women a new mould was being formed. By the forces of their times they were to be urban, self-assertive, and competitive. They were to be critical of inherited patterns and traditions. In increasing numbers they were to accept and to further the widening of the interests of Southern women.

Notes

1. "The Economic Incidence of the Civil War in the South," XIV, 179–191.
2. *American Negro Slavery* (New York, 1918), p. 401.
3. See, for instance, Edgar Gardner Murphy, *Problems of the Present South* (New York, 1904); D. R. Hundley, *Social Relations in Our Southern States* (New York, 1860), p. 91; Gerald Johnson, "The Cadets of New Market," *Harper's Magazine*, CLX, 111–119; and Corra Harris, *The Circuit Rider's Wife* (Philadelphia, 1910), p. 323.

4. Suggestions appear here and there in Alex Mathews Arnett, *The Populist Movement in Georgia* (New York, 1922), and C. H. Otken, *Ills of the South* (New York, 1894).

5. Mrs. Elizabeth Allston Pringle, *Chronicles of Chicora Wood* (New York, 1922).

6. Mrs. Caroline E. Merrick, *Old Times in Dixie Land* (New York, 1901), p. 12.

7. Mrs. Marietta Minnegerode Andrews, *Memoirs of a Poor Relation* (New York, 1927), p. 238.

8. Susan Dabney Smedes, *A Southern Planter* (New York, 1900), p. 237.

9. Elizabeth McCracken, *The Women of America* (New York, 1903), p. 73.

10. Edwin Mims, *The Advancing South* (New York, 1906), Preface, p. ix.

11. Frances Butler Leigh, *Ten Years on a Georgia Plantation* (London, 1883), pp. 193–195.

12. Pringle, *op. cit.*

13. Andrews, *op. cit.*, p. 163.

14. *Ibid.*, p. 204.

15. Smedes, *op. cit.*, p. 244.

16. Amory Dwight Mayo, *Southern Women in the Recent Educational Movement in the South*, Bureau of Education Circular of Information, No. 1, 1892, Whole Number 186 (Washington, 1892), p. 54; Merrick, *op. cit.*, pp. 181–184.

17. John Brevard Alexander, *Reminiscences of the Past Sixty Years* (Charlotte, 1908), pp. 420–421.

18. Harris, *op. cit.*, p. 160.

19. McCracken, *op. cit.*, pp. 391–394.

20. Chamberlain, *Old Days in Chapel Hill* (Chapel Hill, 1926), pp. 199–227.

21. Mayo, *op. cit.*, p. 55.

22. Joel Chandler Harris, *Southern Historical Society Papers*, XVIII, 277–281; Phillips, *op. cit.*, p. 323; Mayo, *op. cit.*, p. 45.

23. Mayo, *op. cit.*, p. 55.

24. Mayo, *op. cit.*, pp. 52–53.

25. I remember as a child puzzling over what became of the two private schools which figured in the stories of my mother's childhood.

26. Pringle, *op. cit.*, pp. 290–310.

27. Mayo, *op. cit.*, p. 137.

28. The average monthly salary for the white teacher in the eighties was $32.74, Mayo, *op. cit.*, p. 202.

29. Mayo speaks of estimates of one million for the period.

30. Gerald Johnson's description of the Woman's College of the University of North Carolina, *Harper's Magazine*, CLX, 115 (Dec., 1929).

31. Mary K. Benedict, "The Higher Education of Women," *The South in the Building of the Nation*, X, 262.

32. M. Carey Thomas in the *Annals of the American Academy of Political Science,* Nov., 1914, Vol. LVI, Whole No. 145. Other universities: Alabama, 1893; South Carolina, 1894; North Carolina, 1897; W. Virginia, 1897.

33. Mayo, *op. cit.,* p. 168.

34. Belle Kearney, *A Slaveholder's Daughter* (New York, 1990), pp. 40–73.

35. Tables derived from census figures—and too bulky to print.

36. *Ibid.*

37. *Ibid.*

38. *Ibid.*

39. *Ibid.*

40. *Ibid.*

41. *Ibid.*

42. Wilbur Fiske Tillett, "Southern Womanhood as Affected by War," *The Century Magazine,* XLIII (XXI, *n. s.*), 1891–1892.

43. Frances E. Willard, *Glimpses of Fifty Years* (Boston, 1889), p. 368.

44. *Ibid.,* p. 373.

45. *Ibid.,* p. 372.

46. *Ibid.,* p. 380.

47. Belle Kearney, *A Slaveholder's Daughter* (New York, 1900).

48. A good example may be found in Colonel William H. Stewart, *The Spirit of the South* (New York, 1908), pp. 175–180.

49. Merrick, *op. cit.,* pp. 141–144.

50. *Ibid.,* chap. XIX, "The Southern Woman Becomes a 'Clubable' Being."

51. *Ibid.,* pp. 216–217.

52. *Ibid.,* p. 217.

53. Andrews, *op. cit.,* p. 204.

54. *Ibid.,* p. 190.

55. Chamberlain, *op. cit.,* p. 274.

56. Merrick, *op. cit.,* p. 144, "Finding that the source of power in my family resided ultimately in the head of the house. . . ."

57. *Ibid.,* pp. 141–142.

58. Mayo, *op. cit.,* p. 54.

JULIA CHERRY SPRUILL

"Conjugal Felicity" and Domestic Discord

Chapter 8 of *Women's Life and Work in the Southern Colonies* (Chapel Hill: University of North Carolina Press, 1938), 163–84, reprinted by permission of the publisher

Almost any chapter in Spruill's classic work could have been included here to mark her part in this extraordinary cluster of studies of southern women. Though her work has not been lost to sight as has that of others represented here, she is such a key figure in this story that it seems appropriate to include a sample from her book.

In our day when social history has attracted so many historians, it is hard to realize just how unusual it was for a southern historian in the 1930s to write not only social history but social history which focused on women. In this chapter as in all the others in her book Spruill brings to bear immense learning derived from close study of virtually all the available primary sources. She writes beautifully, and her evidence is woven together seamlessly. *Women's Life and Work* is so packed with evidence that many readings do not exhaust its capacity to startle even the informed historian.

Once this book was in print generalizations about married life in the eighteenth-century South had to be abandoned. By simply presenting the evidence from newspapers and court records Spruill managed to paint a picture of feisty, outspoken women taking matters into their own hands despite the legal and customary power of men to control them. With this evidence before us no one can believe that either wife abuse or outspoken women are an invention of the twentieth century.

New England and northern colonial women have come in for a

great deal of attention lately in the work of (among others) Mary Beth Norton, Laurel Thatcher Ulrich, and a group of legal historians. Despite the excellent work of Suzanne Lebsock and a few others, it appeared for awhile that there was little interest in further work on southern colonial women. That is beginning to change. A number of dissertations are in progress, and southern colonial women are on their way to a new renaissance. While this new work will certainly go beyond Spruill, it is a test of her thoroughness that her book remains the place to begin.

K EEPING IN MIND the prosaic, businesslike manner in which marriages were often made in colonial days, and considering the immature age of many persons undertaking marital responsibilities, the haste with which a deceased mate was frequently replaced by another, and the numerous ventures often made by the same person, one wonders what was the sequel to this kind of marriage-making. Unfortunately the matrimonial histories of individual couples have not been preserved. But abundant materials at hand reflect the prevailing conception of proper conjugal conduct and throw light upon the general state of marriage.

The subject treated in most detail by seventeenth-century family books was the mutual duties of husbands and wives. Generally it was stated that the husband should guide, defend, and provide for the wife, while she was to serve him in subjection, be modest in speech and dress, and be a good housewife. "A wise husband," declared *A Godly Form of Household Government,* "and one that seeketh to live in quiet with his wife, must observe three rules. Often to admonish: Seldom to reprove: and never to smite her."[1] The commonly accepted idea of the proper treatment of a husband was described by a "well-spoken" wife in *A Looking Glasse for Maried Folks:* "When he lookt at any time very sad, & there were not fit time to speak to him, I would not the laugh & daily with him, and play the tom-boy . . . but I put upon me a sad countenance, and lookt heavily. . . . So it beseemes an honest wife to frame herselfe to her husbands affections. . . . And if at any time he were stired, I would either pacify him, with a gentle speech, or give way to his wrath. . . . This course also I tooke: if he came drunken home, I would not then for anything have him a foule word, but I would cause his bed to be made very soft and easie, that he might sleepe the better, and by faire speeches get him to it."[2]

These views somewhat elaborated were embodied in ladies' books and treatises on marriage throughout the next century, though later writings usually gave more attention to the wife's duties and less to the husband's. She was supposed to exist for her husband, be an agreeable and obedient companion to him, a tender mother of his children, a capable and industrious manager of his house, and a gracious and attractive hostess to his guests. This feeling expressed by an exemplary matron in *The Spectator* was that of the true wife: "I am married, and I have no other concern but to please the man I love; he is the end of every care I have; if I dress, it is for him; if I read a poem, or a play, it is to qualify myself for a conversation agreeable to his taste; he is almost the end of my devotions; half my prayers are for his happiness."[3]

The *Virginia Gazette* offered the "fair sex" these "Rules for the Advancement of Matrimonial Felicity": "Never dispute with him [your husband] whatever be the Occasion . . . And if any Altercations or Jars happen, don't separate the bed, whereby the Animosity will cease . . . by no Means disclose his imperfections, or let the most intimate Friend know your Grievances; otherways you expose yourself to be laugh'd at. . . . Read often the Matrimonial Service, and overlook not the important word OBEY."[4] One "Receipt for the Ladies to retain the Affections of their Husbands" emphasized good humor and discretion as most desirable wifely qualities, and another described the "Good Wife" as one "humble and modest from Reason and Conviction, submissive from Choice, and obedient from Inclination."[5] A North Carolina paper urging upon wives the importance of neatness in dress and a sweet temper, concluded with this advice:

> . . . her Wit must never be display'd,
> Where it the husband's province might invade:
> Be she content sole *Mistress* to remain,
> Nor poorly strive for the *Mastership* t' obtain.
> This would occasion Jars, intestine Strife,
> Imbitter all the sweets of nuptial Life:

Then let her not for Government contend,
But use this Policy to gain her end – –
Make him *believe* he holds the Sov'reign Sway,
And she may *rule*, by seeming to *obey*.[6]

To what extent colonial wives subscribed to these rules and attempted to put them into practice does not appear. Nor is it known whether husbands generally took advantage of their position as "lords of creation." The records show on the one hand a great deal of conjugal affection, loyalty, and happiness, and on the other discord and discontent. As evidence of mutual confidence and devotion, one might point to many wills in which the testator made careful provision for his "beloved wife," to affectionate letters, and to occasional glimpses of happy married life in private papers. Governor William Berkeley of Virginia left his "deare and most virtuous wife" all his estate with this declaration, "if God had blest me with a far greater estate, I would have given it all to my most Dearly beloved wife."[7] Likewise John Smithson of Maryland, in a nuncupative will, declared of his wife, "All I have I leave her, and if I had more she should enjoy it."[8] Some wills included a verbal tribute besides a generous bequest as did that of Benjamin Harrison, who gave his wife handsome legacies besides her thirds and added this explanation, "she hath at all times behaved in a most dutiful and affectionate manner to me and all-ways been assisting through my whole affairs."[9] John Rutledge explained that because of his wife's "good understanding" and tenderness to his seven young children, he was leaving her his entire estate with the right to use or dispose of it according to her discretion.[10] John Randolph made large provision in different kinds of property, jewelry, and money for his "dear and most beloved wife," stating that it was for "her faithfulness affection and prudence."[11]

Scattered through the records are many declarations of tender sympathy and expressions of anxiety at the suffering or grief at the decease of a beloved mate. In 1716 Mann Page of "Roswell" in Virginia wrote in his Bible: "On the 12th day of December (the most unfortunate day that ever befell me) about 7 of the clock in the morning, the better half of me, my dearest wife, was taken from me." At about the same time, grief-stricken William Byrd informed a relative of his "dear Lucy's" death, exclaiming: "Alas! how proud was I of her and how severely I am punished for it."[12] Louis Henry de Rosset of North Carolina declared of his "dear best friend" that her many virtues had so endeared her to him that he "fully enjoyed every conjugal felicity for thirty years."[13] William Stephens of Georgia mourned for a wife with whom he had lived for nearly forty-four years, during the whole of which time, he declared, "a mutual tender affection" had remained between them.[14] Henry Laurens was over-whelmed at the passing of his "bosom friend," whom he praised as "ever loving, cherishing and ready to obey—who never once,—no, not *once*—during the course of twenty years' most intimate connection threw the stumbling block of opposition" in his way.[15]

More convincing evidence of conjugal affection and mutual help-fulness appears in sympathetic and affectionate letters like the following written by General William Campbell of Virginia in 1776:

My Dearest Betsy:

. . .

I received your sweet and most affectionate letter of the 9th inst. by Col. Meredith. The fear you there express for my going to the northward, or against the Cherokees, you may entirely lay aside. . . . If the horse you mentioned please you right well, by all means buy him, though inquire . . . if he is given to stumbling or starting. . . .

I most heartily thank you, dear, for your attention for providing me such necessaries as I stand in need of. I fear you are too solicitous and give yourself too much trouble. You bring to my mind Solomon's excellent description of a good wife. . . . Such is my dearest Betsy. Her worth I esteem far above rubies.

I have now lived about a week in the house where I was first blessed with a sight of my dear Betsy. Little did I at that time think that such superlative happiness was destined for me. From that happy moment I date the hour of all my bliss. I love the place on your account.

. . .

Will see you as soon as I possibly can. . . .

Your most affectionate

WM. Campbell[16]

Letters of James Iredell to his "dear Hannah" reveal a similar affection and esteem. When obliged to be away from home holding court, he wrote her frequently, giving interesting details of his travels, and always lamenting their separation, imploring her to be careful of her health, urging her to write him by every opportunity, and assuring her of his lasting devotion. "O! how long every hour seems to me," he exclaimed while on one circuit. "Never did I feel more anxiety to see you. . . . I will apply day and night to the business at Hillsborough, in order to shorten the time of my further absence from you."[17]

Mutual confidence, loyalty, and devotion were doubtless enjoyed by many other couples. But there were also unhappy marriages. Those who point to the colonial period as a golden age of family relations can hardly be acquainted with the eighteenth-century discussions lamenting the decadence of the domestic virtues, with the suspicion and distrust reflected in private papers, with the large number of public notices of absconding wives and voluntary separations, and with the many complaints by husbands and wives in court records.

"Reflections on unhappy marriages" was a favorite subject of journalists. Among the reasons usually given for the "degeneration of the Married state" were "female extravagance," excessive fondness for dress and display, and neglect of domestic duties. A correspondent to the *Virginia Gazette,* declaring one of the greatest "unhappinesses" of the time was that matrimony was so much discountenanced, suggested as causes of the "interruption of domestic peace" the fact that ladies gave themselves up too generally to an idle and expensive life, and that men, for the sake of beauty or wealth, ran the "desperate hazard" of taking to their bosoms a "fury" or an "ideot."[18] A note familiar to every generation was sounded by a contributor to the *Lady's Magazine:* "If women would recover that empire which they seem in a great measure to have lost . . . they must change their present fashionable method of living, and do what their grandmothers did before them, go often to church, and be well acquainted with their own houses."[19]

Misunderstanding and dissension were reflected now and then in colonial wills, as in this provision made by Willie Jones, prominent North Carolina patriot: "Now, as it is possible and indeed probable that my wife will not be satisfied with the provisions which I have hereinbefore made for her, and consequently could refuse to be bound by this very will. . . . I leave to my wife to do better for herself if she can."[20] Hendrick Sluyter of Bohemia Manor in Maryland left posterity a hint of his domestic problem in this clause, "As my wife, to my sorrow, has always some difference with my friends, it is my desire that she retire to her former home in Philadelphia or elsewhere."[21] A more shameless testator was Colonel John Custis of Virginia, who ordered the following vindictive inscription placed upon his tombstone:

> Beneath this Marble Tomb lies ye Body
> of the Hon. John Custis, Esq.
>
> . . .
>
> Aged 71 Years, and yet lived but seven years,
> which was the space of time he kept
> a bachelor's home at Arlington
> on the Eastern Shore of Virginia.[22]

The seven years which he counted were those after the death of his wife, Frances Parke, with whom he had lived in a turbulent marriage.

Gossip of this eccentric couple must have provided conversation for many Virginia dinner parties. For weeks at a time, it was said, they would not speak to each other, communicating when necessary through the servants. She would say, for instance, "Pompey, ask your master if he will have coffee or tea, and sugar and cream," and he would reply, "Tell your mistress I will have coffee as usual, with no cream." During one of their periods of ominous silence, to her surprise he asked her to go for a drive, and she accepted. Heading his horse into Chesapeake Bay, he drove out into the water. "Where are you going, Mr. Custis?" she asked after a time. "To hell, Madam," he replied. "Drive on," she answered, not the least disconcerted, "any place is better than Arlington." On and on out into the water he drove until the horse was forced to swim, and still the undaunted lady uttered no protest. "I believe you would as lief meet the Devil himself, if I should drive to hell," he announced as he turned again toward the shore. "Quite true, Sir," she retorted, "I know you so well I would not be afraid to go anywhere you would go."[23]

A contract drawn up between this spirited pair now on file in Northampton County suggests that disagreement over financial matters was at the root of their strife. Having brought her husband a large estate at marriage, Frances probably felt entitled to some say as to how it should be used and did not always express her feelings with proper amiability. The immediate bone of contention was some silver plate and damask linen inherited by Frances, which she had removed from the house. She demanded a "more plentiful maintenance" for herself and family and a more businesslike management by him of the estate that was to descend to her children. The text of the contract is revealing as a statement of what were considered proper marital rights in such cases. Frances promised to return the linen and plate and never to take anything else of value from the house without his consent, and John covenanted not to dispose of these articles during her life and to give them to her children immediately after her death. Each agreed to "forbear" to call each other "vile names," to "live lovingly together" and to "behave themselves to each other as a good husband & wife ought to do." She was to avoid meddling with his business matters, and he was to permit her sole control over her domestic affairs. He was to render annually to a third person a true account of his estate, and of the clear profits was to allow her one half for clothing herself and children, for the children's education, and for housekeeping articles from England. Also he promised to contribute certain provisions made on the plantation such as wheat, Indian corn, meats, wool, and flax. All of this was promised on condition that Frances did not exceed her allowance, run him into debt, or break any part of her agreement. Whether she or he or both violated the contract is not known, but it evidently did not, as they had hoped, "end all animositys and unkindness" between them.[24]

Somewhat similar to this covenant was one signed by the Reverend Caspar Stoever, Lutheran minister of the German congregation in Virginia, and his second wife, Maria Magdalena. In their articles of agreement drawn up in 1734, they promised to "totally forget and bury in oblivion" all differences between them. He agreed to provide her with maintenance and clothes according to his station and means, and she to "obey his lawful commandments as a Christian wife ought to do." Also he agreed that if he should travel to some other place and, against her wishes, leave her there, half of his estate would fall to her share, provided she were not the cause of his so leaving her. Provision for her mother and for his children by a former marriage was another cause of dispute. He stipulated to give certain property to his children by a former wife and then leave those by Maria Magdalena his sole heirs, and promised to maintain his mother-in-law and to "shew her all love and faithfulness due from a child." In return, the mother was to be "careful of not giving offense . . . especially to leave off all evil speaking, backbiting & slandering" and to "admonish her Daughter to beware of offending." This provision, inserted "to the end the congregation may not be offended," was duly signed by the mother-in law as well as the husband and wife. Furthermore, it was written into the contract that, if the husband wished it, the mother-in-law was to reside in some place other than with him.[25]

Another marriage possibly more poignantly unhappy than that of the Stoevers or the Custises was the union between Colonel William Byrd III and his first wife, Elizabeth Hill Carter, daughter of Secretary John Carter of "Shirley," The cause of their differences is unknown, but his mother, Maria Taylor Byrd, evidently encouraged her son's dissatisfaction with his wife. Forsaken by her husband then serving in the French wars, deprived of her three oldest boys, who were in England at school, and disparaged by her mother-in-law, young Elizabeth Byrd must have led a melancholy existence at "Belvidere." The older Mrs. Byrd disliked both her daughter-in-law and the girl's mother. She spoiled her son, gave him money, and wrote him flattering letters, in which she insinuated animadversions upon his wife. At one time she complained to him that "the Lady," meaning Elizabeth, had not once been to see her though she had offered her her chariot for the purpose.[26] Again, writing him affectionately of money she had placed with her London agent for his use, she added: "That may help to pay for Mrs. Byrd's [Elizabeth Byrd] Invoice for I hear She has writ one which orders her underclothes to be made & Ruffled in England. I cant but think She had better make them herself. It would be some employment for her. I am sure it is the most extravagant Fashion in the world to have them made in that manner."[27]

In her letters Elizabeth Byrd appears fond though somewhat afraid of her husband.[28] To his command that she send her sick baby to her mother-in-law at "Westover," where the air was supposed to be more wholesome than at "Belvidere," she replied dutifully: "I am very sorry you have limited Poor, sweet Otway, so that he has but a short time to stay with me. Poor dear babe. . . . But Sir, your Orders must be obeyed whatever reluctance I find thereby."[29] After the surrender of the French at Quebec, Elizabeth hoped her husband would return to her in Virginia, but at the end of the war he deliberately went into garrison at Pittsburgh, evidently not desiring to return home.[30] A letter from John Kirkpatrick to George Washington declared: "Colo. Bird I am told has repudiated his Wife, who is now in a Delirium for his Behaviour, and is resolved to make a campaign under Lord Loudon—he has committed his Estate to the Charge of some Friends, & Settled all w[ith] a design never to return to Virginia."[31] The unhappy wife died at the age of twenty-nine in July, 1760, from anxiety and distress, it was asserted by one supposed to have accurate family information.[32] Before news of her death reached her husband, her mother-in-law ordered her children sent at once to "Westover," demanded the keys of "Belvidere" from the deceased wife's own mother, and wrote her son advising that he require a "righteous account" of articles there.[33]

Other domestic troubles are found scattered through private papers. William Fitzhugh of Virginia, consulting the Maryland attorney general in 1681 for some legal remedy for an unhappy relative, explained: "The cruelty of Mr. Blackstone towards my sister in Law is grown so notorious and cruel that there is no possibility of keeping it any longer in private, with the preservation of her life his cruelty having already occasioned her to make two or three attempts to destroy herself which if not timely prevented will inevitably follow."[34] Some time later, writing his mother of the death of his own sister, he expressed a belief that her husband's "unkindness and foolery shortened her days."[35] A more flagrant case of abuse was that of a clergyman, who, according to a letter of Governor Dinwiddie to the Bishop of London, had "very near perpetrated" murder on his wife by "ty'g her up by the Leggs to the Bed Post and cut'g her in a cruel Man'r with Knives."[36] Colonel James Gordon noted in his diary at one time that Robert Edmonds had deserted his wife and at another that Captain Glascock, a family connection, had run away with a young woman, leaving his wife. Again he wrote that the death of a Mrs. Chin, probably a neighbor, was laid to her husband, who was reported to have beaten and abused her.[37] Timothy Ford, a New Englander in South Carolina, wrote of many family troubles there, "especially of the conjugal kind." "I every day hear of unhappy marriages both in time past and present," he declared. He attributed the extraordinary amount of domestic unhappiness to the "sinister views" of the people, who "plumed themselves on rank & fortune, in the making of matches," and to their "confirmed habits of idleness and dissipation."[38]

A cause of much wretchedness of wives must have been the unfaithfulness of husbands, which, though not considered serious by courts or society in general, could hardly have been borne with the equanimity advised in ladies' morality books. These writings usually upheld a different morality for men and women and advised the wife to conceal from everyone her knowledge of her husband's infidelities.[39] A husband might have a practical motive in verifying his suspicion, it was explained, namely, that he might cast off an unfaithful wife. But as a wife could not cast off an offending husband or get any redress, she should not desire to find proof of her suspicions. The inquisitive matron who attempted to pry into her mate's lefthanded connections was held far more contemptible than her philandering husband, so long as he kept his armours private. This attitude is illustrated in a little play in *The Lady's Magazine,* a summary of which follows. Honoria, wife of Morosus, informed by a friend of her husband's intrigue, laid a plot to detect him with his mistress at their rendezvous, the house of a celebrated milliner. She surprised the lovers at breakfast by rushing into the apartment adjoining their bedchamber, and this dialogue ensued:

> *Morosus* (in confusion)   Honoria, Madam, what brings you here?
> *Honoria*   That is a question which ought to be put to you. — I came in pursuit of an ungrateful, too much beloved husband; — you to indulge a lawless flame for an abandoned prostitute.
> *Morosus*   Madam, — Madam, this does not become you.
> *Honoria*   Does it become you, sir, to leave your honest home and wife, — make pitiful excuses for your absence, and skulk in corners with a wretch like this, — this abject hireling of licentious wishes. . . . (Starting toward the mistress).
> *Morosus*   Hold, Madam, hold — this Lady has put herself under my protection, and I will take care to defend her from all insults whatever. (Turning to Honoria) As for you, Madam — you have only exposed me and undone yourself; — I will never see you more.

Then taking his "trembling mistress" by the hand, he led her down the stairs, while *Honoria* followed, catching hold of his arm, and begging him to let the woman go. But throwing his wife aside "with the utmost contempt," he was out of the house and gone. Next day *Honoria* received a letter saying he would never return. "In fine, an eternal disunion must be the consequence of your behavior," he wrote, "nor should the tongues of the angels dissuade me from this resolution;—you will do well to bear it with patience, as the misfortune . . . which has happened entirely through your own fault." *Honoria* begged forgiveness, pleading with him to remember their seven years of happy married life and their children. But he continued determined upon a separation, reminding her thus of the inexcusability of her crime: "During the whole course of the years we lived together, you never had the least shadow of a cause to complain of my want either of respect or tenderness. If I indulged any pleasures, which I imagined would give you disquiet, I took care to be very private in them;—Why then did you suffer yourself to be led by an idle curiosity to pry into secrets, which the discover of must give you pain . . . ?" So, poor *Honoria,* finding her husband inflexible, retired into the country, where she lived "a melancholy example of the ill effects of the officiousness of female friendship and female jealousy."[40]

In the colonies as in the Mother Country, a gentleman's illicit affairs did not prevent his moving in the best society. A South Carolina journalist, lamenting the tendency of parents to accept as proper matches for their daughters men of notorious profligacy, declared that unless a young fellow had killed his man and debauched his woman, he was considered "a spiritless, ignorant milksop."[41] Another correspondent wrote that even "professed Friends to Religion and Virtue" did not hesitate to "make Choice of an abandon'd Fellow, who has been often over-run with a polite Disorder, debauched two or three innocent Virgins or kept half a dozen Negro Wenches in the Face of the Sun."[42]

Men prominent in the history of the colonies were guilty of flagrant immoralities. Thomas, second Lord Culpepper, a conspicuous figure in Virginia affairs, offended even the lax standards of his day by his outrageous conduct,[43] and the records of the Calvert family, the proprietors of Maryland, disclose shocking indecencies— liaisons, illegitimate children, debauchery, and even rape.[44] Colonel Daniel Parke, an outstanding personage in Virginia, was famed for his amorous intrigues as well as his gallantry in war.[45] In Georgia it was reported that General Oglethorpe was living openly with a pretty married woman of bad reputation, and that several officeholders had left their wives for mistresses.[46] Governor Johnston of North Carolina was known to have two natural children,[47] and Henry E. McCulloch, member of the council, kept a mistress by whom he had a son and about whom he wrote quite shamelessly to his young nephew, James Iredell.[48] Cornelius Harnett, Robert Halton, Francis Nash, and Matthew Rowan, all prominent North Carolina gentlemen, acknowledged illegitimate children.[49] A South Carolina law limiting the amount of his estate a husband and father of lawful children might leave to his mistress and bastards indicates that these extra-marital unions were not uncommon in that colony.[50]

Freedom in sex relations was not just a fashionable vice of the well-to-do, but was also found among other classes. Disagreement as to who was entitled to perform the marriage ceremony, the lack of churches in which banns could be published, and often the long distances to be traveled to reach a minister or justice, as well as the excessive freedom of frontier society and the presence of servile women, encouraged the formation of loose unions. Brickell wrote that the "generality" of the Carolinians lived "after a loose and lascivious Manner."[51] An Anglican missionary declared that in North Carolina polygamy was very common, bastardy no disrepute, and concubinage general.[52] A similar situation was described in a complaint before the South Carolina Assembly in 1767 by a group of inhabitants of the upper part of the province. Through the want of churches and ministers, they declared, many persons had been married by itinerant preachers of various denominations, and supposing these unions only temporary had separated and formed new ones whenever they desired, ". . . Swapping away their Wives and Children, as they would Horses or Cattle."[53]

More evidence of lax morality is found in court records, which abound with grand jury presentments of both men and women for adultery and with bastardy cases. These offenders were usually not persons of high social standing, but those without sufficient pride or wealth to make private compensation for their lapses. The justices, who were concerned more with saving the community from charges of dependent mothers and children than with the suppression of immorality, apparently did not trouble themselves with apprehending and punishing the person who voluntarily undertook the responsibility of providing for his reputed child and its mother.[54]

A form of immorality often noted by visitors was the cohabitation of white men with women of colored races. All the southern colonies found it necessary to pass laws against intermarriage or cohabitation between the whites and blacks, and many men and a number of women were brought into court for forming such unnatural unions. These offenders were often servants and almost always of the lowest class. The paternity of a mulatto child was probably not inquired into if there were no danger of his becoming a charge on the community. But though seldom indicted for such crimes, the well-to-do appear to have been partly responsible for the widespread admixture of races. An early Virginia annalist tells of a member of the House of Burgesses in 1676, "a Parson not meanly acquainted with . . . learning," who enjoyed the "darke imbraces of a Blackamoore, his slave."[55] Brickell found a venereal disorder common among the Carolinians, who, he asserted, got it by cohabitation with their Negro servants.[56] Janet Schaw declared that the planters often "honour their black wenches with their attention," chiefly, she believed, to increase the number of their slaves.[57] Josiah Quincy wrote: "The enjoyment of a negro or mulatto woman is spoken of as quite a common thing: no reluctance, delicacy or shame is made about the matter. It is far from being uncommon to see a gentleman at dinner, and his reputed offspring a slave to the master of the table. I myself saw two instances of this, and the company very facetiously would trace the lines, lineaments and features of the father and mother in the child, and very accurately point out the more characteristick resemblance. The fathers neither of them blushed or seem[ed] disconcerted. They were called men of worth, politeness and humanity."[58] To what extent these unions between masters and their female servants were formed is not known, but the many mulattoes mentioned in newspapers and other records indicate that, despite the stringent laws against miscegenation, there was considerable intercourse between Negroes and whites.

Though Indian women, who did not live in such proximity to the whites, were less tempting generally than the Negroes, they were commonly kept as concubines by visitors in the Indian territory. Some white traders remained constant to their temporary wives for several years and helped rear their half-breed offspring, but they usually left these children with their Indian mothers when they returned to their white families. Itinerants formed more transient connections, leaving a half-breed progeny strewn all through the Indian territories. One South Carolinian boasted that he had upwards of seventy children and grandchildren among the Indians.[59] Lawson wrote that traders ordinarily took Indian wives, "whereby they soon learn the Indian tongue, keep a friendship with the savages; and, besides the satisfaction [of] a she bed fellow, they find these Indian girls very serviceable to them, on account of dressing their victuals and instructing them in the affairs and customs of the country."[60] Other journalists observed that it was customary for Indians to offer strangers their young women as bedfellows for the night, which hospitality the white guests apparently had few scruples about accepting.[61] Nicholas Cresswell found it not merely convenient but necessary to take an Indian wife, and wrote quite frankly of his own and other alliances of the kind.[62]

Colonial newspapers furnish abundant evidence of marital friction. Suspicion, anger, and distrust appear in numerous advertisements of their wives by husbands, and in announcements of voluntary separations. In many instances the subscriber states merely that he would not be responsible for his wife's debts, but in numerous others he sought to justify himself and condemn her publicly. Usually he declared she had been so imprudent as to contract debts without his knowledge, had run him unnecessarily into debt, or threatened to ruin him by her debts. Charges besides extravagance were made. George Jones justified posting his wife on the grounds that he and she could not agree in the management of their affairs.[63] John Brown declared that as his Catharine had "behaved in a very imprudent manner," he felt "justifiable in advertising her to the world as an unworthy person."[64] One wife was discredited for behaving "unseemly" to her husband; another for being "highly undutiful and disaffectionate"; and another for being "fond of other men's company."[65] Mary Face refused to "cohabit as a wife"; Martha Beasley went about "scandalizing her husband"; and Delphia Coldwell was a "naughty furious Housewife."[66]

Several husbands renounced their wives in the press. Seth Yeomans advertised "ANNE YEOMANS, who says she is my wife, but with whom I do not cohabit." James Conaway stated that Margaret who went by his name and pretended to be his wife was only his "bought Servant." Another notice declared: "Penelope, who stiles herself the wife of the subscriber . . . hath behaved so indiscreet, that he cannot live with her."[67] These public repudiations usually went unchallenged, but Mary McLaughlin answered her husband's denial of her at once, declaring: "His assertion is false; and altho' I do not think he is worthy the name of husband, yet he is certainly mine; as may be seen by the Registry Book of St. Anne's Parish."[68]

In many notices the subscriber stated that his wife had "eloped from his bed and board," "clandestinely left his home," or "voluntarily separated herself from him." To those believing that marital disunion was a rare occurrence in colonial days, the large number of such advertisements is astonishing. Inserted between notices of stray horses and fugitive slaves, they are almost as numerous as advertisements of runaway servants. The ostensible purpose of the husband was to protect himself from debts with which his absconding wife might charge him, but actually in many cases his evident motive was to vent his exasperation, elicit public sympathy, and wreak vengeance upon his offending spouse.

Besides warning the public against crediting his wife, the deserted husband often cautioned all persons against "harbouring or entertaining" her, threatening that they would do so "at their peril" or "on Pain of incurring the utmost Rigour of the Law." Many also forbade masters of vessels from carrying off the fugitive, and several offered a reward for information of her whereabouts. Like the runaway servant, an eloping wife was sometimes described for identification as in the following notice:

> Whereas my wife Mary Oxendine, hath eloped from me, this is to forewarn all persons from Harbouring or entertaining her, day or night, or crediting her in my name, as I am determined not to pay any debts by her contracted. All masters of vessels or others, are hereby cautioned against carrying her off the province, as they may expect to be prosecuted with the utmost severity.— She is of fair complexion, with light colour'd hair, and has a mark over one of her eyes.[69]

One subscriber advertised his fugitive wife as "a short, thick Woman, of dark Complexion, with black Hair, black Eyes, aged about fifty Years, and has lost one of her fore Teeth."[70]

The subscriber frequently stated that his departing wife had carried off "sundry of his effects," mentioning such valuables as slaves, horses, household furniture, silver plate, his own and her apparel. Elizabeth Sully was advertised as having taken with her eight hundred pounds worth of money, plate, and rings.[71] Elizabeth Home-wood took ten pounds in cash, a new shirt, four silver spoons, a new calico counterpane, new sheets, and some china.[72] Anne Campbell "robbed" her husband of "all her Wearing Apparel, a fine Pair of English Cotton Curtains, a Chintz Counterpane . . . two Pillow Cases, three Diaper Napkins, a large Diaper Table-Cloth . . . and a Side Saddle."[73]

Subscribers to these advertisements apparently felt no indecency in thus exposing their matrimonial partners. Other husbands published the infidelity of their mates in scandalous notices like the following:

> CATHERINE TREEN, the wife of the subscriber, having, in violation of her solemn vow, behaved herself in the most disgraceful manner, by leaving her own place of abode, and living in a criminal state with a certain WILLIAM COLLINS, a plaisterer, under whose bed she was last night, discovered, endeavoring to conceal herself, her much injured husband, therefore, in justice to himself, thinks it absolutely necessary to forewarn all persons from trusting her on his account, being determined, after such flagrant proof of her prostitution, to pay no debts of her contracting.[74]

One announced shamelessly that his bosom companion had brought into his family "an adulterous Child,"[75] and others accused their wives of improper relations with Negro men.[76]

A number of wives eloped with other men, probably for practical as well as romantic reasons. Elizabeth Sellman went away with William Freeman, taking many of her husband's clothes.[77] Mary, wife of Robert Taylor, set out with a man named Cuttings, intending to go to England for some money which she had just inherited.[78] Susanna, wife of Robert Grier, was supposed to have been accompanied in her flight by a former convict who had been freed and entertained by her husband. She took with her her fourteen-year-old son, two Negro children, some silver spoons, chinaware, and other household furniture. Her companion, described as a person with good education, fluent in conversation, and "as genteel in person as insinuating in address," took a horse and valuable books. The husband offered ten pounds reward for their apprehension.[79]

Robert Grier was apparently a man of some means and cultural interests. A few other husbands who advertised their wives appear to have been well-to-do, but a majority were probably of the poorer classes. Those whose professions were given were planters, merchants, apothecaries, silversmiths, overseers, barbers, butchers, tailors, bricklayers, and marines. Quite a number were apparently fathers of grown sons, as they signed their names with a "Sen." Several runaway wives, like Sarah Page, mentioned in her husband's advertisement as "late Sarah Eden,"[80] were evidently brides.

The advertisements as a rule give no clue to the reasons for the wife's leaving home. The husband sometimes stated that she had gone "without any lawful reason," "without any just cause," or "without any Fault in me." John M'Adooe's Anne had eloped "after the most tender treatment of upwards of twenty years."[81] Prudence Cockney was advertised as having deserted her family upon the advice of her friends.[82] Isaac Simmons' Mary left to work in the playhouse at Charles Town.[83] Mark Edwards suspected his Margaret had been "seduced by bad company,"[84] and William Wheat's Amy was supposed to be "disorder'd in her mind."[85]

Occasionally a high-spirited wife published her grievances in answer to her husband's advertisement, as in the following statement by Sarah Cantwell:

> John Cantwell has the impudence to advertise me in the Papers, cautioning all Persons against crediting me; he never had any Credit till he married me: As for his Bed and Board mention'd, he had neither Bed nor Board when he married me; I never eloped, I went away before his Face when he beat me.[86]

Margaret Franks gave the public this "true state" of her "supposed elopement" from her husband: "My now being absent from him was occasioned by his most cruel and inhuman Treatment to me, . . . by his severe Threats, Blows, and turning me out of Doors, in the Dead of Night, leaving me, and a poor helpless infant, whom I had by a former Husband, naked, and exposed to the inclemency of the Weather."[87] Mary Myers explained that her husband had driven her away by "inhumanity and preferring an old negro wench for a bedfellow."[88] Elizabeth Moore's husband had "publickly said his Mother would sooner live in a hollow Tree" than with her, and had himself removed her to her father's house and left her there.[89]

The subsequent history of these absconding wives is not known.

Many probably continued to live separate from their husbands, supporting themselves by whatever employment they could find. Those less capable possibly made their homes with relatives. Others, by court order or voluntary agreement with their husbands, secured separate maintenance. Many dissatisfied wives, after a rest from the monotony of domesticity and a bit of adventure, probably returned home and were welcomed with open arms. Running away seems to have been Susanna Starr's means of getting vacations, for a postscript to her husband's advertisement stated that this was her fourth elopement.[90] Edward Day's Anne absconded in 1757, evidently returned, and ten years later eloped again.[91] Sometimes the husband in her newspaper notice requested his truant mate to return, promising she would be kindly received and supported according to his ability. Samuel Gaither publicly apologized for posting his "beloved Anne," revoked his order against giving her credit, and explained that "all Contentions and Misunderstandings" between them were at end.[92] John Baker, Charles Town merchant, tried a more lordly method commanding his Unice-Mary to return at once to his habitation.[93]

In a number of advertisements the husband stated that as he and his wife had separated by mutual consent and he had agreed to allow her separate maintenance, he would no longer be responsible for her debts. Thomas Barkley notified the Maryland public the he and his wife Isabella had agreed to live apart and that, as she had in her possession free from his intermeddling, her own and her children's share in her former husband's estate, he would not be responsible for her debts.[94] Articles of separation like the following were also published.

COLEMAN THEEDS and ELIZABETH, his Wife, having this Day parted by mutual Consent, and given Bond each to the other, the Subscribers being Witnesses to their Agreement, that they will not interfere with any Estate which shall hereafter accrue to either Party, this Notice is given to the Gazette, that no Person, after this Date, may credit the Wife on the Husband's Account, or the Husband upon that of the Wife's. Given under our Hands, this 12th Day of June, 1773.
RICHARD BEASLEY
JOHN JAMES[95]

A most extraordinary notice was a contract between Joseph and Mary M'Gehe signed by both and published in the [New Bern] *North*

Carolina Gazette, April 7, 1775. Mary admitted having eloped with another man, by whom she was then with child, acknowledged her intention never to live with her husband again, and, in consideration of his having delivered to her "effects" to the value of one hundred and twenty pounds, covenanted never to claim further support from him. Joseph promised to allow her full and free use of these "effects," and agreed never to claim her as his wife, but to allow her to go wherever she chose. By these articles, they declared, they "solemnly agreed before God and the World, to be no longer Man and Wife, but for ever hereafter, be as if we had never been married." This agreement would probably not have been considered binding by the courts, but, according to reports of Anglican missionaries, such divorces were followed by remarriage and were not uncommon.[96]

Occasionally more serious domestic tragedies appeared in the press. The *South Carolina Gazette* in 1736 published news of a husband, who, having been imprisoned for refusing maintenance to his estranged wife, shot himself and died instantly, and later reported the case of another, who, "living unhappy with his wife," committed suicide.[97] In 1751 John Steadman, fifty-four years old, was executed for the murder of his wife, who was found dead in bed with bruises on her body and the marks of a man's fingers on her throat.[98] Two years later, John Barret acknowledged the barbarous murder of his wife, and the death of a prominent gentlewoman, Mrs. Alethia Cook, was laid to her husband, a clergyman, whose "horrid Usage and unparallel'd Barbarity" was, according to the report, "such as Decency forbids us to relate."[99] Another husband, maddened by jealousy, shot his wife as she lay asleep in bed.[100] John Frentz, a Georgia barber, some time after his wife's elopement, went to the house where she was lodged, asked her to make up their differences and go home with him, and upon her refusal shot her, killing her instantly. He was apprehended by neighbors, tried, and executed.[101]

Court records, like newspapers, reveal a surprisingly large amount of general domestic dissatisfaction.[102] While the husband usually proclaimed his grievance in the press, the wife was oftener the complainant in court. There was no tribunal in the South empowered to grant absolute divorces, but courts frequently heard cases of domestic trouble, sometimes ordering a separate maintenance for the wife, but oftener merely requiring the husband to give bond for good behavior to her. Charges usually brought were cruelty, desertion, and nonsupport, probably because these were offences for which justices were most ready to grant a remedy. Many pages of court minutes are filled with altercations, scandalous accusations and recriminations, and patched-up agreements between husbands and wives, which indicate a state of matrimony somewhat out of keeping with the ideals set up by domestic conduct books and other guides to conjugal felicity.

Notes

1. Chilton Latham Powell, *English Domestic Relations*, p. 133.

2. *Ibid.*, p. 141. Sir Thomas Overbury in his *Characters* (1614), describes "A Good Woman" as one "whose husband's welfare is the business of her actions." Her chief virtue is that "Shee is Hee." William Habington in *Castara* (1634), describes the ideal wife's attitude toward her husband: "Shee is inquisitive onely of new wayes to please him, and her wit sayles by no other compass then that of his direction. Shee lookes upon him as Conjurers upon the Circle, beyond which there is nothing but Death and Hell; and in him shee beleeves Paradice circumscrib'd."—Quoted in Myra Reynolds, *The Learned Lady in England, 1650–1760* (Boston and New York, 1920), pp. 24, 32.

3. No. 254.

4. May 20, 1737.

5. *Ibid.*, March 19, 1772; January 21, 1773.

6. *North Carolina Gazette*, July 14, 1775. For other discussions of the wife's duty, see below, Chap. X.

7. *Minutes of the Council and General Court of Virginia*, p. 535.

8. *Archives of Maryland*, IV, 45–46.

9. *Virginia Magazine*, XXXII, 98.

10. *South Carolina Magazine*, XXXI, 10–11.

11. *Virginia Magazine*, XXXVI, 376–79.

12. Stanard, *op. cit.*, p. 107.

13. "The de Rosset Papers." Letters and Documents relating to the Early History of the Lower Cape Fear. *James Sprunt Historical Monograph*, No. 4, p. 18.

14. *Colonial Records of Georgia*, XXII (Pt. II), 424.

15. Wallace, *Life of Henry Laurens*, pp. 180–81.

16. Thomas Lewis Preston, *A Sketch of Mrs. Elizabeth Russell, Wife of General William Campbell, and Sister of Patrick Henry* (Nashville, Tenn., 1888), pp. 11–13.

17. McRee, *Iredell*, I, 380.

18. February 4, 1773.

19. May, 1773, p. 238.

20. W.C. Allen, *History of Halifax County* (Boston, 1919), p. 156.

21. Rev. Charles Payson Mallery, *Ancient Families of Bohemia Manor; their Homes and their Graves.* "Papers of the Historical Society of Delaware," VII, 35–36. The lady here disparaged later married a second, a third, and a fourth husband.

22. *Virginia Magazine*, XXXII, 239.

23. Charles Moore, *op. cit.*, pp. 65–66; Paul Wilstach, *Tidewater Virginia* (Indianapolis, 1929), pp. 194–96.

24. *Virginia Magazine*, IV, 64–66.

25. *Virginia Magazine*, XIV, 142–44.

26. *Ibid.*, XXXVII, 245.

27. *Ibid.*, pp. 249–50.

28. *Ibid.*, pp. 242–43, 246–47, 247–48, 349–50.

29. *Ibid.*, pp. 246–47.

30. *Ibid.*, p. 349.

31. *Letters to Washington* (ed., Hamilton), I, 335–36.

32. *Virginia Magazine*, XXXVIII, 52–53.

33. *Ibid.*, pp. 155–56, 347, 350. Six months later Colonel Byrd married Mary Willing of Philadelphia, who was apparently better able to cope with a spoiled husband and a meddlesome mother-in-law, for, though he wasted a large part of his estate gambling, their marriage seems to have been happy. His affectionate confidence in this wife, and also his later dissatisfaction with his mother and children appear in his will. He appointed his wife executrix, directed that his son Otway be disinherited if he quit the navy, and that his son Thomas Taylor be disinherited if he should marry Susannah Randolph. In distributing his estate among his children, he ordered that there should be deducted from the share of those of the first marriage "such sums as they may claim under the wills of my deluded & superannuated Mother & my ungrateful son, William."—*Ibid.*, pp. 59–61. This harsh reference to his deceased mother indicates that, despite her dislike for Elizabeth Byrd, the old lady left the larger part of her property to Elizabeth's children rather than to those of her son's second wife.

34. *Ibid.*, I, 40–41.

35. *Ibid.*, IV, 418–19.

36. "The Official Records of Robert Dinwiddie," Virginia Historical Society, *Collections*, IV, 696.

37. *William and Mary Quarterly*, XI, 217; XII, 2, 9.

38. "Diary, 1785–1786," *South Carolina Magazine*, XIII, 192.

39. This explanation by a correspondent to the *Lady's Magazine*, August, 1771, was representative of many: "A licentious commerce between the sexes . . . may be carried on by the men without contaminating the mind, so as to render them unworthy of the marriage bed, and incapable of discharging the virtuous and honorable duties of husband, father, friend. . . . [But] the contamination of the female mind is the necessary and inseparable consequence of an illicit inter-

course with men . . . women are universally virtuous, or utterly undone." The most common argument for a double standard, however, was that of Dr. Johnson: "Confusion of progeny constitutes the essence of the crime; and therefore a woman who breaks her marriage vows is much more criminal than a man who does it. A man, to be sure, is criminal in the sight of God: but he does not do his wife a very material injury, if he does not insult her; if, for instance, from mere wantonness of appetite, he steals privately to her chambermaid. Sir, a wife ought not greatly to resent this. I would not receive home a daughter who had run away from her husband on that account. A wife should study to reclaim her husband by more attention to please him."—James Boswell, *Life of Samuel Johnson* (text of 3rd ed., printed in 1927), I, 372. See also II, 205.

40. *The Lady's Magazine,* September, 1771.

41. *South Carolina and American General Gazette,* April 8, 1768.

42. *South Carolina Gazette,* January 26, 1738.

43. Leaving his wife, who had brought him a large fortune, and his daughter, he spent most of his revenue upon Susanna Willis, a mistress with whom he lived openly for many years and by whom he had two daughters. Some months before his death, he settled his estate upon these natural daughters and later by his will confirmed the settlement, leaving the lands acquired with his wife's fortune charged with his debts, a large part of which was contracted for rich household furnishings, plate, and jewels for Susanna.—*Virginia Magazine,* XXXIII, 250–53, 261–62, 266.

44. Benedict Leonard Calvert, who died in 1715 the fourth Lord Baltimore, not only kept as mistress a Mrs. Grove, but treated his wife with barbarous cruelty. Charles, fifth Lord Baltimore, kept the same Mrs. Grove.—*Maryland Magazine,* X, 372–73. Benedict Calvert of Annapolis, whose daughter Eleanor married Jackie Custis, George Washington's stepson, was the illegitimate son of this Lord Baltimore, who recognized him as his son, bestowed lands upon him, and made him a member of the Maryland Council.—Moore, *op. cit.,* pp. 93–94. The colonial newspapers for the year 1768 carried shocking accounts of the atrocious conduct of Frederick, sixth Lord Baltimore, who carefully planned and executed a rape upon a young girl of recognized reputation. Dying without legitimate children in 1771, this last Lord Baltimore made his natural son proprietor of Maryland, giving a reversion to the boy's sister and giving legacies to his own sisters on condition that they assent to the will.—*Letters to Washington* (ed., Hamilton), IV, 113–16; Thomas W. Griffith, *Sketches of the Early History of Maryland* (Baltimore, 1821), p. 63.

45. Moore, *op. cit.,* pp. 61, 62, 67–68; G. W. P. Custis, *op. cit.,* p. 26; *Writings of William Byrd* (ed., Bassett), pp. l–li.

46. *Colonial Records of Georgia,* IV, 344–45, 482, 499; V, 344, 399, 573.

47. [Janet Schaw], *Journal,* Appendix, p. 293.

48. McRee, *Iredell,* I, 42, 43, 51.

49. [Janet Schaw], *Journal,* p. 173.

50. *Digest of the Laws of South Carolina* (ed., James), p. 66.

51. *Natural History of Carolina*, pp. 36–37.

52. *Colonial Records of North Carolina*, VII, 288. See also, I, 767.

53. Fulham MS. North Carolina, South Carolina, Georgia, No. 72. A copy of the petition is given in Harvey Tolivar Cook, *Rambles in the Pee Dee Basin*, pp. 203–5.

54. See below, Chap. XV.

55. "A Narrative of the Indian and Civil Wars in Virginia," *Force Tracts*, I (No. 11), 46.

56. *Op. cit.*, p. 48.

57. *Journal*, p. 154.

58. *Journal*, p. 464. For similar reports, see Anburey, *Travels*, II, 386, Davis, *Travels*, pp. 56, 250, 400, 414; Bernard, *Retrospections of America*, p. 147.

59. Arthur Wallace Calhoun, *Social History of the American Family*, I, 325.

60. *Op. cit.*, p. 301. For similar accounts see Brickell, *op. cit.*, pp. 294–301; Smyth, *Tour*, pp. 190–91; William Bartram, *Travels*, pp. 194–95, 449; Benjamin Hawkins, *Letters*, pp. 18–21, 35–36, 39–40, 44, 45, 47, 54, 56, 57, 83–85, 188, 252, 253, 430.

61. *Writings of William Byrd* (ed., Bassett), pp. 96–97; Cresswell, *Journal*, pp. 105–6.

62. *Ibid.*, pp. 107–8, 109–10, 113–14, 115–17, 121, 122. Byrd attributed the war of the Indians upon the Carolinians in 1713 largely to the abuse of the Indian women by white traders.—*Op. cit.*, pp. 239–40. The Reverend Peter Fontaine declared that many of the colonists' Indian troubles were due to the mistreatment of their Indian concubines by white traders.—Ann Maury, *Memoirs of a Huguenot Family*, pp. 349–51.

63. *Virginia Gazette*, January 30, 1772.

64. *Maryland Journal and Baltimore Advertiser*, November 2, 1779.

65. *Virginia Gazette*, July 26, 1770; *ibid.*, March 28, 1771; *Maryland Journal and Baltimore Advertiser*, September 10, 1782.

66. *Virginia Gazette*, March 22, 1770; *ibid.*, August 24, 1751; *ibid.*, January 21, 1775.

67. *Dunlap's Maryland Gazette; or the Baltimore General Advertiser*, February 20, 1776; *Maryland Gazette*, August 15, 1765; *Maryland Journal*, August 2, 1775.

68. *Maryland Gazette*, July 13, 1748.

69. *South Carolina Gazette*, May 25, 1765.

70. *Virginia Gazette*, October 31, 1751.

71. *South Carolina Gazette*, January 3, 1743.

72. *Maryland Gazette*, February 2, 1758.

73. *Ibid.*, March 16, 1758.

74. *Maryland Journal*, January 20, 1774.

75. *Maryland Gazette*, March 29, 1759.

76. Henry Pratt, *Maryland Gazette*, April 22, 1773, and Walter Skinner, *ibid.*, October 12, 1769.

77. *Ibid.,* September 5, 1750.
78. *Virginia Gazette,* July 6, 1769.
79. *Ibid.,* December 14, 1769.
80. *South Carolina Gazette,* May 9, 1768.
81. *Virginia Gazette,* June 21, 1770.
82. *Maryland Journal,* October 26, 1774.
83. *South Carolina Gazette,* February 5, 1737.
84. *Virginia Gazette,* April 27, 1769.
85. *Maryland Gazette,* April 3, 1755.
86. *South Carolina and American General Gazette,* March 27, 1776.
87. *South Carolina Gazette,* July 12, 1770.
88. *Ibid.,* November 14, 1768.
89. *Virginia Gazette,* May 9, 1771.
90. *Maryland Gazette,* January 29, 1756.
91. *Ibid.,* July 7, 1757; August 20, 1767.
92. *Ibid.,* March 31, 1757.
93. *South Carolina Gazette,* May 27, 1766.
94. *Maryland Gazette,* April 7, 1747.
95. *Virginia Gazette,* February 10, 1774.
96. *Colonial Records of North Carolina,* I, 767; VII, 288.
97. May 29, 1736; *ibid.,* January 1, 1737.
98. *Maryland Gazette,* April 17, 1751.
99. *Ibid.,* November 8, 15, December 6, 1753; *ibid.,* February 1, April 26, 1753.
100. *Ibid.,* August 20, 1759.
101. *Georgia Gazette,* August 5, July 20, 1768; January 11, 1769.
102. For court action in matrimonial cases, see below, Chap. XVI.

GUION GRIFFIS JOHNSON

Family Life

Chapter 8 of *Ante-bellum North Carolina: A Social History* (Chapel Hill: University of
North Carolina Press, 1937), 224–58, reprinted by permission of the publisher

Johnson's book is the most comprehensive social history of North
Carolina ever written, and it has not been matched for any other
southern state. Women, black as well as white, weave their way
through the book, and they are central to this chapter on family life.
Johnson, like Spruill, was a demon for digging out primary material.
She exhibited considerable skill, too, in using the data she had collected. If her writing is a shade less graceful than that of her friend, it
is nevertheless good enough to hold a reader's interest through a
lengthy chapter. Her quotations and anecdotes are admirably chosen
and sometimes startlingly effective. More than fifty years after its first
publication this chapter still merits the most careful study by historians of southern women.

The Family Dwelling

THE HOUSE to which the average bridegroom in North Carolina
took his bride was a humble abode even in 1860. When Thomas
Henderson, editor of the Raleigh *Star,* attempted in 1810 to obtain
information about the general state of society in North Carolina, he
found that the prevailing style of architecture then, as in colonial
times, was the log cabin. William Dickson wrote of Duplin County:

> The first Inhabitants of Duplin and Sampson Counties, built and
> lived in log Cabins, and as they became more Wealthy, some of

them Built framed Clapboard Houses with Clay Chimneys, at Present there are not many good Houses, well Constructed, with Brick Chimneys, and Glass lights, there are no Stone or Brick walled Houses, not any that can be called Edifices in the County—The greatest Number of Citizens yet build in the old Stile.[1]

Dr. Jeremiah Battle said of Edgecombe County: "There are a few well built private houses, some of which have lately been finished. The 'style of building' [in Tarboro] is as it is in the country, generally plain & cheap."[2] Henry Barnard of Connecticut, who visited the South Atlantic states in 1833, said of his trip from Virginia to Raleigh, "The whole aspect of the country is mean—not a decent, painted house, or a neat village the whole way." Later from Salisbury he wrote, "I have visited all the intelligent familys here—and rode 8 or 10 miles into the country in every direction to see the sovereign people in their homes—their log huts, which is the prevading style of building."[3] In 1837 a North Carolinian, William Henry Wills of Tarboro, found the houses along the road from Edgecombe County to Fayetteville "few and poor."[4]

A common type of log house of the better sort was that which had four rooms, two rooms separated by a partition, with a loft above which was reached by a narrow stairway or a ladder, and a small lean-to at the end of the back porch. The chimney, which was usually built of field stone, was frequently ten feet wide and high enough for an ordinary man to stand in it.

In 1851 the *Southern Weekly Post* of Raleigh declared that the average house in North Carolina was neither attractive nor comfortable, and that the people of the State had not improved in their ways of living upon the examples of their ancestors. "How often do we see houses set on the brow of a sandy hill, with not a tree or shrub, or patch of green grass to relieve the eye or refresh the imagination; . . ." In summer they look "like places of penance, bake-ovens whose inmates are suffering all the tortures awarded to the martyred Saints." In the winter, fires "large enough to burn a brick kiln" roared in the immense chimneys, "and the family will be crowding round, scorching and sweating on one side, while the other is shivering with the keen blasts that sweep through open doors and a thousand yawning crevices." "Why do you not," impatiently asked the *Post*, "make" your houses tight, "and in winter close the doors and keep the windows full of glass?"[5]

Two years later, Professor William H. Owen of Wake Forest College declared through the columns of the *Weekly Post*, "It is admitted that there are few things in which we are more deficient than in Architecture. The State is covered with huge squares and parallelograms of painted weather boards, which *might have been* built up into *sightly* and *comfortable* dwellings for one half of what they originally cost."[6] He wished that North Carolinians would take more to the cottage style which was "becoming fashionable."[7]

There were, however, stately homes in North Carolina.[8] In 1807 Joseph A. Brown of Bertie County, described his plantation house situated on the west bank of the Chowan River as "a large comfortable brick Dwelling House, with 6 rooms on the first floor, surrounded with piazzas, situated 200 yards from the river, a court yard surrounded with handsome railed fencing, near two acres of garden, also enclosed by paling, a two story Kitchen, brick store-House, large Barn Stable, Corn Cribs, &c. &c."[9]

The most extravagant type of "mansion house" in the antebellum days was usually approached by a broad avenue flanked with tall elms. The avenue, some four hundred yards long, gradually led up to the house on the crest of a knoll or terrace. About the house were noble front trees with comfortable seats at their bases. The plantation house at "Rich Lands" in Chowan County where James Battle Avirett grew to manhood is typical of "the big house" of the coastal plain region.[10] Including the piazzas, it was sixty feet square and three stories high, built of North Carolina pine and weatherboarded with yellow poplar. It stood on brick pillars about five feet above the ground to avoid dampness. The broad piazzas on the first and second stories extended all around the house. The windows were wide and deep, reaching to the bottom of the floor. Along the walls were rows of bookshelves and hammock hooks, suggesting lazy comfort on a hot summer day. On the right was the large parlor with its piano, mahogany furniture, oil portraits, and heavy carpets. Back of the parlor was the master's bedroom; across the hall, the nursery; and opposite the parlor, the family sitting room. The two stories above were for the older children and guests, while the attic was the family storeroom. To reach the dining room and kitchen one had to pass through the large central hall and cross a piazza, for, as in most antebellum mansions, the kitchen was an establishment separate from the living quarters. In the kitchen the wide fire-place was equipped with a crane for swinging the large pots and with hooks for roasting, for here the family cooking was done.

From the kitchen porch could be seen the pump, sheltered by a covered arbor situated in the center of a broad quadrangle. To the right were three smoke houses where pork was cured, also a "flour house," "coffee house," and a storehouse for groceries. Back of these in a two-acre enclosure were the poultry houses where there were chickens, turkeys, guineas, and ducks and geese, kept especially for making feather beds. To the left as one looked from the kitchen porch was the vegetable garden and below that the weaving room where most of the "negro cloth" was manufactured. Still farther beyond were the "quarters," the houses of the slaves, and not far off the stables.

The type of house intermediate between the mansion and the log cabin was the frame cottage of four or five rooms. The architecture was simple. Usually a wide hall, running the length of the house, separated two groups of rooms; or two rooms and a piazza sprawled out in the rear from two rooms at the front of the house, forming together an enormous L or T. The furnishings were simple. The unpainted floors, often kept scrupulously clean by scrubbing with ashes, were covered, if at all, by hand woven rag rugs. The walls were white washed or, less frequently, papered or plastered. The furniture was made from native wood either by the head of the family or by a mechanic in a local cabinet shop. The dutch oven and frying pan were the chief kitchen utensils even after the stove came into general use in the fifties.

The number of free persons per dwelling in North Carolina in 1790, 1850, and 1860 as reported by the census is shown in the following table:

Number of Free Persons Per Dwelling[11]

Year	Free Population	Number Dwellings	Average Number of Persons to Dwelling
1790	292,554	40,018	7.3
1850	580,363	104,996	5.5
1860	661,563	129,585	5.1

The average number of persons to the dwelling in North Carolina was less than in the more thickly settled states, such as New York and Pennsylvania, and even slightly less than in Virginia, but the extent of overcrowding can be estimated only roughly, for the number of rooms to the dwelling is not available from the census reports.

The Ante-bellum Woman

The qualities often thought of as being peculiar to the Victorian lady were characteristics of the genteel lady long before 1837. Delicacy, innocence, modesty, simplicity, and good nature, "are jewels of inestimable value, in the character of a man or woman," wrote Dr. James Norcom of Edenton in 1810 to his young fiancée, "but in a woman they are everything!"[12] Also in 1810 President Caldwell of the University of North Carolina, addressing the young ladies of the female department of the Raleigh Academy, solemnly assured them that "maidenly delicacy" was the foundation of the social structure. "In the improvement of that delicacy and superior sensibility which it belongs to your nature to possess," said the President, "is found the firmest security for the best state of society which virtue alone can insure and perpetuate."[13]

The ideal woman of ante-bellum days was modest and innocent, graceful in person and gracious in manners. She had a flattering timidity and "modest softness." She was cultivated in the "polite arts" of dancing, music, drawing, and embroidery. She was fond of reading; but, whenever she commenced a work "without having previously been directed by some judicious and thoughtful friend," she would "lay the book aside forever" the moment her eyes fell "upon an impure thought, . . ."[14] Such a ban upon the reading habits of the sex automatically restricted the education of woman to the three R's and a cursory view of a few cultural studies.[15] The well-bred woman did not care to pursue her studies to such an extent that she might be called masculine, for "all those studies and pursuits that qualify women to shine in the society of the learned," tended "essentially to rob them of the attractions" which made them "most fascinating in the eyes of men." The elderly Dr. James Norcom, criticizing a manuscript which a young lady of Virginia had sent him to read, thought the essay would be unexceptionable "were it not . . . a little too masculine," warning her that "estimatable female authors" sought to retain their feminine charm in their writings.[16]

Religion was woman's greatest comfort in life. Indeed, females needed "the hopes, and the prospects of religion, more, . . . than the other sex." It softened "the pains of living . . . by the hope of dying" and made woman able to bear with "patience and submission" the "trials of disobedience," the "weakness of a feeble constitution," and "a husband of acid temper."[17] Having a greater need for religion than men, women also had greater religious responsibility. "How solemn and how awful . . . is their responsibility," wrote a correspondent of the *Western Carolinian* in 1822, praising Miss Fanny Badger who spent her time reading Dwight's *System of Theology* instead of devoting it to "the foolish vanities and licentious practices of the world." Would the female sex "become truly and unaffectedly pious;—the whole moral face of the world would be changed; . . . drunkards, duellists, gamblers, and infidels, would no longer be found in respectable society; and good sons, good brothers, good husbands, good neighbors, good friends and good Christians would every where abound."[18]

In addition to her church work, the well-bred ante-bellum woman might also engage in charity. It was becoming of her to take baskets of food and clothing to the poor, for she should always be a "ministering angel." Above all, however, she should have a regard for "the duties and enjoyments of domestic life." "God in his inscrutable wisdom," wrote Dr. Norcom in 1848, "has appointed a place & a duty for females, *out of which* they can neither accomplish their destiny, nor secure their happiness!!"[19] "The truth is, Miss Mary," he wrote to an aspiring literary female, "that woman, in her proper sphere & office, is the grace, the ornament, the bliss of life. Out of it, she may shine and dazzle," but "she will soon cease to command attention and admiration, if she lack those characteristics of feminine softness & delicacy & modesty which so eminently distinguish her from our rougher sex. If these divine & love inspiring attributes be wanting, the woman disappears, & we behold in her place, . . . an hermaphrodite, a creature acknowledged by neither sex, & a terror & reproach to both. . . ."[20]

Upon the death in 1845 of Mrs. Ann Sellers, wife of Colonel John Sellers of Sampson County, the *North Carolina Standard* declared her to have been "a rare assemblage of all those amiable qualities which adorn" woman. Her "deportment" was that of an "exemplary Christian." "She was kind to her friends, hospitable to strangers, charitable to the poor and afflicted of her neighborhood, forbearing to her domestics and ever ready to do good to all, . . ."[21]

Travelers in the South often commented upon the differences between southern and northern women. In 1852 the *Weekly Post* of Raleigh mentioned one such traveler who was "particularly struck" with the beauty of form of the southern woman, "their symmetrical and harmonious figures," their "exquisite taste" in dress, their "proverbial affability and urbanity." "The southern lady is naturally easy, unembarrassed and polite—You may go into the country, where you please—you may go as far as you please from town, village and post office—you may call at the poorest house you can find, provided you don't get among 'Crackers,' and whether you accost maid or matron, you will always be answered with the same politeness and treated with the same spontaneous courtesy."[22]

Writers both at home and abroad also commented on the "physical delicacy" of the southern female. Most critics, overlooking malaria, typhoid, and the general languor of a sub-tropical climate, saw in it the curse of slavery. Southern women, wrote the *Weekly Post* of Raleigh, "are brought up to be dependent for every little object upon servants, and never acquire the habit and faculty of waiting on themselves. There are many exceptions to this, but it is generally true of those whose circumstances permit the indulgence. This fact has also made an impression upon the minds of the poorer classes, that much muscular exercise is indelicate and ungenteel, and they, too, make as little exertion in the open air as possible."[23]

Certainly by the thirties, it had become definitely unfashionable for a lady to exert herself physically, and she had become what Dr. Norcom thought to be her proper sphere, "the grace, the ornament, the bliss of life." There were many, however, who regretted that the industrious housewife had given place to the "hot-house flower." In 1852 the *Weekly Post* wrote in protest:

> There was a time, when industry and good housewifery were
> reckoned indispensable qualifications among women; and when
> a young gentleman happened to step in where girls were at work,
> his presence seemed to "set a keener edge on female indus-

try." . . . But now the thing is greatly changed. A girl must by no means be seen making a shirt, or sewing on a pair of panta-loons;– . . . the only appearance of work that can be at all allowed in company now, is a slip of fine muslin, with a half-finished flower, which the young lady must by all means declare was begun six weeks ago; or a similar slip of cambric, concerning which we must be informed that three inches were hemmed in a week; or, what is at present bearing away the palm of time-murder,—crotcheting a lady's collar or a spangled purse, concerning the completion of which no definite time can be fixed upon!"[24]

Housewifery

However much the ante-bellum woman chose to appear as a lady of ease, few in North Carolina could actually assume this role. In any successful family whose fortune was built largely upon agriculture, regardless of the number of slaves at their command, "the feeble wife" was no less industrious or economical than "the strong husband." Many a North Carolina husband might have written to his wife as William Atson of Virginia did late in the fifties, "I know that, accustomed to luxury, and capable of shining in society, you have cheerfully worked, economized, and shunned the world."[25] The household duties of a wife, mother to a "numerous offspring," gave her little time for fashionable embroidery, novel reading, and long afternoon naps until she was well passed middle age. Not even the wife of a wealthy planter, with her cook, butler, maid, nurse, and laundress could entirely escape the drudgery. She might not have much of the actual labor to perform, but it was hers to plan and superintend many household industries which today have been taken out of the home.

The housewife's day usually began a little after six if she had servants, at four-thirty or five if she was a yeoman's wife. The efficient housewife was always in the kitchen soon after the cook had arrived and had started a fire in the fireplace or, after the late forties, in the stove. She looked first to the appearance of the cook to see that she was "properly and neatly attired," "bright and glossy in complexion" with hair "combed, braided, or turbaned." She was on hand at the setting of the table, especially if she had recently "installed a new servant." She saw that the butler had a clean napkin to cover the food which he bore across the open passage-way from kitchen to dining room, not only to keep it warm but to protect it from air and flies. She lighted her spirit-lamp to keep tea and coffee hot at the table and then made sure that each person was ready to take his seat before ordering that muffins and batter bread be placed on the table.

After breakfast, "Virginia ladies, who are proverbially good managers," wrote Mrs. Mary Randolph in her Virginia Housewife of 1831, "employ themselves, while their servants are eating, in washing the cups, glasses, &c; arranging the cruets, the mustard, salt-sellers, pickle vases, and all the apparatus for the dinner table. . . . When the kitchen breakfast is over, and the cook has put all things in their proper places, the mistress should go in to give her orders. Let all the articles intended for the dinner, pass in review before her; have the butter, sugar, flour, meal, lard, given out in proper quantities; the catsup, spice, wine, whatever may be wanted for each dish, measured to the cook. The mistress must tax her own memory with all this: we have no right to expect slaves or hired servants to be more attentive to our interest than we ourselves are: they will never recollect these little articles until they are going to use them; the mistress must then be called out, and thus have the horrible drudgery of keeping house all day, . . ."[26]

One of the imperious chores of the housewife's day was to make ready the lighting equipment before dark should fall. If the household burned candles and the wife was a tidy housekeeper, the candlesticks must be cleaned of drippings and polished; the candles replenished. If lamps were used, the wicks must be trimmed, the bowls filled, and, if the lamps had chimneys, they must be polished. Mrs. Cornelia Phillips Spencer of Chapel Hill, godmother of the University of North Carolina after Reconstruction and writer of much spirited comment on her times, in contrasting housekeeping chores of ante-bellum days with those of 1890, was impressed most greatly with the difference in the lighting equipment. "In summer," she wrote, "we had to go across the yard to the kitchen for a *chunk* to light up with. And what blowing and puffing to coax a blue flame to catch upon the candle wick, what dripping of tallow and sperm before this could be accomplished."[26a]

When Janet Schaw visited North Carolina on the eve of the Revolution, she found Wilmington housewives of fashion using in the kitchen the beautiful green bayberry candles made from the native wax-myrtle. They preferred spermaceti candles for the parlor. "The poorer sort burn pieces of lightwood, which they find without trouble, . . ." wrote Miss Schaw.[26b] Lightwood and tallow and sperm candles continued to be used throughout the ante-bellum period. An advertisement in the *Fayetteville Observer* of August 4, 1846, declared that the North Carolina Soap and Candle Factory of Fayetteville made from forty to seventy thousand pounds of tallow candles a year and largely supplied Wilmington, Raleigh, Chapel Hill, and Hillsboro with light.

Various kinds of lamps were also in general use in the antebellum period. The small, vessel-shaped lard or sperm-oil lamp, usually made of iron, was a familiar object on the colonial table. The Argand lamp with circular wick and chimney was manufactured in England in 1782 and immediately met with success. It was devised to burn sperm-oil, but a variant of the lamp was manufactured to burn lard. With the manufacture of camphine from turpentine, special lamps were made to burn this fuel, and after 1845 public buildings in North Carolina and the parlors of the wealthy were brightly illuminated. Some kerosene had been sold as an illuminant as early as 1848, but it was not distilled on a large scale until 1854, and it was not until 1859 that it began to be advertised in North Carolina as "the cleanest, most economical, and best light to be obtained except from gas." By 1860 Raleigh, Wilmington, Charlotte, and New Bern had gas lights. At the close of the period, however, the average family in comfortable circumstances still had one tallow candle on the supper table, two sperm candles or a camphine lamp in the parlor for evening, and a tallow candle to carry about the house.[26c]

Mrs. Mary Mason of Raleigh, writing on "the duties of wife and mother . . . expressly for the benefit of residents of the Southern States, before emancipation, . . ." thought that a mistress should inspect every apartment daily to see that "the whole is swept, dusted, aired, and divested of cobwebs."[27] Bedrooms should be aired daily and beds sunned twice a month. All kitchen utensils should be taken out doors once a week and scrubbed. Chimneys should be swept down every day in the winter before the fires were made and burned out once a month on a rainy day. Closet, cupboard, and pantry doors should be kept shut and locked to keep out cats, mice, and rats, and the mistress herself should carry the keys. If possible, she should strain the milk herself and see that the churns were scalded and aired daily. She should be on hand once or twice a month when the clothes were being sorted in the laundry, when starch was being made, and when bluing was being added to the rinsing water, for "servants have little idea of proportion" and quickly become careless. The mistress should grease the flat irons and later attend to the airing of the ironed clothes unless she had "a careful person in this department." Clothes should be sorted before being placed in the wardrobe and those needing repair mended at once or taken to the seamstress. "Especially your husband's shirts," wrote Mrs. Mason, "should never be put away without buttons, his drawers without strings, or his stockings with holes." This is "one of the greatest annoyances a man can be subject to."[28]

The mistress should begin housecleaning in February, "as vermin begin to lose their torpor about this time, and bestir themselves to prepare for a progeny." "On some bright day, have all your beds moved out into the sun, shaken, dusted, and searched well," advised Mrs. Mason. "While the beds are sunning, search over all your bedsteads. Wipe them over with cold soapsuds, and carefully stop every crack, seam, and screw-hole with hard turpentine soap."[29] General housecleaning did not begin until the first of May, when the prudent housewife removed all furniture from the house, took up carpets, whitewashed all walls and ceilings, washed windows, and scrubbed all the woodwork. A bushel of unslacked lime, slacked in a barrel with boiling water and then whitened with a gallon of flour-paste and a little bluing, was sufficient to whitewash an entire house. One began with the upstairs, doing one room at a time, taking a week or more to finish the job.

Although with servants to do most of the actual labor, the mistress should supervise the soap-making, the poultry yard, and the garden. "Insist on all your wood-ashes being saved to make the family soap," wrote Mrs. Mason. "Let your servants understand at once that you *will not buy soap* when there are abundant materials at home for its manufacture."[30] The fowl-house should be swept clean once a week and fumigated every three weeks with sulphur and tobacco. "Have a hole cut in your hen-house door just large enough for the hens to enter; but keep the door locked that the eggs may be safe." The mistress should also know when to have her garden plowed or spaded, when to add manure, what seeds to choose and how to dry them, how to rotate her little crops of vegetables.[31]

But the most exacting duties which filled the faithful housewife's day had to do with the nursery. She turned over the fatiguing work of "minding child" to a Negro nurse, but she supervised the nursery routine, made a great many of the little garments herself, although with a seamstress at her command, and did much of the actual nursing when a child was sick, as was frequently the case. The nursery itself should be "a moderately large room, high-pitched, and well ventilated, with an open fireplace, in preference to either a stove or grate." It should be aired and swept every morning, have a fender for the fire too high for the little ones to climb over, have scanty furniture to give ample room for the children to play, and be covered with "a good thick carpet" to "save their little heads when they fall."

Children should be dressed warmly in winter and play out in the open air as much as possible. Mrs. Mason strongly advised mothers against "the prevailing custom of extravagant dressing." In winter, children are "arrayed in embroidery and furs, save that the legs, arms, and neck" are "unmercifully exposed to the weather." In summer, infants, "arrayed in an extravagant profusion of laces, ribbons, flowers, and feathers, most uncomfortably placed in a reclining posture, in a beautiful baby's barouche, with the top thrown back, so as to exhibit the beauty as well as the finery of the inmate as much as possible," are sent out with "a thoughtless and foolishly fond, ambitious nurse," to vie with others in the heat of mid-afternoon.[32]

The mother should supervise the children's diet herself, leaving the actual feeding, however, to the nurse if she chose. Milk and well-baked light bread or crackers made an excellent breakfast. A young child should not have green corn or new potatoes in summer or be given cake or preserves at night, but "a little salt herring or ham will sometimes give tone to the weak stomach of a child, when suffering especially with diarrhoea."[33] The mother should also administer all medicines herself, "however you may think you may confide in your nurse." "If it should happen," wrote Mrs. Mason, "that you wish to attend a party at night, and your babe is not inclined to sleep, never administer opiates; forego the party rather, if you have not sufficient confidence in your nurse to leave it in her care while awake."[34]

A southern housewife, in addition to her other duties, had to know how to manage her servants. All lady's books of this period, written by southerners, and even agricultural magazines and newspaper gave hints on this subject. Mrs. Mason thought that a good nurse was one of the greatest blessings which could befall a southern housewife. The nurse should be a healthy, honest, well-tempered middle-aged woman, fond of children, not too self-sufficient, free from drinking, snuff-taking, and the baneful influence of superstition. Some housewives were always more or less in the power of their servants. "It is, therefore, wise to get on the right side of them," wrote Mrs. Mason, "so that they will be less inclined to take undue advantage of you."[35] The cook, who was the real power among the servants, should be healthy, brisk, honest, and not too amiable, "for your very amiable cook" is apt to be "over-indulgent to her fellow-servants. . . ."[36]

In the management of servants, praise was far more effective than censure. "Trust them if you would have them honest," but keep provisions locked up in order not to tempt them to do wrong. "Counsel and encourage, reprove and condemn them, as you would your own erring children, . . . Feed your servants bountifully, not forgetting to include a portion of the dainties with which their ready hands are constantly supplying you. In this way you will always be rewarded by the agreeable appearance of a cheerful, happy, and contented countenance, and a ready alacrity in your service."[37]

Hard was the lot of a young wife who had not been trained in household management. "Do not fancy it unrefined for young ladies to enter the culinary domain," cautioned Mrs. Mason. "No duty is unrefined. . . . Accustom your daughters while growing up, to aid you in culinary matters. . . . Otherwise they may be unhappy, unprofitable wives, and more of a burden than a pleasure and comfort to their husbands."[38] After a visit to his daughter, Mrs. John W. Brodnax, in 1850, Judge Thomas Ruffin wrote of her: ". . . Polly is getting on very well towards establishing a high reputation not only as a good wife and mother, but a choice house-keeper in all branches, house, kitchen, yard, garden, poultry, and the rest; and, withall, keeps her amiable manners, cheerful smiles, and social qualities, and genteel appearance."[39]

It was not easy to keep cheerful smiles when one had a daily round of nursing, cooking, washing, sewing, knitting, weaving, preserving fruits, and canning vegetables in the summer and curing fresh pork in the winter. As Dr. Norcom wrote to his daughter, after he had taken charge of his household a few days because of his wife's illness:

> if it is not managed with great ability, sobriety, & good sense, the duty of house-keeping is dirty, demoralizing & debasing in a high degree. . . . It confines one to a series of low pursuits, a course of filthy drudgery, & disgusting slovenliness, that have but little time for study or quiet meditation, & very little for improving conversation of refined society; & it is altogether unsuited to moral & religious enjoyment. It keeps one in perpetual agitation, anxiety, & apprehension; & has no pleasure equal to the pains, the toil, the privations & the suffering, which it is almost sure to impose.[40]

Perhaps Mary Sawyer had in mind this very thing when she wrote to her young friend, Mary Shepard, later Mrs. John H. Bryan, "One does not always have a great deal of good humour to spare after marriage."[41] Not many years later, Mrs. Bryan complained to her husband, who was then in Washington attending Congress, "You have no idea of the trouble of our numerous offspring, they require such unremitted attention & care, I cannot like many mothers neglect them."[42] Her sister, Mrs. Ebenezer Pettigrew, was having the same difficulty. Although not interrupted by fashionable visitors at her plantation home, Phelps Lake in Washington County, her days were so full of household duties that she found time only on Sundays for relaxation and a little reading. "We have not yet procured another Teacher and I am obliged to bestow some attention on the children, but I find the duties of housekeeping, nursing and teaching are not compatible therefore one of them must be neglected, which is the school, the others being indispensable, my time is always usefully employed."[43]

Some mothers, as in the case of Mrs. Pettigrew, tutored their children in addition to their other duties. The *Carolina Observer* in 1926 thought this number to be few. "It is to be regretted," wrote the *Observer,* "that few mothers are either capable or willing to perform so arduous a task."[44] After the establishment of public schools in 1840, some mothers were relieved of tutoring; but many still clung to the old custom, too proud to have their children educated at public expense. In 1852 Mrs. Rebecca McDowell wrote to her relative, Alexander F. Brevard, concerning her young son, "I have never sent him to school and from his progress I am satisfied to teach him a year longer myself."[45]

Wives of the yeomanry class not only did the work associated with the maintenance of the household, but sometimes assisted with the work in the field. They and their children did the lighter tasks of farm work, dropping seeds, chopping cotton, hoeing corn, worming and curing tobacco, picking cotton, and they even helped with the more strenuous work of pulling fodder.

Woman's Legal Status

Legally, the personality of the wife was merged in that of the husband. She could not sue or be sued alone.[46] She could not hold property separate from her husband even in her savings unless her husband by some clear and distinct act divested himself of the property and thus gave her permission to claim it as her own.[47] She could not make a will disposing of her land unless her husband specifically authorized her to do so, setting forth his authorization in a will, deed, or marriage contract. In 1841 the Supreme Court handed down the decision that "a married women can only make an appointment in the nature of a will of real estate under a power of appointment specially given in some deed, . . . But a married woman, by her husband's consent, can make a will of her personal property."[48] In 1844 the Legislature passed an act providing that a will made by a married woman under such conditions might be probated in the court of pleas and quarter-sessions or in a court of equity,[49] a great concession, some thought, to the property rights of the married woman.

Marriage was itself an unqualified gift to the husband of all the wife was in possession of at the time and all that she should thereafter acquire during coverture whether he should survive her or not. As Chief Justice Taylor wrote in 1827 in his decision of Bryan *v.* Bryan: "It may be a hardship for a married woman who brings a fortune to her husband, to find herself and her children reduced to poverty; but she knew when she married him, that the law gave him an absolute property in all her personal estate. . . . The hardship might have been guarded against by a settlement, and the not making one, is an evidence that she agreed to share his fortune, be it prosperous or adverse."[50]

The property which a woman possessed at the time of her marriage might be secured to her through a marriage settlement, or contract, entered into prior to marriage and registered as any other deed. The contract, however, could secure to the intended wife only such property as she or the bridegroom actually possessed at the time of making the deed.[51] In such instances, it was customary to place the bride's estate in trust for her "sole and separate use."[52] Property settled upon the wife after marriage, by a special wording of the instrument conveying the property, might be secured against the claims of her husband. For instance, William Cain of Orange County bequeathed money and slaves to William Cain, Jr., Willie P. Mangum, and Polly Sutherland in trust for the sole and separate use of his daughter, Mrs. Edward Davis, in order to secure the property against the rights of her husband, and the Supreme Court upheld the grant.[53] The bequest was given for the daughter's use during life and after her death in trust for her children. A third means by which a married woman might obtain control over property was the passage of a private act for her benefit by the Legislature. Such an act secured to her "such property as she might thereafter acquire" by her own efforts.[54]

Several attempts were made in the General Assembly during the early days of the ante-bellum period to enlarge the property rights of married women. In 1804, for instance, Reuben Small of Chowan County presented a bill to secure to married women money arising from the sale of certain household articles.[55] All attempts to alter the status of women in regard to their control of property were resisted, however, until 1848 when an act was passed making it illegal for a husband to sell or lease real estate belonging to the wife at the time of marriage without her consent.[56] This act at once brought up the question of whether it was intended to deprive the husband of his wife's estate by courtesy, but it was not until 1859 that the Supreme Court decided this important question. In Houston *v.* Brown, Chief Justice Pearson gave a blow to property rights which married women thought they had obtained in 1848.

> In the absence of an express provision to that effect, we should be slow in adopting the conclusion that it was the intention of the law-makers to enact so radical a change in the law; because, if such was the intention, it is reasonable to presume it would have been declared in direct terms. . . . The purpose was to

adopt, to a partial extent, the principle of a "homestead law," and to provide a home for the wife during her life, leaving the rights of the husband unimpaired and unrestricted after her death . . . and after her death there is no intimation of an intenton to interfere with his rights according to the common law. . . . The sole object is to provide a home for her, of which she could not be deprived either by the husband or by his creditors.[57]

The first significant change in the property and contract rights of married women did not come until the Constitution of 1868, and it was not until the Martin Act of 1911 that the wife was emancipated "absolutely as to all contracts, except with her husband."[58]

Although in most cases the husband had complete control over his wife's property, the common law permitted the married woman to claim dower. If her husband died intestate or did not make a provision in his will fully satisfactory to her, she might signify her dissent before the county court and be allotted a third part of the real estate including the dwelling house.[59] Nor could the husband defeat his wife of dower by a secret conveyance of property.[60] If the husband chose, he might make his wife executrix or administratrix of his estate and she had the privilege of making affidavit to her inventory before a justice of the peace instead of in open court.[61]

The ante-bellum husband not only had control over his wife's property, but he was also the master of her person. "The wife must be subject to the husband. Every man must govern his household," said Chief Justice Pearson in his decision of Joyner *v.* Joyner in 1862. It was for this reason, he pointed out, that the law gave the husband authority over his wife and, in turn, had adopted proper safeguards to prevent an abuse of this power.[62] According to common law, if a wife should slander or assault a neighbor, the husband was made to pay for it. If the wife should commit a criminal offense, less than felony, in the presence of her husband, he, not she, was held responsible. The husband was subject to the payment of his wife's debts even after she had deserted him unless it could be proved that she wilfully deserted.

But the law also gave a husband "power to use such a degree of force as is necessary to make the wife behave herself and know her place."[63] In 1825 the *Raleigh Register* declared that the general idea was "that a man may chastise his wife, provided the weapon be not thicker than his little finger."[64] Two years later in the case of the State against one Forkner for whipping his wife, tried in Warren County Superior Court, Judge Ruffin held "that altho' in civilized society it was universally considered as dishonorable and disgraceful for persons in elevated situations to lift their hands against their wives, yet the law was made for the great bulk of mankind . . . the only question for the Jury was whether the whipping was excessive, barbarous and unreasonable."[65] In several cases which reached the Supreme Court, the judges discussed the relationship existing between husband and wife. In State *v.* Pendergrass[66] the Court set forth the amount of chastisement which a husband might inflict upon his wife, and in State *v.* Hussey declared that "the wife is not a competent witness against her husband, to prove a battery on her person by him, except in cases where a lasting injury is inflicted, or threatened to be inflicted upon her."[67] In Joyner *v.* Joyner, Chief Justice Pearson reviewed several circumstances in which a husband might be justified in striking his wife "with a horse-whip on one occasion and with a switch on another, leaving several bruises on the person."[68] He held these circumstances to be: abuse in the strongest term and repeated use of the word *liar.*

In 1845 a native of Connecticut, signing himself W.J.F., wrote an essay which went the rounds of the national press, pointing out that there was "no essential difference between the legal condition of the married woman and that of the slave." In publishing the essay, the *North Carolina Standard* said that the writer "fixes upon the mind the undeniable fact, that the wives of Christian husbands are as much slaves, so far as privation of rights is concerned, as the negroes of the utmost South. We have always regarded many of the provisions in our laws in regard to the rights of the married women, as unjust and harsh—as illiberal and tyrannical. . . . The parallel he draws between what the slave *is* and what the wife *might be,* is both striking and complete, . . . We have only to add the hope that the article . . . may not cause a 'rebellion' among the married ladies."[69]

The wife actually occupied a far higher status than that assigned to her by law. Nor can the extent of her control over family affairs be ascertained by a mere glance at her legal status. In 1820 John Y. Mason wrote to his friend John H. Bryan warning him that if he should embark in matrimony he must "be prepared to have his nose occasionally ground, that he must be fond of servant-whipping, and that he must not drink or play cards."[70]

Husbands frequently depended upon their wives to carry on business in their absence; indeed, the law recognized the wife as the business agent of her husband under certain circumstances.[71] In 1828 John H. Bryan, writing to his wife from Washington where he was attending Congress, said to her after discussing the political situation, "You see I am disposed to make you somewhat of a politician but every wife ought to know something about and take an interest in her husbands business & concerns."[72] A year later he wrote, "You had better endeavor to collect the notes of Wood & Bob Lisbon for the hire of the negroes, particularly the latter.— . . . I am very well satisfied with your disposition of the negroes—you are my smartest as well as most trusted agent."[73]

There also existed between some husbands and wives a companionship which arose from mutual interests in things other than domestic affairs. Mrs. Henry W. Conner went fishing with her husband,[74] and Mrs. Rebecca McDowell studied Roman history with hers. "We have spent this winters long nights in the study of Rome," wrote Mrs. McDowell, "And I am engaged in writing down the most interesting events that have occurred and the lives of the principal persons who figured while she was a commonwealth."[75]

In North Carolina as elsewhere in the South wives in genteel families often followed the custom once prevalent among the gentry in England of addressing their husbands formally even in private conversation and correspondence. It is not strange that the custom should have continued in slaveholding areas, where the wife often spoke to her husband in the presence of domestics. Mrs. Ebenezer Pettigrew addressed her husband as Mr. Pettigrew and even in correspondence saluted him as "My dear Mr. Pettigrew" and subscribed herself, "Your dutiful wife, Ann B. Pettigrew."[76] Less frequently a husband addressed his wife formally, but almost invariably he began a letter to her with "Dear Madam" or "Dear Wife." This custom was not so much an indication of the abasement of woman as it was a matter of expediency and a reflection of the formality of the upper classes in the ante-bellum South.

The meekness of a wife depended more upon individual temperament than upon repressive customs. Although Judge John H. Bryan thought that "a woman who abuses her husband to strangers, ought to have her tongue cut out, or slit at least,"[77] examples are not lacking of women who saw fit even to advertise their husbands publicly if they considered themselves as having been grievously injured. As early as 1806 the *North Carolina Journal* of Halifax carried following advertisement:[78]

Notice

WHEREAS my husband James Taylor has behaved towards me in the most dishonorable manner; and did, on Saturday night last, take himself from me, with a certain Pattey Norton, who is of a light complexion, black under the eyes, and extremely homely; his treatment to the subscriber, in various instances has been so infamous, as to induce her to give this caution to the public, that the innocent may beware of the imposter.—It is expected the said Taylor was persuaded to go off by one Clem. Reed, an infamous character, who has acknowledged himself a liar, in as many as four or five different places.

BASHEBA TAYLOR

Halifax county, August 8, 1806

The pattern for this advertisement is to be found, of course, in the custom of advertising runaway wives. After 1810, when the *Edenton Gazette* raised the price of an advertisement for a runaway wife from ten shillings to "five dollars for the first insertion, and two and a half dollars for each continuance" the frequency of such insertions abated considerably although the practice was by no means discontinued.[79]

Woman as a Wage Earner

Many women, even of the upper classes, by frugality and management were able to add something to the family income. Miss Janet Schaw, who visited Wilmington shortly before the Revolution, found Mrs. Cornelius Harnett, the wife of that indefatigable leader of the Sons of Liberty, "a pattern of industry." They tell me," wrote Miss Schaw, "that the house and every thing in it was the produce of her labours. She has (it seems) a garden, from which she supplies the town with what vegetables they use, also with mellon and other fruits. She even descends to make minced pies, cheese-cakes, tarts, and little biskets, which she sends to town once or twice a day, besides her eggs, poultry and butter, . . . all her little commodities are contrived so, as not to exceed one penny a piece, and her customers know she will not run tick."[80]

Prior to 1840, thrifty housewives could by their weaving alone keep the family supplied with many necessities, but after that date, as one woman complained in a petition to the Tennessee Legislature, the existing improvements in carding, spinning, and weaving by machinery reduced "the labor of females in those branches of domestic industry . . . so low, that there is but little inducement to follow them, except to make clothing for ourselves and our household." As she pointed out:

> In by gone days we could, by industry, not only provide clothing for our household, but we could make a sufficiency of domestic manufacture to spare to sell to the merchants to procure other necessaries for our families. This is not the case now; when we manufacture those articles now, and take them to the merchant, we find them supplied with domestic manufacturers from Northern and Eastern manufactories of the Union and at so low a price that ours cannot bear a competition with them.[81]

When this condition arose, some women turned their attention to the culture of the silkworm. As early as 1831 the daughters of Harrison Smith of Wake Forest sold $60 of sewing silk in a few months.[82]

Like Mrs. Cornelius Harnett, many women sold little articles related to domestic industry and their husbands would often permit them to retain for their own use the profits made in consideration of their supplying the family with certain necessary articles. For instance, John Croker, a planter of large estate in Northampton County, gave his wife for her separate use "what money she could make by the use of her needle (she being a good tailoress), the sale of fowls, eggs, butter, and vegetables from their garden."[83] They kept separate accounts at the stores; she lent her money on bond and took the notes in her own name, and her husband even borrowed from her.

Women innkeepers were frequently to be found, and the operation of a boarding house was considered one of the most respectable ways in which a widow might earn a livelihood.[84] In 1840 the *Fayetteville Observer* was of the opinion that the Fayetteville Hotel, operated by a certain Mrs. Brown, was the handsomest hotel in the State.[85] Women frequently owned shops, especially those offering articles of feminine wear. In 1818 a Miss Raley opened a shop in Raleigh with the following announcement:

She has Silk and Sattin Bonnets of the newest fashion; plain and open work Straw Bonnets; Ruffs & Turbans; Ladies Kid Gloves; Band boxes by the dozen, or single ones—also a good assortment of Perfumery. She flatters herself she will be able to give general satisfaction, as her Millinery and Dresses will be made in the newest fashions, having weekly correspondence from New-York, and by keeping up a good and general assortment.[86]

Miss Jane Henderson has a millinery shop in Raleigh for several years and then sold it to the Misses M. A. and S. Pulliam who were patronized by all the surrounding neighborhood. In New Bern, Wilmington, Fayetteville, Greensboro, Charlotte, and Salisbury women owned and operated their own shops.

When factories began to be established in North Carolina, some women found employment as "hands." The Lincoln Cotton Factory near Lincolnton was mentioned in 1849 as employing white girls exclusively.[87] School teaching was another position open to women. In 1853 Calvin H. Wiley, superintendent of common schools, urged examining committees to "encourage as much as possible the very poor, and especially poor females to become teachers."[88] Long before this, however, women were tutoring in private families and teaching in the female departments of the local academies. In 1810 Mrs. Falkner's Boarding School at Warrenton was prosperous and well patronized.[89]

The work most often resorted to by "destitute females" was domestic service, laundering, and sewing. When Mrs. Stephen A. Norfleet, wife of a wealthy planter of Bertie County, became too ill in 1858 to manage her household, her husband employed a Miss Virginia Vaughan whom he paid $4 a month "for Housekeeping," a total of $24 for six months work. In 1859 he paid Miss Renny Wooten a slightly higher wage, $60 for the year.[90] Laundry work and sewing were little better. A "Sewing Girl" described her situation in a letter to the *Southern Weekly Post* in 1851. She was "the elder of five sisters, with somewhat better advantages than generally falls [sic] to the lot of girls of my class, owing to the exertions of a kind father, who died ere the others were old enough to profit by his labor." Her father dead, her mother feeble, how was this young girl to feed six hungry mouths?

Tailors were applied to, and to work I went; pantaloons at seventy-five cents, vests at one dollar; three of the former, one of the latter, were the most I could do in a week; thus making seventeen dollars per month; no allowance made for sickness, &c five dollars of this must go for house rent, leaving twelve dollars for fuel, lights, food and clothing for a family of six.[91]

It was clearly too much for the young girl, and now she was appealing through the *Weekly Post* for a larger field of activity for intelligent young women who were reduced to the sad necessity of supporting their families: "Will our gentlemen merchants take our daughters as clerks? Will you, Mr. Post, and your brother editors, let our sisters set type at your stands, or must the next generation still be doomed to

Stitch—stitch—stitch
In poverty, hunger, and dirt
Sewing at once with a double thread
A Shroud as well as a shirt!

To this appeal "Mr. Post" was silent, but a year later he stated his position with an air of gallantry: "We doubt not our lady readers will pardon us for the opinion that their proper position is not in the full glare of public observation—not in the general practice of what are called the learned professions, nor in any employment which would compel them to violate the delicate modesty in which their virtue is enshrined."[92]

But the movement for "the emancipation of women" was under way even in the South. Free-thinking articles, such as that by the "Sewing Girl," were creeping into the State papers. In 1850 the *Carolina Watchman* published a story called "The Father," which declared that "all young females should possess some employment by which they might obtain a livelihood in case they should be reduced to the necessity of supporting themselves."[93] The work of Mary Wolstonecraft, Hannah More, Harriet Newell, Isabella Graham, even the activity of "those bold hussies," Anne Royall, author of the *Black Book*, Susan B. Anthony, leader in the advocacy of women's rights, Lucy Stone, who wanted married women to retain their maiden names, Sarah and Angelina Grimké, advocates of the equality of the sexes, was leaven in the region where "modest softness" and "flattering timidity" were a fetish.

There are rare instances of women in North Carolina taking an active part in politics long before Miss Anthony's day. In 1795, for instance, Elkanah Watson of Boston arrived in Warrenton while an election was in progress and found the mother of Benjamin Hawkins, formerly a member of the Continental Congress, active at the polls. "I never met with a more sensible, spirited old lady," Watson wrote. "She was a great politician; and I was assured, that she has more political influence, and exercised it with greater effect, than any man in her county."[94]

It was not until the Harrison campaign of 1840 that both political parties made a direct appeal to women to use their influence in behalf of politics. The *North Carolina Standard* loudly objected to "dragging women into politics": ". . . we can scarcely read an exchange paper containing an account of a political assemblage, which does not inform us that it was cheered by 'the approving smiles of the fair.' . . . It is natural that intellectual ladies by reading or conversation, should form some opinions on political topics, it is natural, and it is right.—But our laws confer on them no political power, and therefore, apart from all considerations of social propriety, they should take no political action." Declaring that "the empire of woman is the fireside: her dominion is that of the affections," the *Standard* continued:

> For the vulgar strife of politics, her sensibilities are too refined, and for its fierce contention, her nerves are too delicate. Her weakness is her surest protection, and her softness is her best ornament. We have been pained therefore, during the pending struggle for the Presidency, which has been distinguished for its bitterness, to see our fair country-women unsex themselves, and stepping across the threshold to mingle in the fight.[95]

The next presidential campaign saw almost the same enthusiasm as four years earlier. The "Whig Ladies" of Raleigh had a local artist paint a Whig banner "on fine gray silk" and they worked ardently for Clay.[96] But women's rights had been launched under anti-slavery auspices, and in 1850 when abolitionists joined with advocates of women's rights in the famous Women's Rights Convention in Worcester, Massachusetts, the North Carolina press unanimously condemned the movement. "Woman's sphere is about the domestic altar, and within the tranquil precincts of the social circle," the *Raleigh Register* declared. "When she transgresses that sphere and mingles in the miserable brawlings and the insane agitations of the day, she descends from her lofty elevation, and becomes an object of disgust and contempt, . . ."[97] To the *North Carolina Standard* the convention was a huge joke: "Women made speeches—women acted on committees—and women claimed the right to vote, and in fact, to *be men*."[98] As the movement gained strength at the North, claiming more and more support from the radical abolition element, it came to be condemned more and more in the southern press. "The most ridiculous escapade of this century, is the unwise, foolish, and incomprehensible position assumed by certain trous-a-loon women at the North," declared the Oxford *Leisure Hour* in 1858. "All this originates in a false state of society—in a society that at the South would not be countenanced for one day."[99] Nevertheless, southern women in their writings, their church activities,[100] their education,[101] and their daily work, were beginning also to cry, "Equality!"

The Status of Children

The ante-bellum tradition was one of large families. John Bernard, celebrated English comedian who visited North Carolina about 1800, observed that there were never less than a dozen children in a family, adding that "the women seem to bear them in a litter in these regions."[102] William White, for many years Secretary of State, son-in-law of Richard Caswell, the Revolutionary patriot, had ten children. Judge Thomas Ruffin had fourteen children, only one of whom died before maturity. Judge John H. Bryan also had fourteen children. In 1828 after Mrs. Bryan had given birth to another child, her sister, Mrs. Ebenezer Pettigrew, wrote: "I take this opportunity of congratulating you on the birth of a fine son. I have no doubt but the stock will be increased every eighteen months, very fortunate for us, the breed is so good, so smart."[103] Mrs. Pettigrew was herself bearing one child after another.

Undoubtedly many children died in infancy. The census of 1860, however, lists the number of deaths of children under one for the year ending June 1, 1860, at only 56 in every 1,000 free children.[104] Among the causes of death given, croup, whooping cough, scarlatina, infantile fever, worms, teething, and measles headed the list.

The size of free families in North Carolina as given by the census of 1790 is indicated in the following table:

Size of Families in 1790[105]

Size	Number	Per Cent
1 person	3,519	7.2
2 and under 4	9,237	19.0
4 and under 6	12,973	26.6
6 and under 8	11,245	23.1
8 and under 10	7,460	15.3
10 and over	4,267	8.8
Total	48,701	100.0

In 1790 almost half the families in the State, or 47.2 per cent, contained six or more members. Almost a tenth, or 8.8 per cent, contained ten or more members; while a little more than a fourth or 26.2 per cent, contained less than four members. The tendency toward large families was in keeping with the general trend throughout the United States.[106]

The average size of all free families in North Carolina at three different periods, 1790, 1850, and 1860, as given by the census reports, is indicated in the following table:

Average Size of Free Families

Period	Total Free Population	Number of Families	Average per Family
1790	292,554	52,613[107]	5.6
1850	580,363	105,451	5.5
1860	661,563	125,090	5.3

The average size of free families in North Carolina decreased less from 1790 to 1850, six decades, than in the one decade from 1850 to 1860. By 1900 the average size of families had decreased to 5.1 members.

A midwife functioned far more frequently at the birth of a child than did a doctor, not only because the doctor's fee was higher, but also because doctors were less plentiful. Each community usually had its midwife, and a skilful midwife sometimes practiced in several counties. In 1813 William Hayne wrote to his father-in-law, Alexander F. Brevard, that a friend of theirs was much pleased with the midwife in Columbia, S. C., although she "has not been very long engaged in that business—the former one here being dead."[108] Newspapers usually announced a baby as having been born to the father, as, for instance, "May 18—a son to Peter Warren, Town."[109]

A law requiring registration of births was advocated at various times during the ante-bellum period. In 1829 the *Raleigh Register,* on observing the passage of such a law in Georgia, asked, "Is not such a regulation desirable in this State?[110] In 1850 a bill requiring the registration of births, marriages, and deaths submitted in the Senate by Thomas N. Cameron was finally defeated by a vote of 25 to 17.[111]

Most genteel and middle-class families turned over the care of the children to Negro nurses. In cases requiring the expedient as a means of saving life, Negro nurses even suckled their little charges.[112] In 1825 the *Hillsborough Recorder* protested against the custom of "delivering a child over into the hands of a nurse . . . where it may first learn to lisp vulgarity and obscenity, and from whom it inevitably acquires a pronunciation and accent, such as may never be fully corrected. . . . Many parents are ashamed to introduce their children into society, and well may they," for the child is often "unfit for society; and in the parlour words might be heard from its mouth to put to shame these faithless guardians of its youth." Among the other evils of Negro nurses the writer listed "the propensity to frighten children" and the fondness for telling tales of ghosts and genii. Indeed, he had known of children in whom foolish superstitions had been aroused "which education and even religion have sometimes been found unable to counteract."[113] Mrs. Mary Mason of Raleigh, writing in her *Young Housewife's Counseller and Friend,* declared, "The nursery is the hotbed of superstition. Who does not know that from the very first . . . the inmates of the nursery are controlled by superstitious fear? . . . how often does the nursery-maid still the restless little prattler by calling upon 'the bugaboo to come and catch naughty little Charley!' And further than this the memory of ghost-stories is among the most vivid of early impressions, . . ."[114] In 1847 "Phil," writing a series of articles on children for the *Star,* thought that "one of the greatest evils now in existence, is that of trusting our children to wicked and ignorant nurses."[115] In nonslaveholding families, the babies were usually left to the care of the older children.

Family discipline seems to have been as varied in ante-bellum days as at present. Parents desired obedient children, but many were too indulgent or too absorbed with other matters to give them the necessary training. A newspaper correspondent in 1809 was of the opinion that family government "in spite of the modern whims about liberty and equality . . . must be absolute; mild, not tyrannical."[116] In 1810 a writer lamented, "There are no more children."[117] They "now treat parents, their relatives, their masters, with contempt. . . . Licentiousness, pride and boldness, have superceded mildness, timidity and innocence." In 1832 William Hooper, professor of Ancient Languages in the University of North Carolina, in a lecture before the North Carolina Institute of Education, regretted that parents were "generally so injudiciously indulgent." Some children were allowed to "indulge a violent temper without punishment, to domineer over slaves, to struggle with, and even fight their mothers, when they attempted to control them."[118]

In 1841 a citizen of the town rejoiced that "we have a School in Raleigh at last," because at last a man had been found who could keep the students in check. For the first time in many years boys "who have never been under control at home or elsewhere," sons "of our first citizens," were being taught a little self-restraint. The boys of Raleigh seem not to have been abashed long by the new teacher. In 1845 the *Register* declared, "It is distressing to see so little restraint imposed upon the Youths of our city,"[119] to which the *Carolina Watchman* replied: "We know of no place where the exercise of *Parental Authority* is more needed, than in Salisbury. . . . We have on many occasions had to be put on public duty after night, and were astonished at the number of boys running to and fro through the streets, (children of those whom we thought knew better how to control them) *swearing* like sailors, and *blackguarding* to such a degree, that we know would utterly astonish their parents if they knew." The *Watchman* thought that every father should know "the whereabouts of his Son after sundown. He ought to know whether he is frequenting the *grog-shops*, the *card-table*, or any other place where *immorality* and *vice* is carried on."[120]

Town ordinances, such as the curfew and the regulation of children's games, passed for the purpose of aiding parents in controlling their children, often fell short of the aim.[121] "Is Nash-Square the public property in such a sense, that it may be taken possession of by groups of rude and noisy lads, during the afternoon of the Sabbath, for their sports;—such as dog-fighting—wrestling—marble playing, &c, to the great annoyance of those who dwell in the neighborhood?" asked "A Parent" of Raleigh in 1853. "If such lads are beyond the reach of parental restraint,—or if these are [children of] parents who do not care to control them, lest it should curb their high spirits, is there no other authority that can and will restrain them?" The writer called on the town commission for a special police for juvenile delinquents who should be confined to the guard-house and released only after their parents had paid a fine.[122] In much the same vein the *Weekly Post* had written in 1851: ". . . the worst thing we know of about some villages is the manner in which the children are raised; and on this subject we feel that a great reform is needed. Parents . . . often look on it as evidence of spirit and smartness to see their children rudely insulting the quiet and often humble citizens of the Country, gibing them on the streets, doing mischief to their nurses and vehicles, and making sport of their plain equipments."[123]

In a few instances, the "spirit and boldness" of the ante-bellum youth took extreme forms. In 1805 "a large family of children" attempted to kill their mother because she was too strict with them[124] and in 1854 a Cabarrus County father, over-wrought by his son's misconduct, hanged the boy for his disobedience.[125]

There were parents who demanded that their children treat them with deference, and they seemed to have had no great amount of trouble in exacting it. The letters of Dr. James Norcom of Edenton to his children are an excellent example of the parental attitude which placed, "Honor thy father and thy mother," and especially thy father, above all other commandments. When he sent his young daughter to a boarding school in Philadelphia, he instructed her to begin her letters to him "with any of the following addresses—viz—Dear & honored Father—my dearest Father—my beloved Father, or my best of Fathers."[126] He was constantly reminding his children of their duty; nor did he cease to exact this duty after they were married and had children of their own.

According to common law, the child owed the father certain services which the parent had a right to demand. A child's wages belonged to the father and the father had the right to require certain labor of him in return for his support. In 1815 a father brought action for an injury done to him in the loss of his daughter's services in consequence of her seduction, illness, and death in childbirth.[127] Children of the yeomanry were put to work in the fields at an early age. Some were hired out at specific wages for short periods of time,[128] and others were apprenticed until they arrived at maturity, the apprenticeship usually continuing from five to seven years. With the establishment of factories, children were also employed as factory hands at a rate as low, in some instances, as 12½ cents a week.

The dissenting opinion of Judge Daniel delivered in 1832 in the case of Williams *v.* Barnes foreshadowed the modern attitude toward the relation of parent and child:

> There is a natural and legal obligation on the parent to maintain his child during infancy. The law has fixed the time during which the child shall be considered an infant, to the period of twenty-one years. The parent, during this period, has a right to the services of the child to enable him to fulfil his obligation. But after the period of twenty-one years the parent is released from his obligation, . . . and the law likewise releases the child from the obligation of giving his labor and services to the parent, . . . Therefore when he labors for the parent after the time he arrives at age of twenty-one years, the law raises a promise by the parent to pay as much as the labor of the child is reasonably worth.[129]

Judge Ruffin and Chief Justice Henderson held that such a position would tend to "change the character of our people, cool domestic regard, and in the place of confidence sow jealousies in families."

Upon the father's death, the child was thrown upon the mercy of the orphans' court. By the act of 1762 and the interpretation of this act by several Supreme Court decisions, no one had a right to the guardianship of a child under twenty-one "except as testamentary guardian or as appointed by the father by deed or by the County or Superior Court."[130] The appointment of a guardian was a matter of discretion by the court and the court usually would not rescind an appointment,[131] once made, unless it seemed that injury was likely to result to the orphan's estate. In some counties it was customary for the orphan, on arriving at the age of fourteen, to be permitted to come into court and make choice of a guardian if his father had not appointed one by will or deed,[132] but the choice of the orphan was not binding upon the court.[133] The court was required to take bonds from guardians appointed and the justices of the peace forming the court were held liable for taking insufficient security.

The act of 1762 required the holding of orphans' courts in every county once a year. The court was held for the purpose of examining guardians' accounts, but occasionally the court might discipline an unruly orphan. The Orphans' Court of Edgecombe County, for instance, has on its record for 1800 the following entry:

"William Robertson being brought before the Court for misbehaviour—it is the sentence of the Court that he be committed to Jail, there to remain til tomorrow morning 12 o'clock—Ordered that the Sheriff execute the said sentence."[134]

The large number of orphans' accounts consumed much of the time of a county court and leads to the conclusion that the percentage of orphans in the State was high. In six counties,[135] selected at random from different sections of the State, the average number of accounts proved each year was well over a hundred. In Edgecombe County, for instance, the orphans' court proved from 110 to 126 accounts every year between 1831 and 1835.

The fact that there was mismanagement of orphans' estates and even ill treatment of orphans is indicated by the numerous bills and petitions to the Legislature on that subject.[136] Governor Benjamin Williams in his address to the General Assembly in 1800 urged that an act be passed compelling guardians to return lists of orphans' lands in order to protect orphans against dishonesty.[137]

But the role of a guardian was not always an easy one, and in some instances courts had difficulty in finding persons who would undertake the responsibility. A bill before the Legislature of 1806 declared that "It often happens, that orphans are entitled to considerable estates in woody land, young negroes . . . the income of which will not support them and their sickly constitution will not admit of their being bound out, nor their property allow them to be put on the Parish."[138] In such an instance the guardian had either to support the child himself or sell a part of the orphan's estate. But the procedure to be followed in selling a part of an orphan's estate was subject to complication and delays. The county court had first to determine whether the sale was expedient and then to select the part of the property which could be disposed of with least injury to the ward.[139] Orphans with insufficient property to support them were bound out by the county court to earn their "board and keep."[140] Orphans of this class were usually illegitimate children, and children whose fathers had deserted their families or whose mothers had obtained from the Legislature the right to such property as they might thereafter acquire.

The ante-bellum conception of the family and the laws upon which it was based were built around the husband as the head and ruler of the household. But this ideal was seriously overcast and the laws themselves gradually modified by the extra-legal position of woman. Women engaged in business, and married women found ways of holding and disposing of property long before the Constitution of 1868. Intellectual women had from colonial times taken an interest in politics, and after 1840 it became fashionable to attend political gatherings. Votes for women were being agitated in other parts of the United States and North Carolina did not escape the woman's movement. While the law gave the father unlimited power over his children, he was often prevented from exercising it by the children themselves. The ante-bellum boy was often referred to as "a bold, spirited youth, whose dominion over slaves made him impatient of restraint."

Notes

1. MS in Thomas Henderson Letter Book, "Duplin County"; Newsome, "Twelve North Carolina Counties," *NCHR*, V, 440.

2. *Ibid.*, VI, 82.

3. *Op. cit.*, pp. 321, 338.

4. *Op. cit.*, p. 437. For a description of the houses from Virginia to Fayetteville in the fifties see Olmsted, *op. cit.*, p. 321.

5. December 13.

6. *Ibid.*, October 1, 1853.

7. *Ibid.*, October 15, 1853; see also *Fayetteville Observer*, September 1, 1856.

8. See in *North Carolina Booklet:* A. C. Avery, "Historic Homes in North Carolina—Pleasant Gardens and Quaker Meadows, in Burke County," IV, No. 3; Thomas Blount, "Buncombe Hall," II, No. 8; Col. Burgwyn, "The Groves," II, No. 9; A. L. Devereux, "Historic Homes: Welcome," XI, No. 2; Richard Dillard, "Hayes and Its Builder," II, No. 8; M. H. Hinton, "Ingleside, Home of John Ingles," XV, No. 3; L. T. Rodman, "Historic Homes and People of Old Bath

Town," II, No. 8, and "Residence of John Gray Blount, Esq.," XXII, 46–52; A. M. Waddell, "Historic Homes in the Cape Fear Country," II, No. 9.

9. *Edenton Gazette,* December 2, 1807.

10. J. B. Avirett, *The Old Plantation,* pp. 35–42.

11. U. S. Census Office, *A Century of Population Growth,* p. 102; *Population of the United States in 1860,* p. xxvii.

12. MS in James A. Norcom Papers, February 4, 1810.

13. *Star,* November 28, 1810.

14. *Leisure Hour,* November 18, 1858.

15. *Infra,* pp. 302–8.

16. MS in James A. Norcom Papers; James Norcom, Sr., to Mary B. Harvey, April 24, 1848.

17. "Beauties in Female Piety," D. A. Clark, *Sermons* quoted in *Western Carolinian,* September 19, 1820.

18. Quoted in *Hillsborough Recorder,* November 6, 1822.

19. MS in James A. Norcom Papers: James Norcom, Sr., to Mary B. Harvey, May 25, 1848.

20. *Ibid.;* see also letter of April 24, 1848.

21. July 23.

22. February 28; see also Barnard, *op. cit.,* p. 342. Captain Marryat of Great Britain (*op. cit.,* p. 100) did not confine his remarks on beauty to southern women, but said, "In my former remarks upon the women of America I have said, that they are the prettiest in the world, and I have put the word *prettiest* in italics, as I considered it a term peculiarly appropriate to the American women."

23. July 9, 1853.

24. March 27.

25. *Heart Whispers; or a Peep Behind the Family Curtain,* p. 251.

26. Pp. xi–xii.

26a. H. S. Chamberlain, *Old Days in Chapel Hill, Being the Life of Cornelia Phillips Spencer,* p. 45.

26b. E. W. and C. M. Andrews, *op. cit.,* p. 203.

26c. Sprunt, *Chronicles of the Cape Fear River,* pp. 162–63; Chamberlain, *op. cit.,* p. 45.

27. Mason, *op. cit.,* p. 20. See also *House and Home; or, The Carolina Housewife;* Randolph, *op. cit.;* S. A. Elliott, *Mrs. Elliott's Housewife;* Cotesworth Pinckney (ed.), *The Lady's Token,* pp. 119–20.

28. Mason, *op. cit.,* p. 36.

29. *Ibid.,* p. 27.

30. *Ibid.,* pp. 28–29.

31. *Ibid.,* pp. 48–59.

32. *Ibid.,* p. 73.

33. *Ibid.,* p. 66.

34. *Ibid.,* p. 61.

35. *Ibid.,* p. 11.

36. *Ibid.*, p. 18.
37. *Ibid.*, p. 17.
38. *Ibid.*, p. 120.
39. *Papers of Thomas Ruffin*, II, 294.
40. MS in James A. Norcom Papers, August 19, 1846.
41. MS in John H. Bryan Papers, November 22, 1821.
42. *Ibid.*, January 23, 1828.
43. *Ibid.*, October 20, 1828.
44. February 8, see also Andrews, *op. cit.*, pp. 154–55, for Miss Janet Schaw's observation on the mothers' instruction of their daughters in colonial North Carolina.
45. MS in Brevard Papers, March 22, 1852.
46. But see *Revised Code,* 1855, Chap. XXXIX, sec. 13.
47. Croker *v.* Vasser, 37 N. C., 553.
48. Newlin *v.* Freeman, 23 N. C., 514.
49. *Revised Code,* Chap. CXIX, sec. 3.
50. Bryan *v.* Bryan, 16 N. C., 47; see also Ruffin's opinion in Lassiter *v.* Dawson, 17 N. C., 348.
51. *Sessional Laws,* 1785, Chap. XII; *Revised Code,* 1855, Chap. XXXVII, sec. 25.
52. See Rutherford *v.* Craik, 3 N. C., 262.
53. Davis *v.* Cain, 36 N. C., 304; see also Ponton *v.* McLemore, 22 N. C., 285.
54. *Supra,* pp. 219, 222–30.
55. *House Journal,* December 11, 1804, p. 39; see also report of John Stanly in *House Journal,* December 4, 1821, p. 38.
56. *Revised Code,* 1855, Chap. LVI.
57. Houston *v.* Brown, 52 N. C. 161.
58. For the present legal status of married women see M. P. Smith, *Special Legal Relations of Married Women in North Carolina as to Property, Contracts, and Guardianship,* University of North Carolina Extension Bulletin, VII, No. 9.
59. *Revised Code,* 1855, Chap. CXVIII, sec. 1. Before the act of 1848 (Chap. 101, secs. 1–2), a widow could not dissent from her husband's will by attorney although she was too ill to travel to court to dissent in person.
60. *Ibid.*, Chap. CXVIII, sec. 1.
61. *Ibid.*, Chap. XLVI, sec. 65.
62. Joyner *v.* Joyner, 59 N. C., 322.
63. *Ibid.*
64. August 26; see also *Hillsborough Recorder,* August 24, 1825.
65. *Star,* May 3, 1827; *Raleigh Register,* May 4, 1827.
66. S. *v.* Pendergrass, 19 N. C., 365.
67. S. *v.* Hussey, 44 N. C., 123.
68. Joyner *v.* Joyner, 59 N. C., 322.
69. October 22. For Judge Ruffin's statement as to the similarity of the

status of wives and slaves see Waddill *v.* Martin, 38 N. C., 562. In this connection, it is interesting to note that travelers from abroad when commenting upon the status of woman in the New World, sometimes observed that "the Americans have, in the treatment of women, fallen below, not only their own democratic principles, but the practice of some parts of the Old World." See, for example, Marryat, *op. cit.*, p. 106.

70. MS in John H. Bryan Papers, May 6, 1820.

71. Cox *v.* Hoffman, 20 N. C., 319. "A *femme covert* may become an agent for her husband, and such an appointment as agent may be inferred from his acts and conduct respecting her."

72. MS in John H. Bryan Papers, February 10, 1828.

73. *Ibid.*, January 7, 1820.

74. MS Diary of Juliana Conner.

75. MS in Brevard Papers, December 15, 1851.

76. MS in Pettigrew Papers: Ann B. Pettigrew to Ebenezer Pettigrew, February 1, 1818 (UNC). Rev. Henry Pattillo always referred to his wife as "the old woman."—*Ibid.:* Henry Pattillo to Dr. Andrew Knox, n. d.

77. MS in John H. Bryan Papers, February 20, 1828.

78. August 18. For other advertisements see *Fayetteville Observer,* March 18, 1830; *Carolina Watchman,* September 20, 1845; *Tarborough Press,* November 2, 1850.

79. *Infra,* p. 793.

80. Andrews, *op. cit.*, pp. 178–79.

81. *Raleigh Register,* February 1, 1842.

82. *Ibid.*, October 6, 1831, November 3, 1831, December 31, 1838; *Star,* June 16, 1831.

83. Croker *v.* Vasser, 37 N. C., 553.

84. See *Raleigh Register,* October 10, 1803, November 11, 1805; *Edenton Gazette,* December 9, 1807; *Star,* October 1, 1819.

85. May 8.

86. *Raleigh Register,* January 9, 1818.

87. *North Carolina Standard,* October 31, 1849.

88. *Ibid.*, August 13, 1853.

89. *Raleigh Register,* January 4, 1810.

90. MS in Stephen A. Norfleet Farm Record Book, December, 1858, December, 1860.

91. December 13.

92. *Ibid.*, December 11, 1852.

93. May 16.

94. *Op. cit.*, p. 251.

95. October 28, 1840; see also *ibid.*, January 22, 1841; *Raleigh Register,* January 31, 1841. Michael Francis of Haywood County, after having attempted repeatedly to defeat a bill in the Legislature of 1842–1843 to incorporate the town of Shelby, moved as a last resort to amend the bill so "that the ladies of the

town of Shelby shall have the right to vote in all elections for town officers." See *House Journal*, 1842–1843, p. 979.

96. *Star*, April 10, 1844.

97. November 2, 1850.

98. November 2, 1850.

99. June 10.

100. *Infra*, p. 426.

101. *Infra*, pp. 304–5.

102. *Op. cit.*, p. 204.

103. MS in John H. Bryan Papers, February 18, 1828.

104. U. S. Census Office, *Statistics of the United States*, 1860, p. 44. This estimate is open to question, for in 1890 the infant death rate in Richmond was 186.9 per 1,000 and in Charleston, 200.4.

105. U. S. Census Office, *A Century of Population Growth*, p. 98.

106. The average size of white slaveholding families was slightly larger in 1790 than the average for white nonslaveholding families, as is shown in the following table taken from *A Century of Population Growth*, p. 100:

Comparison of Slaveholding and Nonslaveholding Families

	Number of Families	Number of Members	Average per Family
Slaveholding	14,945	87,121	5.8
Nonslaveholding	33,076	178,077	5.4

107. Estimated for Caswell, Granville, and Orange counties.

108. MS in Brevard Papers, April 27, 1813.

109. *Carolina Watchman*, May 23, 1850.

110. January 23.

111. MS in Legislative Papers, in Senate, December 20, 1850; *Senate Journal*, January 14, 1851.

112. Lyell, *op. cit.*, p. 222.

113. July 27.

114. Pp. 61–62.

115. September 29.

116. *Raleigh Register*, September 14, 1809.

117. *Star*, October 4.

118. *Raleigh Register*, May 30, 1833.

119. Quoted in *Carolina Watchman*, October 11, 1845.

120. *Ibid.*

121. *Ibid.*, April 26, 1845.

122. *Southern Weekly Post*, August 20, 1853.

123. December 13.

124. *Raleigh Register*, September 16, 1805.

125. *Fayetteville Observer*, September 4, 1854.

126. MS in James A. Norcom Papers, July 5, 1836.

127. M'Farland *v.* Shaw, 4 N. C., 200; in McAulay *v.* Birkland, 35 N. C., 28, it was assumed that the father could recover damages.

128. York, *op. cit.,* pp. 13–18.

129. Williams *v.* Barnes, 14, N. C., 348.

130. Long *v.* Rhymes, 6 N. C., 122; Payton *v.* Smith, 22 N. C., 325; *Revised Code,* 1855, Chap. LIV, sec. 1.

131. For examples of removals of guardians, see Edgecombe County Court Minutes, August term, 1802; Cumberland County Court Minutes, August term, 1802.

132. Cumberland County Court Minutes, August term, 1802.

133. Mills *v.* McAllister, 2 N. C., 303; Grant *v.* Whitaker, 5 N. C., 231.

134. Edgecombe County Court Minutes, February, 1800.

135. Carteret, Cumberland, Edgecombe, Orange, Pasquotank, Rutherford.

136. MSS in Legislative Papers. See, for instance, bill for establishing a court for the protection of orphans in each county, 1803; bill to ameliorate condition of orphans cruelly treated, 1812; bill to point out the duty of guardians, 1820; numerous resolutions calling for investigation of laws regulating orphans' estates, 1822; report of Judiciary Committee, 1829.

137. *House Journal,* November 20, 1800, p. 6.

138. MS in Legislative Papers, 1806.

139. Leary *v.* Fletcher, 23 N. C., 259.

140. *Infra,* pp. 703, *et seq.*

ELEANOR M. BOATWRIGHT

The Political and Civil Status of Women in Georgia, 1783–1860

Georgia Historical Quarterly 25 (1941): 301–24, reprinted by permission of the publisher

By the time one has read through Gray, Spruill, and Johnson there are few outright surprises in this essay, though Boatwright's perceptions are often keen and certainly her findings strongly reinforce those of the other three. Her thesis develops in detail insights which are only touched on here, but there is enough in the essay to have led a reader (had there been one with eyes to see) back to the thesis itself.

Eleanor Boatwright's personality shines through her prose. She had a keen sense of the ridiculous and a profound understanding of the complexity and ambiguity of human experience. The final paragraph in the essay is vintage Boatwright: "A married woman's position in Georgia before 1860 was always hazardous, frequently humiliating, and often tragic. Her true status, nevertheless, was far more commonly determined by her character, that of the man she married, their personal relations to each other, the use they made of the laws, and even by public opinion, than by the statutes alone." There is a chance that her thesis will be published, but meantime there is food for thought even in this very spare version of it.

THE PHILOSOPHIES, facts, practices and sentiments governing the political and civil rights of white women in Georgia between the Revolution and the Civil War were confused, fickle, contradictory, and paradoxical. The Constitution would have allowed full political equality, but theory and practice granted none; whereas the statutes denied the civil existence of a married woman, yet permitted her to establish it if she chose and protected it if she did. It seems to have been a system of letting the right hand know not what the left hand did, but public opinion approved the conspiracy and guarded its secrets.

Georgia women were denied the suffrage between 1777 and 1789 otherwise they might have voted from the founding of the colony until the Civil War. The facts were that the original charter had no disqualifying clause, the Constitution of 1777 limited the franchise to males, those of 1789 and 1798 were silent on the subject, and the Constitution of 1861 barred women from the suffrage.[1] This does not mean that women voted nor that Georgia intended that they should. Neither were Negroes explicitly disqualified until 1861. The Constitution of 1789 and 1798 neither say that women may vote nor that they may not. Women are not mentioned. This failure of the framers was not due to masculine liberality but to feminine insignificance. If a woman had taken advantage of the loophole and attempted to vote it is safe to wager public opinion would have left her in no condition to contest the point.

It appears that Georgia men heard, or thought they heard, the rustle of petticoats in the vogue for democracy that came with the Revolution and fortified their prerogative with the Constitution of 1777. The flutterings were so stilled by 1789 that precautions were abandoned.

Nevertheless Georgia women were not wholly negative in politics. They rarely entered into political discussions, in part because they were uninformed, or found it socially expedient to pretend so; in part, perhaps, because the same code which demanded that a gentleman never contradict a lady, expected that a lady should never embarrass a gentleman with a controversial issue. When there was uniformity of public opinion, however, women who enjoyed politics had their innings. James Buckingham, an Englishman who visited the slave states and wrote of his observations, noticed that in "the struggle between the nullifiers of South Carolina and the General Government of the United States" women "took a very important part," and, according to him, long afterwards retained "more of the enthusiastic feeling of that period than the men."[2] This was not surprising. Life was drab for ante-bellum Georgia women unless they were unmarried and young.

Sometimes a woman held political power. Nancy Rumsey did. "This white female," according to her contemporary Garnett Andrews, "levied blackmail on all office-seekers in Elbert county for half a century." She began her career with a traveling restaurant which she made from an ox cart. When court was in session she drove her team into Elberton, hitched at the court house, and opened up for business. Nancy must have been a good cook for her profits enabled her to build a comfortable house called "Goshen" in the Chinquapin settlement near Elberton. There she established her "throne." Her talents were such that politicians sought her support. "Each got her promise of favor and she got money from each." Her practices became well known but her opposition was so feared that office seekers continued to pay their tax. During the last twenty years of her power it was said, "lawyers who were looking up business took care to say pleasant things to her as they passed, and the Judge, as he went by paid his respects."[3]

Feminine good will was considered important enough for women to be "flattered and appealed to by political orators, and by newspapers, whenever the occasion presented itself for so doing with effect."[4] It was common to see the ladies in the gallery of the legislature. A good murder trial was sure to find them present.[5] At one it was reported the ladies "filled the gallery and even took possession of the floor of the Senate."[6] Wives, daughters, and sweethearts were frequently taken to political celebrations, toasted at political dinners, and danced with at political balls,[7] but that was about the limit of their public activities. What political influence Georgia women had was usually individual and was exercised socially. The men of their state rarely acknowledged that any existed.

The political status of women was ignored but the civil received the most unfavorable attention. Both married and single women shared some civil disabilities. Neither performed jury service and the testimony of both, except in criminal cases, was taken out of court.[8] There the likeness stopped. The law allowed unmarried women to contract; to sue and to be sued; to act as administrators of estates and as guardians of children; to hold bequeath, inherit, or purchase property; and to work, keep their earnings, or to spend them as they pleased. All of which they did as bountiful court evidence proves.

The ceremonial pledge of a man to his bride "with all my worldly goods I thee endow" did not have the legal significance of a valentine. For the civil law saw to it that the new-made husband lost nothing of his own at the altar and took away from it all his bride possessed— perhaps even the ring with which he made his vow. For the common law of England gave a man unconditional title to his wife's personal property[9] while the Georgia Act of 1789 guaranteed him her real property on the same terms.[10]

In 1784 Georgia legally adopted all the English common law not repugnant to the State or Federal Constitution.[11] This common law gave a wife no legal civil status. It recognized the husband and wife as one person, suspended the legal existence of the woman, and put her under the protection of "her husband, her baron, or lord." Under the common law a husband could neither grant anything to his wife nor enter into an agreement with her for "the grant would suppose her separate existence, and to covenant with her would be to covenant with himself."[12]

Georgians, following the English common law, wrote into their statutes:

"In this State the husband is the head of the family, and the wife is subject to him; her civil legal existence is merged in the husband except so far as the law recognizes her separately, either for her own protection or for her benefit, or for the preservation of public order."[13]

The estates of husband and wife were mutually responsible for debts existing at the time of marriage until the Act of 1856.[14] It left the husband responsible for his wife's debts only to the extent of the property she brought him and relieved her estate of all claims of his creditors.[15]

After marriage a man's financial obligations were reduced to a legal minimum. He was required to provide his wife with the "necessities suitable to her habits and conditions of life," but for "anything besides necessaries" he was not "chargeable."[16] After his death she was entitled to dower rights in his estate[17] or to her part, under the law, in its distribution if he died intestate;[18] and to a year's support for herself and their children, even though the estate was insolvent.[19]

Otherwise what a wife had was her husband's, free from all rights of survivorship, to sell, dispose of, or bequeath as he wished, regardless of whether his wife's property was derived from parents, relatives, friends,[20] her former husband,[21] the child of a previous marriage,[22] or the profits of her own labor.[23] Even if a husband deserted his wife prior to 1851 he might appear periodically and collect her earnings, those of their minor children, or anything else the family which he had abandoned might have accumulated.[24]

The following wills from Wilkes County are typical of the period. John Bowen left: "to wife Rachel all that her father gave her, a slave boy Adam, the dun mare, and her bed and furniture."[25] And Samuel Jack's will reads: "Whereas at the time of our marriage my wife owned a house and lot at Chambersburg and three hundred acres . . . willed to her by her former husband Alex. Stewart, she shall hold it."[26]

A striking case that came up in the Cobb County Superior Court was that of Penalton & Co. *vs.* Mills & *al.* It is concerned with the ownership of a slave girl. She had been kept by the daughter of a widowed mother for some time. The two women had no clear understanding as to whether the negro was a gift or a loan. All went well until both of them were married. Then the mother's husband sued the daughter's husband for the return of the slave, not because she was his wife's property but because she was his own. Both mother and daughter were left out of the case. It was a question of whose husband owned the slave.[27]

The story of Fanny Kemble, the beautiful and successful English actress who married Pierce Mease Butler during her brilliant season in Philadelphia, is the story of a rebel against the code of her day. Theirs was a clash to two cultures which soon led to unhappiness, separation, and divorce. This niece of Mrs. Siddons with a background of Drury Lane and Covent Garden, with generation of distinguished actors behind her, who was held in adoration by two continents, and who had been married in the Unitarian Church which omitted "obey" from its ceremony, was ill designed for ante-bellum domesticity. Butler may have been bigoted but he was charming, educated, and wealthy. During their whirlwind courtship Fanny Kemble apparently never inquired the source of his wealth—slave labor on Butler's Island at the mouth of the Altamaha.[28]

Fanny Kemble had always disliked slavery. Her disapproval of it blazed into a burning hatred the winter she and her husband visited his plantation. The system which she so violently attacked he as jealously defended.[29] Slavery came to serve as a battle ground for all the differences that lay between them.[30]

Fanny Kemble was English, she spent only one unhappy winter in Georgia, she was an odd pattern for the mistress of a remote rice plantation, and most of her legal controversies were in Philadelphia; still she was the wife of one of Georgia's richest planters. The problem of her rights to earn, to dispose of her earnings, and to retain the custody of her children were the products of the English common law which she would have found as binding in Georgia as it was in Pennsylvania.[31]

One of their early quarrels was over Fanny Kemble's *Journal of a Residence in America*. It was an account of her first tour in this country. She had contracted for its publication soon after she landed here but was married before the proof was ready. When it came from the press her young husband edited and altered it in spite of her violent protest. This was his marital right and Pierce Butler knew his rights. The *Journal* appeared with the marks of his censorship still on it.[32]

It seemed to Fanny Kemble "too beneficient a provision of the law for the protection of male superiority" that "the man whose wits could not keep him half a week from starving" should be entitled to his wife's earnings.[33] But that was possible.

A case heard three times in the Georgia Supreme Court was that of a woman who had made a little money keeping boarders and from renting property belonging to her. Her husband collected her earnings, invested in land, took the title to it in his own name, and subsequently lost the property. The wife protested against the seizure but the courts ruled in favor of her husband's creditors.[34]

In establishing a husband's claim to his wife's property there was one important qualification. He must "reduce it to possession" during coverture"[35] for the wife had the right to her "choses in action."[36] This had its origin in common law. It meant that debts due her—such as rents, legacies, residuary personal estate, money in funds, or shares—which at the time of her marriage were in the possession of a third person, remained there unless her husband took steps to "reduce them to possession"—gain control. To do this he had to show his intentions together with some overt act to give them force—such as receiving payment on a debt due his wife, having stock belonging to her transferred to him, or bringing action for an offence against her property in his name.

In the case of the woman with the boarding house the court held that her earnings had been reduced to possession by her husband's action. He had received and invested the money as though it were his own and had not recognized the title as being his wife's until it was attached. He had then attempted to set up her equity in the property. The decision was that a wife's earnings became her husband's if he invested them, whether he took the money with or without her consent, and "whether such earnings were made from keeping a boarding house or from washing, ironing, or cooking."[37]

In another Georgia Supreme Court case, Oglesby and wife *vs.* Hall, Oglesby had permitted his wife to sell cakes and to put her earnings in the bank in Athens. She added to them with money which she borrowed from her brother and bought a negro woman and her four children. Mrs. Oglesby took the title in her own name, held the slaves as separate property, met the taxes, and paid her debt to her brother with the profits of her baking. Oglesby neither objected to her actions nor attempted to establish his claim. Nevertheless he secretly deeded the slaves away retaining for himself and his wife a life interest only. His action became known, Mrs. Oglesby contested his rights, and brought suit for the return of the slaves. At the trial Oglesby admitted he was ignorant at all times and drunk when he executed the deed, but he said he was prompted by "love and affection." The court held that since he had neither reduced his wife's earnings nor the slaves to possession that the property was hers and the deed void.[38]

The laws governing a married woman's property were harsh. George Paschal found during the panic of 1837 they took a grim toll in Georgia and produced "moral and social" disorders which were impossible for later generations to understand.[39] Yet a Philadelphia lawyer's remark, that the presumption of the law which gave a husband complete control over his wife's actions "in nine cases out of ten . . . resolved itself into fiction,"[40] had some foundation.

The law allowed a woman to establish a separate estate.[41] The object of this, Judge Bleckley said from the Supreme Bench of Georgia, was to guard a wife from the " 'kicks and kisses' especially the kisses of her husband."[42] The separate estate originated in the common law and did not appear on the statute books of Georgia until 1847.[43] It might be created in several ways: by conveyance to a trustee before marriage;[44] by prenuptial agreement between the parties;[45] by postnupital settlement—under which a husband conveyed property to a third person to hold for his wife;[46] and by gift or legacy especially establishing a woman's sole ownership and disavowing her husband's claim.[47]

The common law gave a wife "without aid of statute" control over her separate estate and permitted her husband none "except as he may be trustee by implication." It bound him, even then, to follow her directions and required that he be removed if he failed to do so.[48] In Georgia an agreement creating a woman's separate estate, whether or not in writing could be enforced in the courts of equity. Both judge and jury were inclined to be friendly to the wife's interest, and, in legal controversies, they might be expected to construe the agreement liberally.[49]

Throughout the ante-bellum period the laws to protect a married woman's property were adequate if she had safeguarded her rights in time. The weakness of the system was that it offered no shelter to those who had not. Yet, as Harriet Martineau pointed out, weak and ignorant women were the ones most likely to need legal protection and the least likely to have sought it.[50]

Little by little women in Georgia gained control of their earnings. Beginning in 1851 certain wives who applied to the legislature for "reliefs" were allowed to carry on an independent business. They were called "free traders." During 1851 and 1852 there were four women so recognized, from 1853 to 1854 there were ten, and from 1855 to 1856 the number rose to fourteen.[51] After that a woman who had gained the consent of her husband was allowed to become a free trader by publishing a notice of her intentions in the paper for a month before beginning business.[52] She was then liable for her contracts and entitled to her profits.

Even when the Married Woman's Act of 1866[53] and the Constitution of 1868 insured a wife's unqualified control of her possession the courts did not relax their guardianship. In 1875 Supreme Court of

Georgia decided this legislation had not modified those sections of the Code which prevented a wife from selling her estate to her husband without a court order and which prohibited his creditors buying it under any conditions.[54]

Fanny Kemble saw in the increasing liberality of the law a "possible advantage to the magnanimous sex." For according to her, it enabled dishonest men to settle extensive property on their wives and then to "baffle the claims of the creditors."[55]

In general a woman's share in her husband's estate was for life only. The laws of inheritance favored the male line and the majority of wills seem to have followed the same trend.[56] The laws regulating intestate estates made the husband the sole heir of his wife and excluded her children,[57] but only allowed a widow to choose between a child's portion and her dower. Before 1829 if a husband left no children his widow was entitled to half of his estate. The remainder went to his next of kin.[58] In that year, however, the law was altered and where there were no lineal descendants the wife became sole heir of her intestate husband.[59]

The best legal protection a woman had for a share in her husband's estate was her dower. The courts defined it as the "favorite of the law" and stipulated "neither the husband nor the courts, nor any other human power can compel a wife to relinquish this right."[60] The law restricted a husband's disposal of his property during his lifetime so as to protect the wife's dower rights.[62] This the Supreme Court of Georgia interpreted to mean free of all mortgages that might be on the estate at the time of the husband's death—as though no encumbrances existed.[63] The law permitted a wife to choose her dower property.[64] And it allowed her a year's support for herself and her children even though the estate was insolvent.[65]

The status of a wife under the law was, in part that of a minor whose husband was her guardian. In general public opinion accepted this theory although it was not always practiced. Like a minor her contracts were void;[66] her husband was answerable for her words and her misdemeanors;[67] if through commands, threats, coercion or persuasion he induced her to commit a crime not punishable by death or life imprisonment he must pay the penalty in her stead;[68] and, if she disobeyed he was entitled to administer punishment.[69]

It was explained that inasmuch as the husband was made responsible for his wife's misdemeanors the "law thought it reasonable to intrust him with the power of restraining her by domestic chastisement in the same manner that a man is allowed to correct his apprentice or children." There was a time when, for some offences, a man was permitted to "beat his wife severely with scourges and sticks," but in England the "politer reign of Charles II" brought this power of correction into "doubt,"[70] and in Georgia the law required that the stick be no larger than a man's thumb.

Husbands of the upper class in Georgia did not use the lash but women were expected to obey. Something of a code of honor reinforced a husband's discipline. Probably the young ladies of LaGrange College had been reminded of their responsibilities many times before Robert Charlton told them "a woman ought not to speak what she pleased," because her husband must answer for her words "either by fight or by law—the first threatening his person, and the last invading his purse."[72]

Yet Georgians could say with their English ancestors "the lower ranks of people . . . still claim and exert their ancient privileges"[73] for here too husbands continued to give disobedient wives corporal punishment. Public opinion was increasingly hostile, however, and sometimes it intruded. Only a broken rail and cool headed intervention prevented a lynching when the husband of one of the mill girls in Columbus attempted to beat her.[74]

In 1857 the law made beating or mistreating a wife a penal offense. It carried a possible six months sentence and allowed the wife to testify in her own behalf.[75] But public opinion still found cause for complaint. When a husband in the factory region of Augusta was fined only "5.00 for whipping his wife" the *Evening Dispatch* strongly protested against the "cheapness of the luxury."[76]

A wife was the property of her husband to this extent: he had the right of action against another for abducting, harboring, seducing or beating her. These were actions at common law for which the husband might collect damages.[77] Many husbands advertised their fugitive wives, and warned against "dealing with, harboring, or concealing" the runaways under the penalty of the law.[78]

Women were expected to accept their lot as part of the punishment visited upon Eve, to continue the "even as Sarah obeyed Abraham" teachings of the Jews, and to "reverence their husbands" in accordance with the theology of Paul.[79]

When Pierce Butler was preparing for his divorce he, with the aid of his lawyers, drew up his *Statement* to be used as testimony. In it he cited as "perhaps the fundamental" reason for the failure of his marriage the "peculiar views which were entertained by Mrs. Butler . . . she held that marriage should be a companionship on equal terms—partnership, in which if both partners agreed all is well—but at no time has one partner a right to control the other."[80] He claimed the things to which his wife objected were "the customary and pledged acquiescence of a wife to marital control—nothing more."[81] Pierce Butler asserted that "nothing is required to show the error of this principal of equal rights in marriage. . . . No one who is not morally astray can fail to see the heedlessness of the pretension."[82]

A man was the head of his family. His wife and his minor children were his wards. The common law provided that "a mother as such is entitled to no power but only to reverence and respect," but that "the Empire of the father continues even after his death."[83] Both the statute law[84] and public opinion supported the father's authority. And this authority, Fanny Kemble discovered, "endowed" the father with the power of "supreme torture."[85] Yet she accepted her husband's right to the custody of their children.

Her acceptance is significant of the code under which she lived. Fanny Kemble was not lacking in daring. There was no doubt of her devotion to her children. Her personal conduct was unquestioned. Yet she possessed adequate proof of her husband's infidelity and made no use of it. He divorced her in 1849 and got the custody of the children.[86]

Butler himself admitted "her care and management of our children was admirable we have never disagreed once about them."[87] But both he and his wife regarded the children as a species of the father's undisputed personal property and behaved accordingly.

Fanny Kemble was planning a separation when their second child was expected. She wrote her husband that she could reach England in time for it to be born there and "if you will appoint the means for your child being brought over to you, I shall of course observe them."[88] In considering his wife's determination to leave him Butler questioned the welfare of the children without her, his own ability to care for them, and her happiness if separated from them, but not the possibility of the mother being given the guardianship of the children.[89]

The father had the right to will away the custody of his children. He might, and frequently did, name their mother as their guardian. This was the only way in which she ever gained complete control over legitimate children. If the father died without providing for their guardianship the mother was eligible for appointment by the courts, but on remarriage her authority terminated. She might be reappointed or dismissed at the discretion of the court and the father's next of kin, the new step-father, or someone else named by the court replace her.[90]

A widowed mother's estate was divided among her children but under the Act of 1804 she was entitled to nothing from an intestate legitimate child whom she might have survived. If such a child had no descendants, father, brother, and sisters shared his estate. Whole or half blood on the paternal side inherited equally. If the father was dead and the mother had remained a widow she was entitled to her husband's part of the estate, but if she had remarried the father's next kin inherited his share.[91]

The Act of 1843 was less harsh. Remarriage still barred a mother from participation in the estates of all children except her last or only one. This she might inherit unconditionally.[92]

This law took an odd turn in the settlement of the estate of William Harrell, a posthumous child who died before he was three years old. His mother had married again and by that marriage had had a daughter, Mary. When the girl was two days old the boy died. Since he had inherited considerable property from his father the disposition of it became a matter for the courts. The case finally reached the Supreme Bench. It defined the "last child" as being the last surviving child of the mother and named Mary as the sole heir. Thus she inherited the estate of her mother's first husband, through a half brother, who never saw his father and who was probably never aware that his sister had been born.[93]

Illegitimate children had "no blood except that given them by the law."[94] Under it they belonged to the mother and, unless the father legally adopted them,[95] it was as though he were dead and his relatives had never existed. An illegitimate child shared equally in the estate of its mother with a legitimate one. If it died intestate, provided there were neither wife nor lineal descendants, its estate was divided alike between mother, brothers, and sisters. If none of these existed the property went to the mother's legitimate children.[96]

The law of 1793 provided that both man and woman accused of misconduct should be indicted but the Supreme Court of Georgia left no room for doubt that the "primary object of the act . . . was to protect the county from the charge of bastard children."[97]

The mother of an illegitimate child might choose between naming the father and giving security for its support. If the father were known he was forced to provide for the expenses of the child's birth and its maintenance. Whomsoever the mother accused was held guilty unless proven innocent. The father's offence was not his paternity but his failure to pay the bills. This was held to be a misdemeanor.[98]

The fate of such children was always sad but the taxpayers were determined to protect their pocket books if possible. Most of the Bastard Bonds seem to cover the care of the child until it was fourteen years of age,[99] but among the court records are items such as: "Lucy Sheet, illegitimate child of Anna Shorter, four years old bound to Joseph Barker,"[100] which tell their own story.

With Protestantism both Church and State accepted marriage as a civil contract and divorces became permissible. They were avoided, however, if possible for there had lingered a fondness for the sacramental marriage doctrines of the Catholic Church and the causes for which divorces were allowed placed a stigma on them for either sex. And for a woman a divorce might prove socially and economically disastrous.

The Georgia divorce code was brought from England and, in theory at least, was severe for it still bore the marks of the canon law which did not recognize divorce. The Catholic Church prohibited marriage under certain conditions. If these were not observed Rome declared the marriage void, but if both parties were qualified only death could dissolve the bond. This plan the English incorporated in their civil law—even though the recorder of the common law was "led to wonder that the same authority which enjoined the strictest celebacy to the priesthood should think itself proper judge in causes between man and wife."[101]

The English code classified divorces as complete and partial. Complete divorces were given only to parties who had not made a legal contract. They were not allowed for any causes which arose after a legal marriage—not even when "it became impossible for the parties to live together; as in the case of intolerable ill temper or adultery." Partial divorces were granted for infidelity and cruel treatment. They permitted separation from "bed and board" only and prohibited remarriage.[102]

In Georgia the same distinction existed[103] but as the State Constitution of 1798 provided that divorces should be granted on "legal principles" and these were not defined by the Supreme Court for almost fifty years there was a lack of uniformity in the degree and the causes for which divorces were given. Judge Floyd, in the case of Head *vs.* Head, put a stop to the "flagrant facility" with which divorces were being granted and restricted them to the grounds recognized in the laws which the colonies had brought from England.[104]

The decision necessitated a revision of the divorce code. The amendment of 1849 gave the General Assembly the right to determine the grounds for divorce.[105] The Act of 1849 recognized all divorces allowed before the decision and relieved the parties who had remarried of any possible charge of bigamy.[106] And the Act of 1850 assigned inability of the parties to contract as defined by law, incontinence, and desertion as reasons for total divorce; in cases of cruel treatment or habitual drunkenness the jury was empowered to determine whether the decree should be final or separation from bed and board only; and all other grounds permitted partial divorce only.[107]

Nevertheless the divorce code remained in confusion. The first divorce procedure in Georgia required action by both courts and legislature,[108] but in 1833 the General Assembly amended the Constitution and vested sole authority in the courts.[109] Georgians, however, did not seem to be fully aware of the change for the Legislature continued to receive frequent applications for divorce and sometimes acted upon them. Governor Brown said only one such petition had been granted since the amendment and that was to complete action begun before the alteration of the Constitution. Yet he was called upon to veto a divorce bill in 1859.[110]

The law prohibited the guilty party to a divorce suit from remarrying,[111] but the Legislature by granting a "relief" could remove the disability. It was said on the floor of the House that no petition of this character had ever been denied. In 1859 came a call for a repeal of the restriction. The discussions of the bill show that Georgians had become more charitable toward divorce. One representative dared say, "God does not put his eternal sanction on everything done by preachers and justices of the peace," and to pronounce, "continued cohabitation under the coercion of law, where there is no affection legalized adultery."[112]

As the years went by the divorce rate increased in Georgia. Oliver H. Prince counted 291 divorces granted between 1798 and the close of the legislative session of 1835. He found they averaged about four a year from 1800 to 1810. The next ten years the rate doubled— eight a year. Between 1820 and 1830 it more than doubled again— eighteen a year. And from 1830 to 1835 Georgia granted an average of twenty-eight divorces a year.[113]

By 1833 the weight of divorce legislation had become so great that the General Assembly stepped out from under the load and added a constitutional amendment which included their grievance in its preamble.[114] And by 1859 Representative Wallace of Taylor estimated the state had spent $200,000 on special divorce legislation.[116]

The divorce laws placed the same value on the character of the husband as they did on that of the wife, but public opinion differed. As Judge Floyd pointed out, in his Head *vs.* Head decision, society accepted the delinquency of the husband with greater grace than it was willing to allow his wife. He found this was being justified by presuming the failings of the wife to be more injurious to the home than those of the husband. Judge Floyd denied this theory and refused to believe it was "illustrative of the high esteem placed on feminine virtue." He held that the double standard was owing to the "prevelence of vice among men." And, though he deplored it, he charged that wives were required to "meekly endure" what husbands were "justified in making a good cause for loathing, contempt, and repudiation."[116]

In an unhappy marriage the unsurbordinate status of women was likely to prove tragic. It is true the law granted alimony. The amount was conditioned on the wealth of the husband and the separate estate of the wife.[117] Any part of her property which he might have lost or squandered previously was forgotten by the law. There was the forlorn Elizabeth Harper, for example. She wrote of her husband to the Brothers and Sisters of Mars Hill Church, "he have taken my property and gave it to another and now is sporeting with my carecttor." But she could only be "sory" she had been driven out of her home with nothing but "a little flower and a small piece of meat" and forced to seek "sheltor" with the neighbors. There seems to have been no comfort for her destitution.[118]

Elizabeth Harper's social position was not responsible for her unhappy situation. Women of the aristocracy played with loaded dice too. There is a Charleston gentleman's own record. It appears he had killed his wife's reputed lover, probably in a duel in Georgia. Later with the full connivance of Georgia gentlemen of equal rank he attempted to secure letters which his wife had written to the dead man and which would incriminate her. He wanted them not only as testimony should he decide to sue for divorce and to exhonorate himself should he be extradited for trial, but also because there was a possibility of his "unfortunate" wife inheriting "seventy thousand pounds sterling" from her father's estate. If she did, he made no secret of his plan to use the proof her letters contained of "her behavior and feelings" toward him to "so impress the Court of Chancery with her unworthiness as to induce them to settle the entire fortune on her children."[119]

It was common to find a husband who advertised that his wife had "left his bed and board without the least shadow of provocation,"[120] and to "forewarn all others from trading with or trusting her" as he was no longer responsible for her debts.[121] It is possible these husbands were frequently as poor risks as the wives they advertised. At least the Southern Banner seems to have been suspicious. Beginning in 1842 and continuing for years it charged for "announcing candidates for office $5.00—payable in advance," and for "husbands advertising their wives . . . $5.00 *invariably* payable in advance." All other patrons got twelve lines of advertising for $1.00—on credit.[122]

Taken all-in-all the political status of women in Georgia from 1783 to 1860 was of microscopic importance and their civil status was capricious. That of the unmarried woman was secure but, in theory at least, a husband spoke from a burning bush and a married woman had no legal civil status. In fact, however, the law was flexible. It never intruded but if solicited it could give substantial protection to married women.

The statutes governing the relations between husband and wife were based on a mixed concept. In regard to property they were feudal—she, the vassal, surrendered all she possessed to her overlord in return for protection; in regard to a wife's conduct her relations with her husband were those of guardian and ward; and, if a wife was stolen, damaged, or abused, the law regarded the husband's loss as though his wife were his personal property and allowed him to collect damages.

A married woman's greatest legal liability was her lack of property rights. But here again she played hide-and-seek with the law. The law permitted her marriage vow to confiscate her possessions but did not hesitate to shut one eye, help her establish a separate estate, and maintain it during her husband's life. After her husband's death she was entitled to a year's support and to her dower. In case of divorce there was alimony. The courts were inclined to be friendly to a wife's financial interest, but expected her to keep her marriage contract and were not inclined to show mercy if she failed.

Due to the English heritage and American custom, the tendency was to keep estates in the male line. So women were in the red there. But during the antebellum period public opinion was was slowly crystalizing into laws more beneficial to women. While children were the property of the father, here too a slight change in favor of the mother was in progress.

A married woman's position in Georgia before 1860 was always hazardous, frequently humiliating, and often tragic. Her true status, nevertheless, was far more commonly determined by her character, that of the man she married, their personal relations to each other, the use they made of the laws, and even by public opinion, than by the statutes alone.

Notes

1. Walter McElreath, ed., *A Treatise on the Constitution of Georgia* (Atlanta, 1912), Charter of the Province, 212–237; Constitution of 1777, Art. IX, 232; Constitution of 1789, Art. IV, sec. I, 247; Constitution of 1798, Art. IV, sec. I, 264; Constitution of 1861, Art. V, sec. I, 296.

2. J. S. Buckingham, *The Slave States of America* (London, 1842), II, 182–183.

3. Garnett Andrews, *Reminiscences of an Old Georgia Lawyer* (Atlanta, 1870), 37.

4. Buckingham, *Slave States*, II, 182–183.

5. I. S. Bradwell to Adam Alexander, May 31, 1820, in mss. Letters and Papers of Adam Leopold Alexander, Washington, Georgia, in Duke University Library.

6. Milledgeville *Daily Federal Union,* Nov. 17, 1859.

7. Buckingham, *Slave States,* II, 182–183.

8. *Acts of the General Assembly of the State of Georgia, 1829,* p. 94 (Hereafter referred to as *Acts of Georgia*); Foster Blodgett, Jr. to David L. Roath, Jan. 18, 1860, in mss. Letters of David L. Roath, Augusta, Georgia, in Office of the Ordinary of Richmond County.

9. William Blackstone, *Commentaries on the Laws of England,* with Analysis of Contents by Thomas M. Cooley, ed. by James DeWitt Andrews (Chicago, 1899), Book II, sec. 434–436.

10. Oliver H. Prince, comp., *A Digest of the Laws of the State of Georgia* (Athens, 1837), Act of 1789, p. 225; Royston *vs.* Royston, 21 Georgia 161.

11. Prince, comp., *Digest,* Act of 1784, p. 570.

12. Blackstone, *Commentaries,* Book I, sec. 442.

13. R. H. Clark, T. R. R. Cobb, D. Irwin, comps., *The Code of the State of Georgia* (Atlanta, 1861), sec. 1700. (Hereafter referred to as Clark, Cobb, and Irwin, comps., *Code of 1861.*)

14. *Acts of Georgia,* 1856, p. 229.

15. Clark, Cobb, and Irwin, comps., *Code of 1861,* sec. 1705.

16. Blackstone, *Commentaries,* Book I, sec. 443.

17. Thomas R. R. Cobb, comp., *A Digest of the Statute Laws of Georgia* (Athens, 1851), Acts of: 1768, p. 163; 1807, p. 228; 1824, p. 228; 1826, p. 171; 1839, p. 230; 1850, p. 231.

18. Prince, comp., *Digest,* Acts of: 1804, p. 233; 1829, p. 253.

19. Cobb, comp., *Digest,* Act of 1838, p. 296; John Silcox and others *vs.* John Nelson and others, Richmond County Superior Court, 1842 Term, in *Decisions of the Superior Courts of the State of Georgia,* Part I (Augusta, 1842), 24–25. In De Renne Collection, University of Georgia Library. (Hereafter referred to as *Georgia Superior Court Decisions.*)

20. Penalton & Co. *vs.* Mills & *al.,* Cobb County Superior Court, 1843 Term, *ibid.,* Part II (Augusta, 1844), 116–117; Royston *vs.* Royston, 21 Georgia 161.

21. A. Edwards and wife *vs.* B. Leigh and W. Leigh, Richmond County, Superior Court Records: Minute Book, 1805–1811, April Term, 1818, p. 246. Mss in Richmond County Superior Court Office.

22. Cobb, comp., *Digest,* Acts of: 1804, p. 291; 1845, p. 294; Uriah B. Holden and wife *vs.* David Harrell, 6 Georgia 126.

23. Gorman *et al. vs.* Wood, 68 Georgia 524, 73 Georgia 307; Wilson *vs.* Wilson Sewing Machine Company, 76 Georgia 104.

24. *Acts of Georgia,* 1851, p. 237.

25. Grace G. Davidson, comp., *Early Records of Georgia, Wilkes County* (Macon, 1932), I, 47. (Hereafter referred to as Davidson, comp., *Wilkes County Records.*)

26. *Ibid.,* 85.

27. Penalton & Co. *vs.* Mills & *al.*, in *Georgia Superior Court Decisions*, Part II, 116–117.

28. Leota S. Driver, *Fanny Kemble* (Chapel Hill, 1933).

29. Frances Ann Kemble, *Journal of a Residence on a Georgian Plantation* (New York, 1863), *passim.*

30. Driver, *Fanny Kemble*, 92–114.

31. Pierce M. Butler, *Mr. Butler's Statement, Originally prepared with the aid of his Professional Council* (Philadelphia, 1850).

32. Butler, *Statement*, 22–24.

33. Dorothie Bobbé, *Fanny Kemble* (New York, 1931), 170, citing letter to Harriet Martineau (n. d., n. p.).

34. Gorman *et. al. vs.* Wood, 68 Georgia 524, 73 Georgia 370; Wilson *vs.* the Wilson Sewing Machine Company, 76 Georgia 104.

35. Sayre & Sayre *vs.* Flournoy, adm'r and others, 3 Georgia 541.

36. Blackstone, *Commentaries*, Book II, secs. 389, 397.

37. Gorman *et. al. vs.* Wood, 68 Georgia 524.

38. Oglesby and wife *vs.* Hall, 80 Georgia 386.

39. George Paschal, *Ninety-Four Years, or Agnes Paschal* (n. p., 1871), 97.

40. Augusta *Georgia Constitutionalist*, June 8, 1846.

41. Clark, Cobb, and Irwin, comps., *Code of 1861*, secs. 1724–1729.

42. Humphrey *vs.* Copeland, 54 Georgia 543.

43. Cobb, comp., *Digest*, Act of 1847, p. 180.

44. Lydia C. Pepper and Alexander Fawnes, Chatham County Superior Court Records: Minute Book "2F," Follo 107. Mss. in Chatham County Court Office.

45. Joseph Welcher and Ann Miller, *ibid.*, Book "Z," Folio 507.

46. Clark, Cobb, and Irwin, comps., *Code of 1861*, sec. 1730.

47. Will of William Lowden, Chatham County, Inferior Court Records: Will no. 50. Mss. Chatham County Court Office.

48. Blackstone, *Commentaries*, Book I, sec. 444 (note).

49. McBride *vs.* Greenwood and others, 11 Georgia 379: Kempton *et al. vs.* Hallowell and Co., 24 Georgia 52; Hicks *vs.* Johnson, 24 Georgia 194.

50. Harriet Martineau, *Society in America* (New York, 1837), II, 238.

51. *Acts of Georgia*, 1851–1852, pp. 515–518; 1853–1854, pp. 527–529; 1855–1856, pp. 512–514.

52. Clark, Cobb, and Irwin, comps., *Code of 1861*, sec. 1708.

53. *Acts of Georgia*, 1866, p. 146.

54. Humphrey *vs.* Copeland, 54 Georgia 548; Clark, Cobb, and Irwin, comps., *Code of 1861*, secs. 1783, 1785.

55. Frances Anne Kemble, *Records of Later Life* (London, 1882), I, 28.

56. Davidson, comp., *Wilkes County Records*, I, II, *passim.*

57. Prince, comp. *Digest*, Act of: 1789, p. 225; 1827, p. 251.

58. *Ibid.*, Act of 1804, p. 233.

59. *Ibid.*, Act of 1829, p. 253; Clark, Cobb, and Irwin, comps., *Code of 1861*, sec. 2452.

60. Royston *vs.* Royston, 21 Georgia 161; Blackstone, *Commentaries,* Book II, sec. 129; Clark, Cobb, and Irwin, comps., *Code of 1861,* sec. 1714.

61. Cobb, comp., *Digest,* Acts of: 1760, p. 161; 1768, p. 163; 1785, p. 165; 1842, p. 179.

62. *Ibid.,* Act of 1826, p. 171.

63. Green *vs.* Causey, 10 Georgia 485; Dennis *et. al. vs.* Green, 20 Georgia 886.

64. Cobb, comp., *Digest,* Acts of: 1830, p. 230; 1850, p. 231.

65. *Ibid.,* Acts of: 1838, p. 296; 1850, pp. 297–299; Hopkins *vs.* Long, 9 Georgia 261.

66. Blackstone, *Commentaries,* Book I, sec. 443–445.

67. Smith *vs.* Taylor and wife, Louise Lynch *vs.* same, 11 Georgia 20.

68. Blackstone, *Commentaries,* Book I, sec. 445.

69. Cobb, comp., *Digest,* Penal Code of 1833, Div. I, sec. VIII, 779.

70. Blackstone, *Commentaries,* Book I, sec. 445.

71. Orville A. Park, comp., *History of Georgia in the Eighteenth Century as Recorded in the Reports of the Georgia Bar Association,* reprint from the Annual Report of the Georgia Bar Association (Macon, 1921), June, 1921, 90.

72. Robert M. Charlton, *Address,* delivered at the commencement of La-Grange Female College, July, 1853 (Savannah, 1853).

73. Blackstone, *Commentaries,* Book I, sec. 445.

74. Augusta *Daily Constitutionalist,* July 14, 1847 citing *Muscogee Democrat* 1st inst.

75. *Acts of Georgia,* 1857, p. 126.

76. Augusta *Evening Dispatch,* Feb. 1, 1859.

77. Blackstone, *Commentaries,* Book III, sec. 139–140; Clark, Cobb, and Irwin comps., *Code of 1861,* sec. 2949.

78. Augusta *Chronicle and Gazette of the State,* Oct. 14, 1797.

79. Mary S. Benson, *Women of the Eighteenth-Century America* (New York, 1935), 184–185, citing David Ramsey, *Memoirs of the Life of Martha Laurens Ramsey,* 41–42.

80. Butler, *Statement,* 9.

81. *Ibid.,* 9–10.

82. Bobbé, *Fanny Kemble,* 247.

83. Blackstone, *Commentaries,* Book I, sec. 454.

84. *Ibid.,* secs. 447–452, Clark, Cobb, and Irwin, comps., *Code of 1861,* sec. 1744.

85. Fanny Kemble to Harriet Martineau, Sept. 22, 1846, in Kemble, *Records of Later Life,* III, 137.

86. Driver, *Fanny Kemble,* 114–156; Butler, *Statement, passim.*

87. Pierce Butler to Mrs. Sedgwick, May 31, 1839, *ibid.,* 33.

88. Fanny Kemble to Pierce Butler, 1838, in Butler, *Statement,* 27.

89. Pierce Butler to Mrs. Sedgwick, May 31, 1939, *ibid.,* 38.

90. Cobb, comp., *Digest,* Acts of: 1792, p. 309; 1828, p. 327; 1842, p. 335.

91. Prince, comp., *Digest,* Act of 1804, p. 233.

92. Cobb, comp., *Digest,* Act of 1843, p. 297; Clark, Cobb, and Irwin, comps., *Code of 1861,* sec. 2452.

93. Uriah B. Holden and wife *vs.* David Harrell, 6 Georgia 126.

94. Clark, Cobb, and Irwin, comps., *Code of 1861,* sec. 1751.

95. *Ibid.,* sec. 1750.

96. Clark, Cobb, and Irwin, comps., *Code of 1861,* secs. 1751–1752; Cobb, comp., *Digest,* Acts of: 1816, p. 293; 1850, p. 299.

97. Locke *vs.* the State, 3 Georgia 534.

98. Cobb, comp., *Digest,* Act of 1793, pp. 148–149; Penal Code of 1833, Div. X, sec. XXIX, 1818; Clark, Cobb, and Irwin, comps.; *Code of 1861,* secs. 4640–4643.

99. Richmond County, Inferior Court Records: Bastard Bonds.

100. Davidson, comp., *Wilkes County Records,* I, 145.

101. Blackstone, *Commentaries,* Book III, sec. 93.

102. *Ibid.,* Book I, sec. 440–441.

103. Prince, comp., *Digest,* Act of 1806, p. 188.

104. Head *vs.* Head, 2 Georgia 191.

105. McElreath, *Constitution of Georgia,* Constitution of 1798, amendment to Art. III, sec. IX, 278.

106. Cobb, comp., *Digest,* Act of 1849, p. 227.

107. *Acts of Georgia,* 1850, pp. 151–152.

108. McElreath, *Constitution of Georgia,* Constitution of 1798, Art. III, sec. IX, 263.

109. *Ibid.,* amendment to Art. III, sec. IX, 274.

110. Milledgeville *Daily Federal Union,* Dec. 15, 1859.

111. Prince, comp., *Digest,* Act of 1806, p. 188.

112. Augusta *Daily Constitutionalist,* Dec. 11, 1859.

113. Prince, comp., *Digest,* 187.

114. Cobb, comp., *Digest,* Preamble to the amendment of 1833, Constitution of 1798, Art. III, sec. IX, 1123.

115. Augusta *Daily Constitutionalist,* Dec. 11, 1859.

116. Head *vs.* Head, 2 Georgia 191.

117. Cobb, comp. *Digest,* Act of 1810, p. 226; Clark, Cobb, and Irwin, comps., *Code of 1861,* secs. 1676, 1688–1699.

118. Elizabeth Harper to the Brothers and Sisters of Mars Hill Church, Nov. 12, 1818, in mss. Letters and Papers of Edward Harden, Athens, Georgia in Duke University Library.

119. John Rutledge to Robert MacKay, Feb. 11, 1804, in mss. Letters and Papers of Robert MacKay and W. H. H. Stiles, Savannah, Georgia, in University of North Carolina Library.

120. *Athens Gazette,* June 16, 1814.

121. Milledgeville *Georgia Patriot,* July 11, 1826.

122. Athens *Southern Banner,* June 13, 1842.

Epilogue

THIS HAS BEEN the story of the first generation of historians of southern women. But what, the reader may well ask, happened next?

"Generations" are in any case an artificial construct. By the time all five of the pioneers were publishing, the first member of the next generation was enrolling for graduate work at the University of North Carolina. Elizabeth Taylor arrived in Chapel Hill in 1938, but it is doubtful that she met any of them. If she had they would have offered sympathetic understanding when she realized, as she later wrote, that the professors "did not conceal the fact that they preferred male students and . . . favored men in placement."[1] Taylor finished a master's thesis on the convict lease system in Georgia and went off to teach at a small college in Marion, Alabama. It was there that she discovered the six-volume *History of Woman Suffrage* and began to realize that until that moment she had not been aware that there was a history which included women. In 1941, as men went off to war, the Vanderbilt University history department offered her what may have been the first graduate fellowship it had ever awarded a woman. She arrived already determined to study the suffrage movement in the South and persisted despite the surprise and polite puzzlement of her professors and the open skepticism of other graduate students whom she quoted as asking, "How can you write a dissertation on a subject like *that?*"

She could and did, but getting published was another matter. When she submitted an article on woman suffrage to a regional journal in 1943 it was rejected with the comment that the editors did not consider the subject appropriate for a scholarly journal. It was 1951 before her first article was accepted, and six more years passed before she found a publisher for the book based on her dissertation: *Woman Suffrage in Tennessee.* Meantime she found a job at a normal school (now Texas Woman's University) and moved along to what became her lifework: a state-by-state study of southern suffrage movements. In 1951 at the annual meeting of the Mississippi Valley Historical Society she presented a paper on woman suffrage in Texas, which may have been the first paper in southern women's history ever presented to a learned society. Two of her reflections as she looked back from 1987 are relevant: "Women with doctorates taught only in women's colleges or teachers colleges," and "I still considered myself merely a historian who worked on topics relating to women, not a women's historian. . . . I did not consider myself part of a network. Historians of women had not found a collective identity."

In retrospect it seems to me a little eerie that in 1958 I should find myself in Chapel Hill where Johnson, Mendenhall, and Spruill were all living, and where Virginia Gray was nine miles away. I had just begun to think seriously about southern women as a subject for research. In the process of writing a dissertation on southern progressives I had come across what was then to me a surprising number of activist women, disfranchised women who were astute politicians working through their own voluntary associations. In the winter of 1959, as a temporary part-time instructor in history at the University of North Carolina I found myself invited to present a paper to the monthly faculty seminar. It occurred to me to take another look at the women who had come across my line of vision during the dissertation research.

In 1961 Professor George Tindall of the University of North Carolina invited me to give a paper at the annual meeting of the Southern Historical Association and I chose to go on with the subject; it may have been the second paper on southern women's history presented to a learned society. That essay was published, by another strange coincidence, in the *South Atlantic Quarterly* which so many years earlier had given Gray and Mendenhall a hearing. The editor in my day was William B. Hamilton of the Duke University history department, who assured me that because he was a student of English history he knew that there had been women in the past.[2]

By the time I went to teach at Duke University in 1961 things were beginning to change.[3] I continued to work on southern women with help and encouragement from Spruill, Johnson, and Gray and published several papers before 1970 when *The Southern Lady* came out just as a new wave of feminism was creating a great demand for books in women's history. If it had been ready to publish in 1965 it might well have followed Spruill's book into relative oblivion; timing means a great deal, but in this case the timing was accidental. Students were demanding courses in the history of women, and I was ready to oblige. The new edition of Spruill's book brought new recruits, and a number of able younger scholars began to give papers at historical meetings and to publish in historical journals.

In 1968 when Arthur Link and Rembert Patrick edited a volume surveying the historiography of the South from the beginning of European settlement "women" appeared in the index three times; two of the references were to footnotes. In 1987 a successor historiographical volume contained a fifty-page essay summarizing the historiography of southern women.[4]

To be sure the millenium has not arrived: few of the other essays in that second volume exhibited awareness of work in women's history which would have been relevant to their subjects. Women's history is still often seen as a thing off by itself rather than as a way of looking at any part of the past that sees both sexes. It is still rare for a male historian to think of using women's documents to build a case.[5]

In the realm of professional opportunity, however, things are remarkably better. Most southern history departments now routinely hire the best candidate without regard to sex, and there is serious competition for the most able women. Careers are being built. I have been astounded to find myself serving as president, first of the Organization of American Historians in 1984 and then of the Southern Historical Association in 1989. In each of those years a woman served as chairman or co-chair of the program committee. The Southern Association of Women Historians is a powerful network, and becoming more so. Its triennial meeting now rivals that of the Berkshire Conference of Women Historians in interest and quality of papers. We may now properly say to young historians: "Look southward: the land is bright."

Notes

1. A. Elizabeth Taylor, "A Lifelong Interest," in Ruthe Winegarten and Judith N. McArthur, eds., *Citizens All: The Woman Suffrage Movement in Texas* (Austin: Ellen C. Temple, 1987).

Epilogue

2. "The 'New Woman' in the New South," *South Atlantic Quarterly* 61 (Autumn 1962): 471–83.

3. My own academic history is outlined in "A Historian's Odyssey" in *Making the Invisible Woman Visible* (Champaign: University of Illinois Press, 1984), xi–xvii.

4. Arthur S. Link and Rembert W. Patrick, *Writing Southern History: Essays in Historiography in Honor of Fletcher M. Green* (Baton Rouge: Louisiana State University Press, 1965). The successor was John B. Boles and Evelyn Thomas Nolen, *Interpreting Southern History: Historiographical Essays in Honor of Sanford W. Higginbotham* (Baton Rouge: Louisiana State University Press, 1987). The essay is Jacquelyn D. Hall and Anne F. Scott, "Women in the South," pp. 454–509.

5. Clarence L. Mohr, *On the Threshold of Freedom: Master and Slaves in Civil War Georgia* (Athens: University of Georgia Press, 1986), is a notable exception. By using the records created by plantation mistresses Mohr was able to upset the conventional wisdom and to present his subject in a more complex and believable way than had been done before.

For Further Reading
on Academic Women and
the Spirit of the Times

Some of these books and articles are cited in the text but for an interested person the whole document is illuminating.

Annals of the American Academy of Political and Social Science 143 (May 1929), especially Willystine Goodsell, Ph.D., "The Educational Opportunities of American Women—Theoretical and Actual," pp. 1–13; Chase Going Woodhouse, "Married College Women in Business and the Professions," pp. 325–38; Elsa Denison Voorhees, "Emotional Adjustment of Women in the Modern World and the Choice of Satisfactions," pp. 368–73.

Nadya Aisenberg and Mona Harrington, *Women of Academe: Outsiders in the Sacred Grove* (Amherst: University of Massachusetts Press, 1988).

Carol K. Bleser, ed., "The Three Women Presidents of the Southern Historical Association: Ella Lonn, Kathryn Abby Hanna, and Mary Elizabeth Massey," *Southern Studies* 20, no. 2 (Summer 1981): 101–21.

Susan Carter, "Academic Women Revisited," *Journal of Social History* 14 (Summer 1981): 675–99.

Penina Migdal Glazer and Miriam Slater, *Unequal Colleagues: The Entrance of Women into the Professions, 1890–1940* (New Brunswick, N.J.: Rutgers University Press, 1987).

Jacqueline Goggin, "Challenging Sexual Discrimination in the Historical Profession: Women Historians and the American Historical Association," *American Historical Review* 97, no. 3 (June 1992): 769–802.

William B. Hesseltine and Louis Kaplan, "Women Doctors of Philosophy in History," *Journal of Higher Education* 14 (1943): 235–59.

Emilie J. Hutchinson, *Women and the Ph.D.: Facts from the Experiences of 1,025 Women Who Have Taken the Degree of Doctor of Philosophy since 1877*, Institute of Women's Professional Relations Bulletin No. 2 (Greensboro, N.C., December 1929).

Edward and Janet James, eds., *Notable American Women*, 3 vols. (Cambridge: Harvard University Press, 1971). A topical breakdown at the end of vol. 3 lists twenty-four women as historians.

For Further Reading

Guion G. Johnson, "My Exploration of the Southern Experience," *North Carolina Historical Review* 57, no. 2 (April 1980): 192–207.

Margaret Judson, *Breaking the Barriers: A Personal Autobiography by a Woman Educator and Historian before the Women's Movement* (New Brunswick, N.J.: Rutgers University Press, 1984).

Mabel Newcomer, *A Century of Women's Higher Education* (New York: Harper and Brothers, 1959). See especially chap. 10.

Marjorie Nicholson, "All the Rights and Privileges Pertaining Thereto . . . ," in *A University between Two Worlds: Michigan, 1837–1937* (Ann Arbor: University of Michigan, 1938).

Margaret W. Rossiter, *Women Scientists in America: Struggle and Strategies to 1940* (Baltimore: Johns Hopkins University Press, 1982).

Joan W. Scott, "American Women Historians, 1884–1984," in *Gender and the Politics of History* (New York: Columbia University Press, 1988), 178–98.

Kathryn Kish Sklar, "American Female Historians in Context," *Feminist Studies* 3, nos. 1, 2 (Fall 1975): 171–84.

Barbara Sicherman and Carol Hurd Green, *Notable American Women: The Modern Period* (Cambridge: Harvard University Press, 1980) includes ten women historians. Of special interest as members of the generation covered in this book are Catherine Drinker Bowen, Esther Forbes, Constance McLaughlin Green, Beatrice Hyslop, and Muriel Wright.

Barbara M. Solomon, *The Company of Educated Women* (New Haven: Yale University Press, 1985).

David D. Van Tassell, "The American Historical Association and the South," *Journal of Southern History* 23 (1957): 466–82.

Mary Roth Walsh, *Doctors Wanted: No Women Need Apply: Sexual Barriers in the Medical Profession, 1835–1975* (New Haven: Yale University Press, 1983).

Thomas Woody, *A History of Women's Education in the United States,* 2 vols. (New York: Science Press, 1929).